"**Remarkable . . . Fascinating . . . Impossible to put down.** In my practice as a psychologist and hypnotherapist for 25 years, I worked with more than 400 people who appeared to have had close encounters with extraterrestrials. In approximately 50 percent of these cases, there were healings. . . . After completing *Celestial Healing*, one is left feeling that all illnesses can be healed and with the hope that one day we, too, will have the technologies that are unavailable at this time to cure diseases and save lives."

—Edith Fiore, Ph.D., author of *Encounters*

"*Celestial Healing* is **an important contribution** to our understanding of the extraterrestrial contact phenomenon. Aronson's exploration into the healing aspects of alien contact challenges the widely accepted notion that UFOs and their occupants are evil or self-serving. Her research supports my own conclusions and those of a growing number of researchers that the phenomenon known as 'alien abduction' is in reality part of a cosmic plan to evolve human consciousness to a higher, more profound level. One cannot read *Celestial Healing* and come away feeling a victim of alien manipulation. **Bravo for Virginia Aronson** and her many sources who were willing to go on record with their ET experiences!"

—Joe Lewels, Ph.D., author of
*The God Hypothesis: Extraterrestrial Life
and Its Implications for Science and Religion*

(Continued . . .)

"Whatever you make of the author's contention that human beings can be healed by extraterrestrials, this book presents compelling evidence and moving testimony that many people have indeed been the beneficiaries of remarkable and conventionally inexplicable cures that may have otherworldly sources. At any rate, *Celestial Healing* is **a must read** for everyone interested in the case that can be made for a *positive* take on the role of extraterrestrial intervention in human affairs."

—Kenneth Ring, Ph.D., author of
The Omega Project and *Lessons from the Light*

"Is it ETs? Mind over matter? Universal healing forces? Regardless of attempted rationalizations by experiencers, the medical 'healings' reported here in the context of ET contact are **interesting and important** in their own right. An understanding of them **could revolutionize medicine.**"

—Richard Hall, past chairman,
Fund for UFO Research, author of
Universal Guest and *Testing Reality*

"**Coherently, compassionately, and courageously,** Virginia Aronson reviews the healing experiences of many persons, with assistance from Extraterrestrial Entities. Are these events unusual, or a sign of what we humans can learn to develop?"

—R. Leo Sprinkle, Ph.D., president of the
Academy of Clinical Close Encounter
Therapists (ACCET)

CELESTIAL
HEALING

Close Encounters
that Cure

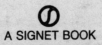

Virginia Aronson

A SIGNET BOOK

SIGNET
Published by New American Library, a division of
Penguin Putnam Inc., 375 Hudson Street,
New York, New York 10014, U.S.A.
Penguin Books Ltd, 27 Wrights Lane,
London W8 5TZ, England
Penguin Books Australia Ltd, Ringwood,
Victoria, Australia
Penguin Books Canada Ltd, 10 Alcorn Avenue,
Toronto, Ontario, Canada M4V 3B2
Penguin Books (N.Z.) Ltd, 182–190 Wairau Road,
Auckland 10, New Zealand

Penguin Books Ltd, Registered Offices:
Harmondsworth, Middlesex, England

First published by Signet, an imprint of New American Library,
a division of Penguin Putnam Inc.

First Printing, December 1999
10 9 8 7 6 5 4 3 2 1

For J.P. and Mel,
my main sources for all healing.

Contents

Contents

Part III: More Celestial Healings

Part IV: It Could Happen to *You*

Part V: What *Is* Happening?

ACKNOWLEDGMENTS

I wish to acknowledge the kindness and generosity shown to me by various people during the writing of this book, including Preston Dennett, ufologist and resource person in the field of extraterrestrial encounters, notably healing ET encounters, who assisted me in connecting with experiencers and healers; Barbara Lamb, regression therapist, who was willing to share her years of work with experiencers; David Miller, channeler of extraterrestrial and spiritual energies, who sent blue light and explained why and how; Dan Wright, director of MUFON's Abduction Transcription Project, who assisted me despite his own contention that the majority of UFO/ET "abductions" constitute "a destructive force" more painful and traumatic than healing in nature; Budd Hopkins, who offered helpful tips; John Mack, M.D., and Karen J. Wesolowski, executive director of PEER, who referred their clients to my project; Leo Sprinkle, Ph.D., who sent words of wisdom and good cheer; Jean Mundy, Ph.D., who shared her UFO cartoon collection and fine sense of humor; Helen Burstin, M.D., who checked the celestial healing cases for medical validity; and Robert Willix, M.D., who saved my neck, literally.

I would also like to thank the following ufologists and therapists for their encouragement and support: Phil Imbrogno and Marianne Horrigan; Richard Hall, chairman, Fund for UFO Research, Inc.; Kenneth Ring, Ph.D.; Edith Fiore, Ph.D.; Joe Lewels, Ph.D.; Grey Woodman, M.D.; Bruce Fox, Ph.D.; Aphrodite Clamar, Ph.D.; Virginia Bennett, CCHT; Scott Mandelker, Ph.D.; Dr. James A. Méade, Meade Institute for Hypnosis Research; Jackie Satchel, CTH, LPN; Joe Nyman; Bob Pratt, journalist, Globe Communications; Brian Crissey, publisher, *Contact Forum*; and Dennis Stacy, former editor, *MUFON Journal.*

I am indebted to all the experiencers who shared their stories, medical intimacies, and personal insights, the brave, honest people who have been willing to risk public ridicule in their attempt to tell others what they know to be true.

Before she passed away suddenly in September of 1997, Connie Clausen, my agent and friend, raved about the concept of this book. Without her enthusiastic endorsement, the project would never have been launched. I must also thank Mary Tahan and Stedman Mays of Connie Clausen & Associates for delivering the manuscript into the capable hands of Danielle Perez at Dutton Signet, who is so open-minded and savvy that she was able to quickly recognize the importance of and potential for such a controversial book. And I am forever grateful to my editor Cecilia Malkum Oh for her essential input and support.

Judy Faro of WORDS, etc., provided lots of input and enthusiasm, as well as her exceptional professional word-processing services. She also tracked down experiencers on the Internet, a gift to me way beyond the call of duty.

Caren Neile, fellow writer and trekker on the uphill climb to selling a book, continuously reassured me that "everything will work out fine." She was right, and her conviction pushed me ahead during the rocky moments when my confidence flagged.

Judy O'Brien, Ph.D., encouraged me to expand the boundaries of my consciousness. She planted the seed and it continues to sprout.

My family has remained totally supportive from the inception to the completion of this book project, despite their bouts with nightmares and weird nocturnal events, eerie side effects of venturing into the unknown with me. We took the journey together. I could not have gone forth without them at my side.

PROLOGUE

It Happened to *Me*

"The more we scientize life, the more we try to find causal reasons for everything, the more fearful we become. The more afraid we become."
—FRED ALAN WOLF, PH. D.[1]

"You have a little cancer in your thyroid."

My mind reeled, even as I snorted at the surgical oncologist's odd choice of words. A *little* cancer? What exactly was a *little* cancer? Was this supposed to reduce my fear, the idea that only a *little* tiny smidgeon of cancer was invading my neck, *my body*? Like a little green monster instead of . . . Instead of what? Instead of what my cancer would surely grow into, if it didn't kill me first?

My mind skittered and balked as the physician on the other end of the phone line droned on about surgery, medical tests, drugs, everything I was devoted to avoiding. I hadn't even reached for an aspirin in years! I'd reluctantly agreed to the biopsies only after two years of pleading by my best friend, a Harvard physician. She was worried about the two tiny lumps that had appeared in my neck and on my breast after my pregnancy. I had simply chalked them up to hormonal changes. After all, I was a healthy person, I'd always *been* a healthy person.

What the doctor on the phone was prescribing didn't apply to *me*. How could it?

In the years since I had left my job at Harvard's School of Public Health, where I wrote books and textbooks, newspaper columns and magazine articles on healthy living, my attitude toward the medical system I once supported had gradually changed. Despite my conservative training as a nutrition educator, schooled in the sovereignty of the four basic food groups, I found myself shopping at health-food stores for organic products, avoiding meats, drinking herbal teas. And when I was eight months into my pregnancy, my husband and I left our obstetrician in favor of a midwife, who calmly delivered our ten-pound baby boy in the comfort of our family room.

In my evolution away from the medical establishment, I found I was not alone. A lot of my fellow baby boomers, elderly people I knew, savvy twenty-somethings, seemed to be thinking along similar lines. We were not radical, just disillusioned. The medical system could not guarantee us the health and vitality we desired. Perhaps it was up to us to take more responsibility for our bodies, to take our health into our own hands.

So there I was, a committed convert to self-help health, listening to a cancer specialist's report on my biopsies: "The breast lump was benign. The lump on your neck, however, was malignant."

What an ugly word, *malignant*. I felt overwhelmed with guilt. Had I caused my ugly cancer to appear on my neck like some overgrown barnacle? Was I a malignant personality harboring some sick, unconscious wish for premature death? If I was responsible for my good health, was I also creating this disease?

The surgeon put me on hold. As I waited for his secretary to pick up, to schedule yet another appointment at our local South Florida cancer center, I remembered the strange woman I had met there on the day of my biopsies. The psychic woman, who appeared to know things about me, things I didn't know about myself. "You are perfectly healthy," the gravel-voiced, middle-aged stranger in the starched lab coat informed me, as if I had asked for her diagnosis rather than simply wandering into her vicinity in front of the treatment facility. "*They* will fill you with fear. Don't listen to them, it's just their business. *You* are the one who creates your reality. And *you* are fine."

At the time, I had no idea who this rather intrusive person was, or whether she was even sane. Yet, her words instantly relaxed me. I was bone-chilled and shaking after undergoing the two outpatient biopsies, even though the surgeon had appeared unconcerned. He reassured me that the pea-size breast lump was a common, benign "fibroadenoma" from breast feeding (which I had been doing quite relentlessly for almost two years). And he was almost certain the swelling of the lymph node in my neck was a side effect of delayed dental work, postponed during my pregnancy (when novocaine was a no-no). But the invasiveness of the procedures, the cold steel of the operating table, the aloofness of the doctors chitchatting about taxes as they cut into my trembling body, all of this had driven me outside the building, seeking the warm embrace of tropical humidity and the calming whisper of palm trees.

And that's where I met her: Nancy sat alone on a plastic bench, dragging on a cigarette and jangling the dozen bangle bracelets on her tanned wrist as she tossed her smoking filter to the ground. I wondered how she could work at a cancer center and avoid feeling hypocritical about her nicotine intake. Later, I would discover that Nancy did not believe in most of the tenets of her employer, nor of the world of organized medicine. In fact, Nancy does not believe most of what our world holds to be true. She doesn't even believe she is *from* our world. She claims to hail from a different world entirely, another planet, a healing planet with a race of people who have come here, to Earth, to help *us* heal. To help us save our bodies, ourselves, from self-destruction.

Nonsense, you say. Ridiculous! Who would listen to some nutcase pseudo-alien in a lab coat when a highly qualified surgical oncologist tells you that you must treat your "papillary carcinoma of the thyroid" with:

- Major surgery—removal of the entire thyroid gland, a butterfly-shaped organ attached to the esophagus;
- Hormone replacement—a lifelong intake program of synthetic thyroid hormones;

- Radioactive dye—ingested (after surgery) to destroy circulating thyroid cells;
- Chest X rays and full-body scans—on a regular basis; and
- Checkups—weekly, progressing to biannually.

As I write this, I am perfectly healthy. But I chose not to undergo the battery of tests and aggressive procedures advised by the surgical oncologist for my "little cancer." Instead, I chose a different path to health. A very, *very* different path.

You can read about my unusual healing experiences in Chapter 17. Nancy, who became a kind of guide for me into the "other world," was only the first person I would meet from what I discovered to be a surprisingly large subgroup of the population who believe in the presence of otherworldly beings here in our midst. Some of these believers have had contact with otherworldly beings, some initiate such contact, and some—like Nancy—feel that they are *of* this other world. "Starseeds" is the popular term for these people, individuals who sense that they may have lived out lifetimes on other planets or in other dimensions before being born on this Earth. Starseeds may suddenly, dramatically come to such a self-revelation, or they can gradually begin to realize this spiritual self-truth. Most believe that they have a "mission" to accomplish during this Earth-bound lifetime, typically through being of service to other people. Many healers are starseeds, or so they believe.

On the day I first met Nancy on the hospital bench under the coconut palms, I had never heard of starseeds. But I instinctively felt as if I could trust the exotic-looking woman with the dangly earrings shaped like golden hands and the warm, throaty laugh. I didn't trust modern medicine, but I trusted Nancy when she advised me that it was I, not the frightening and complex world of modern medicine, who held my future in my own hands.

Nancy ground the cigarette butt under the heel of her navy clog, waved good-bye with a jingle of bracelets, and disappeared through the tinted glass doors of the cancer center. The things she had said made sense to me, they just *felt right*. Eventually, I would discover that her way, the otherworldly, spiritual path, was indeed the *right way for me*.

I took a risk in selecting the otherworldly path. A big risk. My physician friend thinks I'm crazy. But the way I look at it is this: Doctors are not gods. They can treat our bodies, we must cure our own souls. And my cancer was, I believe, a cry from my soul, which manifested in physical form as a means to capture my attention, to open my eyes to *a new way of being*.

There were things in my life that needed attention at that time, *desperately*. But I was ignoring all of the signals, the anger and restlessness, the building resentment. For the first time in almost twenty years, I was not writing. I was breast feeding on demand, and the demand was continuous. I became preoccupied with the physical body, mine and my son's:

What did I eat that made him colicky? Was he eating enough; was I? Was he coming down with something, getting enough fresh air, sleeping well . . . In obsessing over the physical details involved in being the "best mother on Earth," I had forgotten about my *spiritual* life and the role of our spirits, mine and my son's, in our everyday lives. No wonder I felt trapped, stifled, ready to scream. Disgusted with myself that I was not one of those placid "Earth mother" types, I tried to ignore my growing unhappiness.

But I could not ignore the cancer diagnosis.

Suddenly, I was *forced* to take a good, hard look at my life and ask the ultimate existential questions: What am I doing here? What *is* my purpose anyway? Is there some other way for me to live? Do I have a spiritual path, and if so, how do I get on it?

I took action: I went to see a family counselor with a spiritual approach to therapy; I networked with the alternative health people, talking to nutritionists and herbalists; I obtained a second, third, and fourth opinion from my physician friend's colleagues at Harvard; I read the latest medical research on my particular diagnosis, all of the pertinent studies on the treatment options for this type of cancer; I made an appointment with an alternative doctor, a former cardiovascular surgeon who had studied with Maharishi Mahesh Yogi, following in the footsteps of Deepak Chopra; I experienced celestial healing.* And

---

*For the sake of clarity and inclusiveness, I will use the terms "celestial(s)" and "celestial healing(s)" to refer to extraterrestrial, extradimensional, mystical, and spiritual entities and sources.

I began to question the "coincidence" of a cancer diagnosis at age forty-one, *the exact age my mother was when she learned she had terminal cancer.*

There were many factors contributing to my disease. If I went ahead and had my thyroid gland removed while continuing to ignore the psychospiritual issues that needed my attention, how long would it be before *another* illness appeared? Probably not long. And I knew that I would spend the interlude between diagnoses mesmerized by fear—of cancer, of death, of my own future.

My therapist helped me to separate my own life from that of my mother, with whom my *fate as a mother* had become confused. The alternative health network informed me about noninvasive remedies for cancer, while the research studies and doctors' reports clarified my understanding of the physiological causes of my particular type of cancer. (As I had originally suspected, the hormonal changes of pregnancy and breast feeding had undoubtedly played a role in the multiplication of cancerous cells in my thyroid gland, which the swollen lymph node was attempting to collect and dispose of; this was why it had enlarged to a noticeable degree.) I began to accept that I had cancer while learning to live with that knowledge—without succumbing to the mind-numbing influence of abject fear.

Through Nancy, I experienced my first "celestial healing." My thyroid gland was scanned and a cobalt blue light of high vibrational frequency was utilized during a channeled session of extraterrestrial (or ET) healing energy conducted by both Nancy and her healer friend, Ingrid [see Chapters 11 and 12]. Nancy also referred me to a trance medium, a "conscious channeler," who specifically channels some celestial healers known as the Arcturians. [You can read a transcript of my healing session with these beings in Chapter 17.] After these brief, painless, and rather intriguing sessions of celestial healing, I visited the alternative physician for my first checkup. Following a thorough exam, the doctor, a burly, bearded man with the build of a weight lifter and the bedside manner of a psychotherapist rather than one of the busiest M.D.s in South Florida, wrote out a list of "prescriptions." My self-administered therapy was to include daily meditation, prayer (to any deity or Universal Force of goodness), several herbal preparations, and a few vitamin supplements. We also discussed my career and family situation, and the doctor provided some rather lengthy personal advice that I can best summarize as "Get a life" and "Do what you love." When I asked what I needed to do about my thyroid gland, the doctor regarded me with his cool blue eyes. "There is nothing wrong with your thyroid gland," he said matter-of-factly.

Nancy had predicted this amazing new diagnosis. "If a doctor examines your thyroid gland," she informed me following the blue light scan she had conducted with Ingrid during their channeled celestial healing, "he won't see anything wrong with it. *Nothing.*" Once again, Nancy's words rang true. I felt sure at this point that I was on the right path, the *best healing path for me*.

Following the doctor's prescription, I learned to meditate using the Transcendental Meditation (TM) method, and I began meditating twice a day. I began to pray daily, too, teaching my son his own special prayer to say before dinner. I drank special herbal teas, and gulped down spoonfuls of an herbal nectar that resembled black peanut butter. I took my vitamins. I stopped breast feeding. (My son, nearing his second birthday, took it like a "big boy.") I started to write again, rearranging the house to create office space for myself. I went out for long walks, enjoying the surreal blue sky and marveling at the lush greenery of a tropical spring. I laughed a lot more, obsessed a lot less. And I came to terms with my mother's premature death, an issue I had carefully avoided confronting for over twenty-five years. I finally realized that if I failed to deal with the psychological imprint of that devastating childhood trauma, then *it* would deal with *me*—in a way that was redundantly, even fatally devastating.

I continue to see the alternative M.D., and the reports are consistently good. I consider myself to be cancer-free, and very, *very* lucky. Not only because I am healthy, but also because *I have changed my life*. I stopped ignoring the inner voice, the cry of my soul. And I have opened my eyes: There is a *lot* more to "see" when you shed the blinders and old fears and look beyond the obsessions of everyday life.

Many strange events have occurred since I met

Nancy and opened up my life to the possibility of extraterrestrial communication and contact. I cannot say that I have been as brave as I might like to be about this. In fact, there was a span of time in which my family and I felt *very* frightened, awakening every night to inexplicably loud humming noises, blinding lights without any visible source, and dreamlike apparitions. But I have also experienced some wildly incredible, extremely vivid dreams and visions involving strange but *nonfrightening* beings. I once would have referred to such experiences as weird flights of imagination. Now I am not so sure, and am tempted to classify such experiences as extraterrestrial, rather than fantastical, in origin. [I include a checklist for readers in the Appendix, for those interested in determining if they, too, might be extraterrestrial contact experiencers.]

So, did I crack up, go nuts, lose my *mind* due to the stress of the cancer diagnosis? Is all of this extraterrestrial business a bizarre method for me to deny the threat of a horrible, possibly fatal disease? Perhaps. Yet, in embarking on this alternative, *very* alternative healing path, I am not alone. Along this revolutionary road to good health *and transformed consciousness*, I have met others like myself. In fact, I have discovered that people all over the world are finding a new healing path *as part of an otherworldly journey*. I am but one of many.

Now, I did not simply place myself naively in the hands of a bunch of extraterrestrials. First, I very carefully researched the topic of medical healings associated with UFOs and/or contact with extraterrestrials or celestial beings. Since I had had absolutely zero interest in the topic of UFOs prior to this, I began my studies with an open, if uninformed, mind: I had never watched *The X-Files*, I was not a fan of *Star Trek*, I had avoided reading science fiction (except for a few of the classics like *Brave New World* and *On the Beach*), I had never even *heard* of the popular TV show on UFOs, *Sightings*, and I purposely avoided seeing the smash-hit movie *Independence Day*. No interest.

But once I began to read through the available *scientific* literature on UFO history and accounts of contact with extraterrestrials and celestial beings, I became convinced that *something is going on*. There are too many well-documented cases in which upstanding, intelligent, sane people have reported sighting a UFO and/or experiencing some sort of interaction with beings that are quite obviously from somewhere else, some other world. And a number of these people have reported healings, finding themselves cured of various medical conditions ranging from the most minor cuts and burns to fatal diseases such as cancer. [See Chapter 16 for brief recounts of some of these amazing healings.]

I was intrigued, and curious about these people who had experienced healing visits from otherworldly beings. Had *all* of these people cracked up, gone nuts, lost *their* minds, too? I decided to find out.

In the fall of 1997, I began to search for people willing to be interviewed about this, people who claimed to have been healed of physical ailments or dysfunctions by encounters with UFOs and/or celestial beings. It was easier than I thought it would be to find such people, everyday people like ourselves, normal folk who have experienced some *very* abnormal things—and found themselves healed afterward. I was surprised that mainly through word of mouth, I was able to meet more than a dozen such people within a short period of time. I also found that a number of these people *had become healers themselves,* an ability they attributed to their contact with the otherworldly beings. [See Part I.] I met other people with unusual healing skills as well, people who were working directly with what they called "extraterrestrial healing energies" in order to help others heal. [See Part II.] I talked to the experts, ufologists and therapists who work with people who believe they have experienced contact with beings from other planets, other galaxies, other dimensions—and, as a result, have been cured of various ailments. [See Chapters 14 and 15 for interviews with two of the leading experts.] The experts are convinced, too, that *something is going on.* In fact, some believe that *millions of Americans are extraterrestrial contact experiencers,* all experiencing (but not all reporting) similar symptoms, signs, and situations. The ET contact phenomenon is *worldwide,* and people all over the globe have reported experiencing ET-related healings.

Still, no one seems to know: Exactly *what* is actually going on for the growing numbers of people who seem to be "experiencers" of healing extraterrestrial, otherworldly, and/or spirit world communications and experiences? Theories abound [see Chapter 19], but the answer is far from clear. Even the experiencers themselves claim to have only *part* of the answer to a question that may dominate and dramatically change their lives.

I cannot say that I learned "the truth," or discovered exactly how I was healed or why others are experiencing inexplicable medical recoveries through what they believe to be celestial intervention. But in researching this book, I did find that all of the experiencers I talked to had stopped being afraid—of illness, of the unknown, of their own futures and the fate of our world. The experiencers I met had been *healed from fear*. So I knew that I had something very important to learn from them.

The celestial healing phenomenon is a potentially rich source of information about our physical bodies and our spiritual selves, and about our role in the universe as healthy beings. But we must be ready to acknowledge that we really do not understand how nature works, and recognize that we are not privy to many of nature's secrets. After all, we have yet to fully understand the mechanisms for sleep and consciousness, pain and healing. Nor do we know the full power of our own self-healing forces, our inner natures and their recuperative abilities. As a secular society and a science-worshiping culture, we are in denial regarding the existence of *one fundamental healing force*. Instead, we turn to thousands of little "cures" found on the shelves of pharmacies and health-food stores.

The cases of celestial healing I share with you in this book bring all of our modern medical practices into question: What *really* creates healing? It would be tempting to try to squeeze the celestial healing phenomenon into a small-minded conventional explanation, which may feel comfortable, if inadequate and incomplete. Otherwise, we must accept the idea that life includes far more than we once believed. If we push ourselves even further, stretching our minds to encompass a larger, more cosmic worldview, we can actually pass through the boundaries of fear that limit our growth as spiritual beings and restrict us from a fuller perception of reality.

An attempt to accomplish this psychospiritual challenge is daunting, possibly scary or deeply troubling. All spiritual growth is disturbing, however, once we actually acknowledge the reality of the nonmaterial world, rich with the unknown—including otherworldly beings and new domains of existence.

In completing my research on the matter, I have come to believe that the celestial healing phenomenon is the most fascinating and inexplicable example of psychosomatic cure, comparable only to spontaneous remission. By psychosomatic, I mean that the process involves the utilization of one's own inner psychospiritual forces to alter the function and/or integrity of the physical body. I believe that whether or not it will one day be proven to be "real," celestial healing is certainly worthy of our attention. If it is indeed literally true, that is, hundreds or even thousands of people have been healed of medical conditions by extraterrestrial or extradimensional forces, the discovery will be world-shattering in its effect on science and medicine—as well as every other aspect of contemporary civilization. But even if it is *not* literally true, that is, the individuals who have been healed are simply creating their experiences in their own minds, the phenomenon can still be seen as highly remarkable. What does this ability say about the human potential for self-healing through a simple belief in a more intelligent healing force? What does it tell us about our own potential for healing ourselves?

Over the past few years, I have enjoyed a unique opportunity: I have talked at great length with a number of extraterrestrial encounter experiencers, individuals who have been healed and/or have become healers due to what they believe is contact with otherworldly beings. They have shared their extraordinary stories with me, and agreed to be included in this book. And *every one of these experiencers chose **not** to keep their identity a secret*, although some asked to preserve the privacy of a spouse or work place. I see these brave, honest individuals as *a representative sample* of the many, many cases that have occurred throughout history, which includes a secret UFO history full of healing extraterrestrial encounters.

That people believe they are healed is, for me, adequate clinical validity. I have not attempted to "prove" that their experiences really happened. I am simply presenting them to you as case studies, accounts of people who have experienced what they believe to be "celestial healings." You can, after reading these reports, make your own conclusions.

It is my personal belief and strong hope that these inspirational stories of celestial healings will trigger a public outpouring of similar stories, events kept hidden for fear of ridicule, incidents ignored or forgotten for years. Until now. Because *now* is the time for all of us to admit, remember, or at least consider the broader perspective: a new millennium overview of reality that includes more than the limited, three-dimensional, socially sanctioned way of seeing ourselves, our bodies, our health, and our lives.

People everywhere in ever-increasing numbers are experiencing and talking about celestial healing. You just might find yourself wishing it could happen to you, too. [If so, Chapter 18 provides guidelines for inviting celestial experiences into your life.] At the very least, these interviews might inspire you to change your life a "little." As I have.

PART I

It Happened
to *Us*

"They who dream by day are cognizant of many things which escape those who dream only at night. In their gray visions they obtain glimpses of eternity, and thrill, in waking, to find that they have been on the verge of a great secret."
—EDGAR ALLAN POE,
"Eleanora"

CHAPTER 1

Lynne Plaskett:
Cancer Cure

A resident of New Smyrna Beach, a lovely coastal town just south of Daytona Beach, Florida, Lynne Plaskett is a respected leader in her community, where she is known for her activism in the preservation of natural resources. She is also a vocal advocate for the less fortunate and has served on a number of community service committees including the Council on Aging, Commission on the Status of Women, and Habitat for Humanity. Lynne was elected a county councilwoman for Volusia County in 1994. For the past ten years, she has worked full time as the assistant director of Community Development for the nearby city of Edgewater.

An artist and writer, Lynne has published poetry and songs. She co-authored a play that was staged at the Los Angeles Performing Arts Theatre. She is currently writing a memoir. With husband Bill, a journeyman lineman, Lynne has six children. She is forty-seven years old.

Lynne was the first experiencer I interviewed for this book. Over a long weekend in 1997, my family and I drove up the east coast of Florida to Lynne's log cabin-style home nestled in a forested glen a few miles from the interstate highway. I felt nervous, unsure as to what this woman would be like. In 1996, there had been quite a bit of publicity throughout the state while Lynne was running for reelection to her county council seat because she had appeared on national television, openly discussing her UFO experience and celestial healing. At the time, I was not very interested in extraterrestrial matters, but I remembered Lynne's bravery and willingness to risk her career. (She lost the election.)

As soon as Lynne opened the screen door, my anxiety about meeting an ET experiencer rapidly diminished. A warm, energetic woman, Lynne welcomed us into her cozy home, introducing us to several talkative children, her smiling husband, two large dogs, and, later on, some hyper turkeys and cuddly bunnies kept in big pens in the spacious backyard. While my son played with her six-year-old on a huge blue trampoline under the massive oak trees, Lynne and I talked. Here is her story in her own words.

I am the eldest of six children, and my mother raised all of us on her own. We were pretty poor, but we were happy and did not realize that we were poor.

When I married the father of my oldest child Clifford, we moved to Santa Barbara. The marriage didn't work out, so we separated. My mother, brother, and sisters had moved to Long Beach, where my sister Kathy and I decided to get an apartment together. Kathy was working the night shift in a doughnut shop, and I was going to school full time during the day to learn mechanical engineering. My sister is a wonderful person and she loved Clifford, so our living arrangement worked out real well.

In May of 1975, when I was one month shy of my twenty-fifth birthday, I went to the walk-in clinic at UCLA Medical Center to get my annual Pap smear done so that I could refill my prescription for birth control pills. It was a zoo, swarming with people, a gray place with a cold and uncaring roll-'em-in-and-roll-'em-out atmosphere. I thought, *Thank God I only have to go through this once a year.*

One day soon after, I received a postcard in the mail indicating that there was something wrong with my Pap test results and that I needed to contact my doctor right away. I went back to the clinic, where they did a biopsy, taking a little sample of tissue from the cervix.

The results were conclusive. I had cervical cancer.

I was pretty frightened. The doctor explained that they would do a procedure called a "cone biopsy," excising a large section of the cervix (shaped like a cone), hopefully to remove all of the cancerous material. But just in case the cancer had infiltrated my womb, the doctor said to prepare myself for a possible hysterectomy.

"How do I do that?" I asked. I was twenty-four years old! Even though I didn't want any more children at the time as I was a single mother, I still felt confused. When somebody tells you they're going to take all you have, you start having second thoughts. I got *really* frightened, and went home feeling dazed and sorry for myself.

My sister Kathy agreed to watch Clifford, who was only three, for the time that I would need in the hospital. I checked in early and underwent chest X rays, blood tests, a physical exam, another physical exam, and another . . . We were scheduled to go into surgery the next day, but the doctors came into my room and asked me some strange questions.

"Have you been feeling tired lately?" one asked. When I said, "No, not really," they all looked at each other.

"How long have you had that lump in your neck?" another doctor asked. I said, "What lump?" I hadn't noticed it, the swollen lymph node just above my right collarbone, because it was just under the skin and barely visible.

"We see something unusual in your chest X ray," one of the doctors told me. "So we're going to postpone your operation for a couple of days. We need to make sure you're otherwise in good health before we perform surgery." I thought, *What else could possibly go wrong?*

Two days later, they performed the cervical cone biopsy and took a sample of the lymph node at the same time. Then they rolled me into a room with five other female patients. One woman had had her stomach and part of her bladder removed. Another had had brain surgery. My case seemed minor in comparison.

The doctors dropped by during their rounds. An intern introduced himself and another doctor, the chief oncology resident, who said, "Lynne, we have some good news and some bad news. What news do you want to hear first?" I said, "The good news, I guess." So they told me that they did not need to perform the hysterectomy, that all of the cancerous tissue was removed with the cone biopsy. Tears filled my eyes as I thanked them. "But the surgeon indicated you will never have children due to extensive ovarian scar tissue," they added.

Then they told me the bad news.

The biopsy of the lymph node indicated that I had *another* cancer of some sort. And when a specialist looked at my X rays, there was a malignant tumor in my lungs. Other tests showed cancer in my kidneys, spleen, liver, and bone marrow. They concluded that I had a then-rare form of cancer called "convoluted T-cell lymphoma."* They said it was typically a childhood cancer, and they had never seen it in an adult before. The three cases they were aware of were infants at New York Children's Hospital. The doctors indicated that they would contact the New York doctors to try to figure out how to treat my case.

"In the meantime," I said, "I've got this *disease*. What are you going to *do* for me? What are my *chances*?" The intern responded, "To be perfectly

---

*Also known as lymphoblastic lymphoma and convoluted T-lymphoblastic lymphoma, this is one of several varieties of lymphomas in which cancer infiltrates the lymphatic system. Currently less rare and more treatable than in 1975, this cancer occurs most commonly in young people and typically has resulted in an average life expectancy of one year. New treatment protocols have led to improvements in the overall prognosis of this type of cancer.[1]—Au.

honest with you, we think you have about three months left."

I said, "*What?*"

The doctors explained that the cancer had progressed and that it was a very aggressive type of cancer. It had already infiltrated my entire body except for, possibly, my stomach and brain.

"Wait a minute," I said. "I just came in here for some birth control pills and you're telling me I have *three months to live*? Are you sure you don't have the wrong person? I have no symptoms. I'm not tired. I don't feel sick. I just don't understand! This is too much for me to fathom."

They were very considerate. They explained a lot of it to me, or tried to. And they said they needed to get a protocol set up for me, to see if they could do *something* for me, at least to prolong my life a *little*.

I was thinking, *My God!* Of course, I started crying. The intern sat and held my hand. He actually had tears in his eyes. I think it was the first time he'd had to tell somebody as young as I was that they were going to die. He sat with me for quite a while, comforting me, talking.

Then I told him I had to go home. He said, "Lynne, you *can't* go home. You need to stay in the hospital. You're a very sick woman." I told him I had a three-year-old son at home: "I've got arrangements to make for my son, things I need to clear up. And I'll need to grieve in private. I can't sit here and grieve in a room full of strangers. I need my privacy right now."

Of course, it was against hospital regulations. I would have to sign out against medical advice. He said, "You've really got to let us try to help you. If you leave, your chances are slim to none."

I said, "But I need to go home for *just one night*." I was begging him. He said he would see what he could do.

When he returned later, he told me that I could go home for the night. But I had to promise to return early the next morning. "You have to promise me that you'll return before the 7:00 A.M. shift change," he said. I guess there was a certain time period for "outings," and if the patient was gone for longer, they would be automatically discharged from the hospital.

So I promised. I called my sister and told her I was coming home, that the cone biopsy had been "a success." I decided to tell her the rest in person when I got there. I was thinking that I would just go home, sit down and explain everything to Kathy, and we would work something out.

When I got home, nobody was there. I started pacing around the apartment. I was really beside myself. I sketched a picture of myself, of how I felt inside. I sat and stared out the window. I felt so *lonely*. Finally, I went into the bedroom I shared with Clifford, to lie down and wait for them.

The bedroom was small, just big enough for twin beds, a small table, and a dresser. There was a large sliding-glass window, maybe two by four feet wide, which was open. I began to cry. Hard. Then I was moaning. I have never cried like that in my entire life, before or since that day. It was coming from the depths, the bowels of my soul.

At first, I was crying for myself. I was thinking, *What have I done to deserve this? I'm a good person. Things like this aren't* supposed *to happen to people who have a good heart and try to do the right thing.*

After I finished crying for myself, I began to cry for my son. I looked at his empty bed, the neat array of stuffed animals. I was thinking, *What about* him? *He's too young to understand. When I die, all he's going to remember is that I left him. And I'm all he has! It is just so unfair.*

I probably cried for several hours. I was completely exhausted. It was getting dark by the time I was all cried out. I just lay there, feeling numb.

Then I became aware of a humming sound, an electrical buzzing type of noise. It seemed to be emanating from the wall behind my head. It sounded like a small generator or other piece of machinery. I assumed it was one of the neighbors, working on something.

The room began to fill up with foglike smoke. It was gradual, so I lay there thinking, *Maybe I need to get up and close the window.* But as the fog thickened into a dense white cloud, I realized that my body was paralyzed. I couldn't move; it was as if I were frozen in time. It was weird because I knew something was happening to me—I didn't understand what it was, but *I wasn't afraid.* I felt *completely* relaxed. There was no fear whatsoever.

By this time, the whole room was engulfed in this cold white fog. I tried to focus on the ceiling light fixture, but I couldn't see it. The next thing I knew, my body was levitating off the bed! I levitated up around a foot.

All of a sudden, something came in through the window. It was a disk-shaped object, about eight to ten inches across, four to six inches tall, with a slightly raised top. It looked like a Frisbee, only much thicker. It had little rectangular openings like windows around the edge, which were radiating different colors: yellow, red, blue, green. The disk was gyrating slowly in a counterclockwise direction. It was just above my head, hovering.

I was looking *right at this thing* and it was stationary for a moment. Through the little windows, I could see these soft lights. Then the disk began to move, slowly. It moved from my head down to my feet, almost in a scanning motion, then it moved back up again. It scanned from head to toe and back again three times, but never actually touched me.

For some unknown reason, there was no sense of fear, anxiety, or even concern. I felt so completely *relaxed*.

After scanning my body, the disk left through the window, just the way it had come in. The smoke dissipated, and I was gently lowered back onto my bed. The humming sound vanished.

All sense of time had completely escaped me. I had no idea if hours had passed or mere seconds. But a kind of "veil of security" seemed to fall upon me. I felt tranquil, serene. So, I just rolled over and went to sleep. I knew everything was going to be all right.

I woke up the next morning and went out onto the balcony. The sky was azure, the most exquisite shade of blue I'd ever seen. The air was fresh, fragrant with flowers. I felt revitalized, and humble in the face of nature's beauty. I also felt completely refreshed.

Kathy and Clifford had not returned. I telephoned my mother, who said they had spent the night with her. I asked her to meet me at the hospital, where the doctors could explain everything to her. Then I rushed back to the hospital. I didn't want to get the intern in trouble.

When the oncologist came by on his rounds, I told him, "You know what? I'm not going to die. I'm telling you right now, *I am not going to die.* I'm going to be fine."

He looked at me carefully and said, "Yeah, okay, Lynne." He was just pacifying me, as if to say, "Whatever works for you is fine. And now we're going to proceed."

Perhaps I didn't recall at the time what had happened the night before, because I'm sure I would have shared that with him. Years later, when I asked the oncologist if he remembered me telling him about my experience, he said no. I thought I *had* told him, but he certainly would have remembered if I had. He *did* recall that I said I wasn't going to die.

The doctors got a protocol of drugs from New

York Children's Hospital. It was chemotherapy, so some of the drugs had been used with other types of cancer. But some of the drugs they were going to try on me were purely experimental. They warned me about some of the complications that might occur.

So I asked them, "If I take all of these experimental drugs you want me to take, how long are you going to give me to live?" And they said that, based on the chemotherapy results with the babies in New York, I could possibly live almost a year.

A *year*? *But*, I thought, *what do I have to lose*? I agreed to take the drugs. All of them.

Within two days of the night I'd spent at home, the tumor in my chest had been drastically reduced. But the doctors did not tell me this. I began some of the chemotherapy a few days later.

Within four months, I was in complete remission.

Some of the drugs they used made me so *sick*. It was as if I'd been abducted by the American Medical Association! It was as if they had, with my permission, abducted me and were performing experiments on me. And I was getting *deathly* ill from the drugs they were giving me. I had never felt sick at all from the disease! But the chemotherapy was making me sicker and sicker. I lost all my hair. My reflexes were gone . . . But, within a four-month period, I was in *total* remission.

The doctors were extremely surprised. They were pleased. After four months of their horrendous treatment, I asked the oncologist if the chemotherapy had cured me. And he said, "Lynne, I have to be honest with you. In my professional opinion, 99.9 percent of your cure was your mental attitude toward the disease. Because you said early on that you were simply *not* going to die."

I went back to school full time. I graduated in the top ten of my class, and the California State Department of Rehabilitation gave me an award: Rehabilitant of the Year. I was totally surprised.

My life returned to normal. I entered the work force, remarried in 1978, and moved to Florida. Bill and I had two more children (Bill had three when we met, so we raised the six kids together). I had been told over and over that I would not have any more children, so the doctors couldn't figure it out.

One evening in 1981, I was sitting in my living room reading a book. The TV was on, and I was half listening to some magazine program. There were two gentlemen on the show who claimed they had been abducted by a UFO. They also claimed to have made a tape recording of what they called the "mother ship," which had hovered over their boat while they were fishing. They played the tape on TV.

I sat straight up in my chair. It was the *exact same sound* I'd heard in my bedroom that night back in May of 1975. And then I knew: I said, "Oh, my God! *That's* what it was!" And this was the very first time I had connected what had happened that night to any sort of reality whatsoever. That was when I finally realized the disk was an unidentified flying object, or *something extraterrestrial in nature*.

Until that night in 1981, I had no idea what my

experience with the disk was about. When I'd told other people, family members and a few friends, they had said, "Maybe it was an angel," or "Maybe it was God, coming to you in the only form you would accept." I was open to all *kinds* of explanations, because I had no *idea* what it was. Until that night in 1981: The connection was made *instantaneously* at that point, and I knew *exactly* what had happened. It was like the lightbulb came on. And I said, "Oh, so *that's* what happened to me."

Kathy later confirmed that she had heard the humming sound, too. She had returned to the apartment with Clifford and, opening the front door, heard a "loud, electrical type noise. And *something* told me: DON'T GO IN," Kathy explained. "So I said to Clifford, 'Let's go over to Grandma's.'" We had never talked about this because it had simply never come up.

I cannot say that I know why the UFO healing experience happened to me. But I do know there's a reason. And since that night in 1975, other things have happened to me. Things have happened over the years that I did not connect to that experience until recently. Now, with all the research I have done on this topic, I realize that *I was given a gift*. I was *saved, for a reason*. Part of that reason is, I believe, to share my story with the world.

My experience was a very positive one, but I told very few people about it. How do you tell people you believe you've been cured of cancer by a UFO without having them think you're crazy? In 1996, a producer at the *Maury Povitch Show* called me. They were doing a show on abductions and begged me to appear. I said, "Look, I'm in the middle of a reelection campaign for the county council. I *really* don't think it would be a good time for me to appear on your show." But I discussed the idea with my family, and everyone encouraged me to do it.

In September of 1996, I went on the show and told my story. I "came out" publicly because I know that if it had not been for my UFO experience, I would not be here today. I know that in my heart. In my case, I know that my experience was 99.9 percent responsible for my recovery from what was, at that time, a rare and fatal form of cancer. I was given a *gift*.

People ask if I have any way of getting in contact with these beings. (I hate the word "alien." It's so degrading.) But I never saw any beings. I saw this disk. And I cannot say what it was, except that I now know it was extraterrestrial in essence because some wonderful things have happened to me as a result of that experience. I was healed. I also developed an ability to "see" things in order to help people. For example, when a person is missing something, I know where their lost things are. I can tell a person whether or not they will get a job they've applied for. I can do things like this. I don't make it a practice, or do it for just anybody. But I was given this gift of "sight" in conjunction with the healing experience. And it has helped in a lot of circumstances.

Another gift is a healing *ability*. For example, if one

of my children had an ear infection, I'd lay my hand on them and concentrate. And *take the pain away*. For so long, I thought this ability to heal was a natural ability that *all* mothers had. Now I see it as a gift as well.

A couple of months ago, I went to the doctor for a chest X ray. I'm a healthy person, considering the fact that I smoke. (Well, I know it's not good for me. But I've been smoking cigarettes since I was twelve years old.) The doctor showed me my X ray. He said, "Look at this. There is no scar from the malignant tumor.[2] And there's no indication here that you smoke. No sign whatsoever."

I am learning more and more every day about the gifts that have been bestowed on me since the healing experience almost twenty-five years ago. And I believe that coming forward to tell my story is not the end for me, there's still something else that I'm supposed to do. I'm not sure yet what that is. What I do know is, it's not over yet!

CHAPTER 2

John Hunter Gray: "Medical Boosts"

John Hunter Gray is a sociologist, community organizer, and well-known specialist in race/cultural relations and UFO/ET encounters. The former chairman of the Indian Studies Department at the University of North Dakota, Gray's career has encompassed multiethnic organizing, civil rights organizing, and community organizing for American Indians. His father was Micmac/Abenaki/Mohawk Indian, his mother Scottish.

In the 1960s, Gray, then known as John R. Salter, Jr. (he legally changed his name in 1995 to honor a Native American ancestral name), served as the organizer of Mississippi's "Jackson Movement," one of America's first massive nonviolent civil rights protests. As chronicled in the 1996 movie *Ghosts of Mississippi* (and Gray's own book, *Jackson, Mississippi*), the movement was beset by violence, leading to the murder of civil rights leader Medgar Evers. One of the last to see Evers alive, Gray himself was the target of violence, beaten four times by police and local whites, his house shot up by "night riders." At the famous Woolworth sit-in in 1963, Gray, who was on the faculty of a nearby black college, and two of his students were beaten and smeared with condiments at a breakfast counter while FBI agents looked on.

Gray has received numerous honors and awards for his social justice work, including the North Dakota Martin Luther King, Jr. Award for Social Justice Activities. He speaks regularly at colleges and universities and is frequently interviewed in the media about social justice issues, Native American history and sociology, and occasionally UFOs and ETs. A native of Arizona, Gray now lives in Idaho with his wife, Eldri. They have four children and eight grandchildren. He is sixty-four years old.

These days, John Gray is exceedingly careful about agreeing to conduct interviews on the subject of his personal experiences with ETs. He feels he has been too often misquoted and misrepresented in the media, so he usually restricts his public discussions on celestial matters to academic forums and a few select media appearances. When I first contacted John, he politely refused to be interviewed for this book. Only after I reassured him that the focus of the book and the UFO/ET experiences discussed would be positive and healing in nature did he agree to participate. A soft-spoken man, John Hunter Gray combines the engaging storytelling of a good teacher with the analytical skills of a sociologist when he recounts the credible, incredible events of his own celestial healings.

I state candidly at the outset that I see the ET visitors, the so-called alien humanoids, as friendly and with positive motivations and beneficial effects. I am inclined also to see them as essentially one race, quite similar to ourselves in many ways, but a good jump ahead evolution-wise. Based on my own experiences and on direct and collateral contact with hundreds of other experiencers, I view the ETs as friendly but understandably cautious given our "challenging" world.

As a long-term community organizer, I can see that like all good organizers the ETs are working at the grassroots level. I very much believe they are involved in a long-term endeavor that involves:

1. Helping some people on Earth "keep on keeping on" in the save-the-world business, sharpening our social justice sensitivity; and
2. Sensitizing humanity on a step-by-step basis to the presence of friendly ET life in our solar neighborhood with whom we will ultimately interact.[1]

But let me say that if you had asked me on the morning of March 20, 1988, if I thought there was "something out there," I would have said, "Probably, maybe; but I don't really know." *I didn't really give a damn about it* one way or the other.

On March 20, 1988, I left North Dakota with my then twenty-three-year-old son, John III, for a speaking trip in Mississippi and Louisiana. Several days before our departure, I had, quite uncharacteristically (because I am *always* a straight-line, no-dallying driver), decided to proceed through the lonely, isolated, narrow and winding roads of the rugged Mississippi River hill country of southwestern Wisconsin. In retrospect, it was clear that the route I had picked some days before for the first day of our junket was certainly *not* logical.

When we were at LaCrosse late that first afternoon, we were fully awake, vigorous, well fed, with myself driving. Our firm and clear intent was to keep on the chosen route. But then, once into that isolated setting, episodes of gentle, double amnesia began, and we were further diverted onto roads even more illogical and eventually obscure. Matters culminated in the late afternoon and early evening with ninety minutes of missing time in the darkened woods near Richland Center, Wisconsin.

The next morning, we had a close-up and fully conscious sighting of a UFO spacecraft five miles east of Peoria, Illinois. At 10:14 A.M., there was no traffic around us or ahead of us in either direction. And it was then that we both saw a bright, expanding light coming toward us from the sky above and directly ahead of us. Immediately, we realized it was an incredibly bright object, glowing with extraordinary shimmering silveriness. (The closest analogy I can make is the glowing coals of an oak fire, moving back and forth.) It was two-thirds the size of the full double highway. When about two hundred yards from us, it swerved slightly and rose over our pickup truck at an angle. We could now make out its saucerlike form and, I think, slight dome. Then, with incredible speed, it was gone.[2]

At that point, my son and I had several simultaneous thoughts: We saw this sighting as a deliberate appearance for our benefit, and ours alone; we saw it as quite friendly; and we felt that it somehow explained the bewildering occurrences of the previous night.

I then remembered the only UFO situation I had ever read a bit about: the Betty and Barney Hill encounter of 1961, which I had read about primarily because I was interested in the interracial nature of their marriage.* At the time, I was only casually interested in their UFO experience but, impressed by the first-rate character of the Hills, I always remembered their friendly encounter with ETs.[3] (Soon after our own experience, I wrote to Betty Hill and she has since become a close friend of our family.)

It is obvious that these encounters of ours—and I believe this to be the case with most, if not all, people—were specifically selective, anything *except* random, and necessitated a good deal of careful planning and gentle maneuvering by the ETs.

About ninety days after the March encounters, I began a spontaneous recall, which moved forward in a vivid and orderly fashion. In due course, my son's recall commenced. Our respective recalls, which mesh with and complement one another's, clearly indicate that the bulk of our ninety minutes of missing time involved the following events:

---

*Perhaps the most famous of the UFO abductees, Barney was black, a member of the New Hampshire Civil Rights Commission, his wife Betty a white social worker. Their abduction story first appeared in *Look* magazine in 1966, and later that year as the book *Interrupted Journey*. (See References, page 317.)—Au.

As the four-lane highway ends and total amnesia envelops us, we are gently but firmly forced off the highway onto a very narrow and extremely rough road. We park the pickup near the upper far end of this winding, timbered road.

Then we are standing, John III and I, not far from the passenger's side of the pickup. It is almost dark. Completely at ease, I can see two or three small humanoid figures climbing on the back bumper looking at the gear in the back of the truck. Up close, they are four to four and one-half feet tall with thin bodies and limbs, but with comparatively large heads and conspicuously large quasi-slanted eyes. There are several of these small people around us, perhaps six or seven; and a taller, humanoid figure almost as tall as I (six feet) and not as proportionately thin as the others.

Our communication with them is telepathically specific. John III sits down. Three of the small humanoids gather around, viewing him with as much fascination as he does them. Everyone is very pleasant.

Now we are walking through the darkening woods, up a ravine and over a small ridge to the UFO that is in a rather secluded clearing some distance from the pickup.

Throughout this entire (and still-continuing) recall process of mine is the clear, persistent, definite sense of a brightly lit room illuminated with a kind of white light, and a deep blue glowing panel. An implant is placed very carefully up into my right nostril and well beyond . . . There is now an injection into my neck at the thyroid area, and then an injection into my upper center chest (thymus gland).*

The feeling is very powerful that the meeting has gone very well indeed—from everyone's standpoint. Our tall humanoid friend walks with me back through the woods to the pickup. I feel an extremely strong, poignant sense of farewell toward the tall figure, sensing equally strong reciprocity. The tall figure and I tell each other that we will see one another again in another place in another time. I know that I have a very special relationship with the tall humanoid. (Let me point out here that whenever races and cultures begin to come together, half-breeds play very important, often very critical, intermediary "go-between" roles. I'm a half-breed Indian myself.)

Now John III and I are by ourselves in the pickup. We wait. Very shortly, from his window, John III watches the brightly lit UFO rise and move diagonally up into the dark clouds and beyond. We drive a short distance to the end of the road, and take the highway back to the road into Richland Center.

We both feel that double amnesia was briefly induced once again at that time in order that we, still somewhat somnambulistic, would pass through the

*The thyroid gland, located in the front of the neck, produces hormones that maintain normal growth and metabolism. The thymus gland, located below the thyroid in the upper chest, helps to regulate the body's immune system and may be involved in the aging process.—Au.

business section without stopping and perhaps attracting negative attention.[4]

Since then, there has been another encounter that involved John III and myself, this time in Montana. In early July of 1997, my son and I took the first long trip that we had taken together, just the two of us, since the March 1988 encounter. We traveled from Grand Forks to Idaho, where I have many family roots and connections. I purchased an excellent home way up on a mountain slope, then we headed back to Grand Forks.

By the time we passed through Billings, Montana, it was 11:35 P.M. I was driving, feeling wide awake. Some very strange things began to occur after that, among them an odd light that followed us from about one-half hour out of Billings onward. I became dazed, and John worried about an impending UFO encounter. We both felt very strange during this time.

Suddenly, I noticed that according to the road signs we were making extremely poor time, even though I was driving between fifty-eight and sixty-five mph, mostly sixty-five. And somewhere in all of this was a weird blue light in the trees above the highway.

We pulled into a rest stop and I checked my watch: 1:45 A.M. We knew that an ET experience had occurred, someway, somehow. We both felt good about it, although I had an upset stomach that persisted well into the next day. We continued on to North Dakota. Later, in checking, we found that it had taken us two hours and ten minutes to travel seventy-one miles!

Both John and I now feel that an encounter began about a half hour out of Billings, around the time the odd light appeared, and that this encounter lasted for about an hour. It probably took place on one of the several little rural roads off of the isolated section of the interstate we were traveling on. We have reason to believe there were cursory physical exams and medical boosts, resulting essentially in a strengthening of the beneficial effects from the 1988 encounter.

In a very clear, vivid recall dream I experienced six months later:

> John and I are meeting with several ETs, one taller than the rest, all wearing white. We are outside of the pickup truck on a darkened dirt road. For a moment, I am apprehensive, but only moderately so. Then I feel an extremely powerful sense of friendly well-being coming from them.

We are both fine now, couldn't be better. And we continue to see the ETs as friendly, sensitive, and considerate.

In due course, it became clear to me that I had had three previous close encounter experiences: late May 1957, in rural Arizona when I was twenty-three; early August 1952, in rural Arizona when I was eighteen; late summer 1941, in rural Kansas when I was seven. As far as we know, my son John III had not had any encounters prior to our experience in 1988. Since the 1988 UFO encounter experience, a great deal of recall has occurred for me. Some of this has involved the three previously submerged encounters. John III has also had much recall. We both see all of this, including the ETs, their motivations and their effects, as very positive. We certainly hope and expect to see them again.

After the 1988 encounter, a number of physiological changes occurred in me. These changes began to unfold in 1988, and all have continued to this day. My son has experienced several of these changes as well. In addition, he grew more than an inch (despite being twenty-three years of age at the time of the ET episode). We both see all of these physical changes as positive, good indeed. In fact, I have not needed the professional services of any doctor for these past ten years, and have had no colds or flu of any substance.

Here is a list of the physical changes I have experienced, and it is still current:

1. My head hair grows much faster than my previous normal rate—at least twice as fast.
2. My eyebrows have grown much thicker, and darker.
3. Hair has grown over my previously hairless (or almost hairless) body areas—arms, legs, stomach, chest—and continues to grow still, at a slower rate.
4. I now have a very dark beard (i.e., "five o'clock shadow") that I did not have in any sense before 1988, but that occurred rapidly; I noticed it by late in that year.

5. My fingernails and toenails are growing two to three times faster than my previous normal rate; now I must cut my fingernails at least once a week.

6. I have grown about one-half inch taller. (Also, my feet grew a full size from 13D to 14D in the months following the 1997 encounter.)

7. Cuts and scratches clot almost immediately and heal very fast; my gums bled every day from 1984 until soon after the 1988 encounter, when they cleared up for good.

8. Residual disfigurement on the right side of my face (which stemmed from an auto wreck in 1963 when there was an attempt on my life during the Jackson Movement) completely faded as of the spring of 1989.

9. My skin tone improved quickly, most skin spots disappearing completely, along with several scars.

10. I've never had many wrinkles, but those I did have faded completely and did not reappear.

11. My skin is much healthier in general; plus, my face and neck area have slimmed (as has my entire body to some extent) without any sagging skin.

12. My circulation has improved dramatically.

13. My eyesight—always good at a distance, not so good as the years passed with regard to reading—improved slowly after the encounter and is still improving.

14. After more than thirty-five years of heavy

smoking, I quit (in May 1989) with no physical or psychological difficulties of any kind.

15. Interestingly, my protein needs increased substantially, as did my desire for green vegetables, especially peas and broccoli; my fondness for buttermilk also increased.

16. After 1988, I have had much more energy.

17. My immunity is greatly heightened, especially with respect to colds and flus (heavy stuff in North Dakota and Idaho!), and I have had *no illnesses* since the 1988 encounter.

18. I had suffered from a bad sinus condition, which cleared up soon after the 1988 encounter and became a very minor problem.

Another change is this: Ever since I was very small, I have felt "psychic," and my abilities in this regard have been noticed by many people throughout the years; ever since the 1988 encounter, my psychic abilities—telepathy, clairvoyance, precognition, telekinesis—have all increased dramatically. The most dramatic jump in psychic abilities after each of my encounters has been in the telekinesis dimension. But all of these abilities increased with each encounter, and are still increasing.[5]

After the 1988 encounter, I began talking openly about my UFO experiences. Most of the people I met or heard from who had experienced convincing UFO close encounters shared my positive view. In fact, virtually all of the many persons from whom I've heard since I began speaking about my own encounters, probably about 225 contacts, have been *overwhelmingly positive* in their perceptions of the ET encounter experience, and see their encounters as quite friendly. So I am certain that the ETs' motives are positive. They like us. But, like us, they do have their own self-interest. To them, we're the bad kids on the block. They're doing some social work here.

Physically, emotionally, and intellectually, the ETs are, I believe, very similar to ourselves. (Obviously, they are ahead of us in an evolutionary sense.) So there is much racism being exhibited in the public fear of UFOs/ETs. "Gloom and doomers" use the term "abduction" with regard to encounters—on television, in print, etc. Some "abductees" refer to the "aliens" as "so ugly." This reminds one of just how racist some human views can be.[6]

It seems very probable that the social/political system or systems of the ETs are democratic and strike a balance between collective and individual well-being, drawing from the best of the group and from the best of individual creativity. They could never have accomplished what they have attained and are attaining if there existed a totalitarian mentality, or an individualistic mentality of the cutthroat fashion. They are distinctive individual personalities, working together to achieve common goals.

There is no question in my mind about a relationship, an encouraging relationship, between my ET encounters and my social justice work. Most of the close encounter experiencers I've heard from are also involved in meaningful social justice pursuits, that is, enhancement of the human condition with respect to material, libertarian, and spiritual factors; environmentally and ecologically positive activities; formulation of nonviolent approaches to human problems. Of course, many people involved in social justice have never had ET encounters, and some experiencers are not given to social justice endeavors. At least, not yet. But one should not wait for a UFO encounter to do justice work. And one's labors need not be dramatic.

Ultimately, the ETs can offer us many things, among them health advances and much longer life spans, which in turn will help the human race to mature. One of the most valuable gifts from the ETs would be insight into balancing collective and individual well-being. And we can, I'm sure, offer *them* many worthwhile gifts, both tangible and intangible. Those of us who have been fortunate enough to have experienced UFO close encounters should not focus primarily on what these experiences have done for us as individuals, but on how we can take what we have been given, what we are and what we are becoming, and use all of that to make things better around us.[7]

CHAPTER 3

Mary Kerfoot:
"Alien Psychosis"

A systems analyst for a large international corporation, Mary Kerfoot holds graduate degrees in psychology and mathematics. She helped to found and now coordinates a support group for close encounter experiencers in the Chicago area. She is also the executive director for Operation Right to Know, a political activist group that pushes for public disclosure of government-withheld UFO information. The mother of two grown children, Mary is fifty-six years old and lives in a suburb of Chicago.

When she heard about this book project from another experiencer, Mary was immediately interested in participating and telephoned me at once. I was impressed with her intelligence, wit, and generosity: She agreed to conduct our interviews late at night, after her ten-hour workdays had ended. Somewhat sleepy, I listened carefully as Mary struggled to choose the right words to express her complete thoughts on spirituality, sanity, and healing the body and soul.

My contact experiences have not been of the nature that you read about in many of the popular books on UFO close encounters. I have not experienced, as far as I know, any kind of medical exams or experiments. And I have not been taken against my will. I have used hypnosis every week for a couple of years, and *nothing* like that has come out. I can't remember anything even *remotely* like an abduction.

Healing incidents are *very* common with UFO experiencers. People report them all the time. But certain researchers do not want to hear this. They want to believe that it is like the "Stockholm syndrome," that we are "identifying with our captors" and simply want to *believe* we are being healed. But the medical profession *is* acknowledging these kinds of "miracle healings," recognizing the fact that they are significant even though we may not understand them.

I can recall having three different healing-type experiences. The first one I see as a preventative type of healing, and it is very complicated. It occurred when I was a child and is part of the first memories I have of life. The other two, more recent incidents are much simpler.

The first fairly recent incident was in June of 1994, after my right eye was removed in a Chicago hospital because of a series of traumas to it. From about the age of sixteen, I exhibited symptoms of keratoconus, a disorder in which the cornea of the eye pokes out. It is like when you put your finger inside a balloon and the balloon projects outward. The vision is very distorted. The only way the vision can be corrected is with contact lenses, and after that a corneal transplant may be required. I had *four* corneal transplants, due to graft rejections. Then I was pruning some lilac bushes one day, and I leaned forward and ran into a bulb. I lacerated the cornea and iris, so I needed *another* corneal transplant. But the eye just gave up. It was shot. It began to atrophy and it was looking horrendous. I required a new eye.

After surgery, I was brought from the recovery room into my hospital room. I began to notice these puffs of air that seemed to be delivered to the eye socket. I remembered some instructions I'd been given, instructions not to be alarmed when I felt the puffs of air. So I figured the doctors were doing this to help the healing process. Then I began to hear a ticking sound inside my head. That *really* alarmed me because, I thought, *I don't remember* any *instructions about an alarm clock.* But I thought, *Well, maybe it's something to keep the puffs of air delivered at regular intervals.* It never occurred to me that I might possibly be hallucinating, because I was very alert.

A day later, I was released. I went back to the hospital the day after that for a checkup. Now, the way they do artificial eyes nowadays is that they put some sort of acrylic ball in the socket. A plastic shell rests on that, and the eye muscles are attached to the ball. In my case, they took a section of tissue from my hip and placed it in front of the acrylic ball and attached the muscles to that. The theory is that the blood vessels in the tissue will vascularize this ball, because it is porous, and it will all knit into one integrated piece so that the muscles will work the ball.

Well, the oculoplastic surgeon was quite amazed at the degree of healing that had taken place. He looked at the ball and the tissue and said, "This is a miracle! The ball is eighty-five percent vascularized. It generally takes three *weeks* to progress this far."

I said, "Oh, I think that's because of your instructions about the puffs of air." And he said, "What puffs of air?" I said, "Well, there were these puffs of air . . ." And he said, "No, we didn't give you any puffs of air. And I didn't give you any instructions either."

I remembered then that the instructions had come to me in some kind of faraway state, and I began to realize that the otherworldly beings were somehow responsible for the puffs of air. I asked the surgeon, "If doctors were to devise some way of delivering puffs of air or oxygen to the eye socket, would healing be promoted?" And he said, "Yes. *Dramatically.*"

The doctor believes that my experience was an hallucination associated with the anesthesia used during surgery. But I know the experience was real.

I still have the keratoconus in my left eye. The right eye is doing all right, but I'm having a hard time getting a good fit with an acrylic shell. Plus, there was a loss of fatty tissue around the orbit, so I needed plastic surgery to build that up. But I'm getting along fine.

The other recent incident took place in November of 1996. Three of us—two other experiencers and myself—decided to try to make contact with the beings. These other two people have had a lot of conscious awareness of their encounter experiences, as I have. We had been wanting to make contact for some time. We all finally decided to do it. We felt we were at the point where we were ready to *initiate* contact and not just be acted upon. And it worked remarkably well! We were astounded at everything that happened, it was like one thing after another that evening.

Now, leading up to that contact session, I had acquired this rash. I'd had it for about a year prior to that encounter, but it would come and go, getting much, much worse in times of stress. Even if it was not inflamed, it would always be there as a reddish, raised place on my inner arms and the tops of my forearms, and on my neck. And that night, I was scratching like crazy. I had actually mutilated my arms, they were bleeding and very badly scratched. And I kept scratching them that night.

I guess I was feeling a lot of anxiety because the presence of the beings was really *very* apparent, even before we started the contact session. My dog was showing signs of nervousness, exploring the house with her little tail between her legs. And the bird was very, *very* hyper. I have a cockatoo named Toby. He was pacing back and forth on his perch saying "UFO" (a word he picked up somehow) and making this kind of undulating sound. He was anticipating the appearance of the beings.

We tried to stay awake all night, but either dozed

off or went into altered states from time to time. About 3:30 A.M., we all began to concentrate again on communicating with these beings. Very shortly after that, I started to go into an altered state. I felt the floor begin to vibrate, and I felt as if I were moving. One of the other people was almost being dragged away and I felt very worried for him. The other person was just staring straight ahead, she was totally zoned out, and there was an orange ball of light over her. I was awake, but I was in an altered state, a very strange state.

From the perspective of the man, what he saw was an orange bubble that had encased my upper body— shoulders, arms, neck, and head. Even though my eyes were open and I was awake, I was not aware of a bubble being over me. What happened when we all came out of the altered state was a very remarkable thing: After coming out of this bubble, it was like *I had new skin.* All of the scratch marks and bleeding, *everything* was cleared up. It was just like baby-soft skin!

So, *something* happened. I don't know *what.*

The rash eventually came back, after a couple of weeks. So that was not a permanent cure. And the unfortunate thing is, I don't know how any of this works. Just that it happens.

My early healing-type experiences are complicated, and have been more like a training in nature. Starting at about the age of two and one-half, these training experiences dealt with learning reality for *this* time and place. It sounds unusual, but it was a training to learn *this* reality, in *this* time, and to stay focused on *this* place, this *reality*. That way, when I was shown something that was not real or not defined as real by that experience, I knew how to know the difference and to hold on to what *is* real. I haven't heard anybody talk about *anything* like this, but this is what my early experiences were about.

I always came away from these experiences with a sense of what I called "the real one." I talked about "the real one" a lot. I was afraid that if I did not learn reality and how to stay focused, I would go mad. I was afraid of this even as a two-and-one-half-year-old!

"The real one" wasn't a person, but signified the real versus a pale imitation. From time to time when I would be outside playing, as a child younger than five, I would suddenly see a little boy and girl about my own age on the sidewalk. I called them "the wooden people" because they had no affective state, no emotions. And I just *knew* they had not learned reality and they had not learned how to be human. I was terrified. It was like a lesson in what would happen if I did not learn how to be human and learn how to stay focused on *this* reality.

What seemed to happen to me as a child is that impressions from a past existence were bleeding through. Apparently, the memories were not closed off for me, unlike for most children. But I *knew* I had to be normal. And that I had to *work* at it. BUT . . . I got assistance. I got assistance from these beings, who drove the point home for me: *I had no option* but to be normal. Normal in *every* human way.

Mostly, I don't remember what they looked like. But I remember seeing actual beings from time to time. The very first incident, when I was around two and one-half, occurred when I was in bed. I was lying there, facing a tall window, when suddenly a bright white light appeared. And there was a figure out there. I instantly went into this conditioned terror response. It's a really unique kind of terror that I only experienced as a child confronted with either the bright white light or some kind of figure.

The next thing I remember is being *shown* a raggedy old man looking in the window at me and holding up a lantern that gave off a pale yellow glow. I was supposed to believe *that* was what I had seen, instead of the other figure and the bright white light. But what I was to learn was the *difference* between my real experience and this imitation experience I was supposed to believe. It was like a training in differentiating screen images from reality, learning the difference between the pale imitation and "the real one," and staying focused on reality.

Then, about three years ago, I was driving home in my car when I suddenly began to relive what it was I was afraid of as a child: I was so terrified of that madness that I would have done *anything* to avoid experiencing it. When I actually relived it, I understood why, and why it had been such a motivating and driving factor for me. It was an *undescribably* horrendous state. If you were to take all of the different kinds of abnormal psychological states and subject a single person to all of these, the experience would pale in comparison to this kind of madness. And I experienced it for only a few *seconds*. But I felt the aftereffects for *weeks*. I called it an "alien psychosis." Because it was not human.

Yet, I knew it was mine. I knew that at some prior time I had been in that state of madness. And it was just horrendous. I felt as if I were a grain of sand in a huge, immense nothingness, with a sense of not being anchored to anything, free-floating with nothing else except myself as this microscopic *thing*. It is so hard to describe how absolutely *terrible* this madness, this alien psychosis, feels.

I've actually given up trying to tell people about it. Because every time I have, they've assumed what I'm trying to say is that I'm *psychotic*, or fear that I'll *become* psychotic, or that I've *been* psychotic. And that isn't the case at all.

Now, as an adult, I've come to realize that I *am* normal and I don't have to fear this madness. I'm not even sure that a human being *could* experience such a mental state. Because *it isn't human.*

In the last few years, I've gotten into consciousness research, which led me to research on neuroscience and the brain, which led to research on schizophrenia. In reading about the symptoms of schizophrenia, I've begun to see just how many of the experiences that close encounter experiencers report sound exactly like the reports coming from schizophrenics. I've been trying to figure out what the difference is between the two. The typical schizophrenic patient seems to be experiencing a heightened sense of everything that comes into their mental framework. *Everything* they sense is very heightened, very accentuated. Even when drugs are used to tone this down, their experiences may not be as exaggerated, but are still, at times, very bizarre. I feel that the schizophrenic patient is open to input from *all kinds of realities*, not just this one that we call "now" and "here." But I have no way of proving this.

This research, however, did help me to realize what the beings were assisting *me* with. Because when I was young, I seemed to be much more open to everything coming in, too. Not just from the past, but from all kinds of other dimensions and realities. Even now, as an adult, I've been aware from time to time of myself coexisting in this dimension and in another simultaneously. But I can still see that I am *here*. I can differentiate *this* reality from others that may be impinging on me. For the schizophrenic, even if the input is toned down with drugs, it's still bizarre, because they don't seem to have the built-in sense of differentiation. And if I had not had my training, this very *rigorous, intense* training throughout my childhood, I could have ended up like that, too.

In August of 1991, this yellow light came into my bedroom. Up until that point in time, I really did not want to remember any more about my encounter experiences than I already knew. After that night, however, my life changed 180 degrees because, in the morning, I *had* to remember. I felt as if I had to *immerse* myself in it. I read everything I could about the topic, and I joined MUFON (Mutual UFO Network) and other groups for UFO experiencers. And in 1994, I started organizing "Awareness" programs in Chicago to promote public awareness of the facts about UFO-related issues, bringing in well-known speakers and talking to the media. As executive director of Operation Right to Know, I help to get petitions out to our Congress people and to the president, demanding that the government release information on UFOs to the public. We demonstrate quite a bit, too. We were at the White House in the summer of '92 and the spring of '93, and we're making plans for '99 now.

I've slowed down recently. Now I'm researching and writing. I've done a lot of research on modern physics, consciousness, and the connection with extraordinary experiences. My own set of experiences and all the questions I have about them has led me to do a lot of reading in physics, especially the physics of higher dimensional space. I've studied Riemann's theories of higher dimensional space. Georg Friedrich Bernhard Riemann was a very brilliant mathematician in the early to mid-1800s. He proved the existence of ten dimensions, and as far as I know, that proof still stands. Most of the research in modern physics these days deals with problems in dimensional space. There's a branch of mathematics, too, that deals with the behavior of objects in higher dimensional space.

Many of the extraordinary experiences I've had dealt with making connections or relationships with other life forms in other dimensions and other realities. I am using the theories of Riemann and modern physics that deal with hyperspace in order to show how they build a bridge to consciousness because, during so many of the experiences I have had, I've been aware of my consciousness *going*, and going into *some other reality*.

This has caused me to think about dissociative disorders, too. For the most part, mental health professionals will use this diagnosis without any understanding of where the person is *going* when they dissociate. I have been very aware of my consciousness—whereas a lot of people have never felt their consciousness take flight—and this has provided me with input that I primarily see as relative to schizophrenia, but also possibly to multiple personality disorder and other dissociative disorders. I want to establish the basis for other dimensions and flights of consciousness. Once I can establish a scientific foundation for this, then I can provide experiential material to illustrate as practical applications of these theories of physics.

For example, in May of 1994, there was an incident involving an otherworldly being. For a day before the incident, I had been experiencing a lot of anxiety in response to a letter from my friend "Ed." The day of the incident, my anxiety level was extremely high. All I could do was to get into bed that night and just curl up into a ball. I just lay in bed, awake.

I was facing the windows and watching the full moon rise. It eventually rose out of sight. Shortly after, another moon took its place. This object resembled the first one *in every way.* Now I'm not even sure the first object was a real moon. I'd assumed it was, because it was a full moon night.

I was startled to see the second moon, but I was able to convince myself that maybe the moon *could* come back. It is so easy to do this at times. When your reality is *seriously* challenged, you can believe the most ludicrous things! Your mind tries to keep everything in balance.

The object began to move from pane to pane, and began moving closer. Then it began to expand and contract. I was beginning to get the sense that although it was identical to the first object, it *couldn't* be the moon. And suddenly, it shot right through the window at me. It was like a white-hot baseball that passed through the glass and the window fan, passing through just like they weren't there.

At first, I held up my arms to protect myself because the light was coming right at me and I thought it was going to hit me. But then, I *recognized* it. I definitely recognized this white light. I don't know as *what*, now. But it was like something that I had dealt with a lot. And I began to embrace the light. Only, I could get just so close. There was like a force field emanating from it, and intense pressure, so my arms could only get so close.

I began talking to the intense white light. I just

started saying, "Please take care of 'Ed.' Please take care of 'Ed.' Thank you, thank you, thank you."

As I said, "Thank you," all of the horrendous anxiety I had been suffering from just instantly drained away. Instantly! Never in my life have I felt like such a whole person. I was in a world where nothing existed besides myself and the light. There was no rest of the world. There was only me and the light. Physically, we were in the bedroom. *But we were not in the bedroom. We were in a place within a place.*

Then there's a gap. I don't have any awareness of how I moved into this next scene. But the next thing I knew, there was this small, golden ball of light about three feet from my head. Just staring at me. And I thought, *Yeah, I think that's "Ed."* Isn't that odd?

There have been instances reported by people who have also had these white-hot baseball-like lights shoot toward them. And then, the light or the ball sort of unfurls into some sort of being, like a light being of some kind. If I hadn't lost consciousness, perhaps I would have seen this being.

I did ask "Ed" about it later, and he didn't notice anything. So the only person who was helped was myself, which is kind of strange. But I *have* noticed that when one is concerned about others and is seeking help for someone else, often the beings will appear. And if you want something for yourself, often they won't.

One day not too long ago I was walking into my bathroom when I suddenly remembered and began to actually relive what it was like to be in the presence of what I call the "higher beings." It was very extraordinary. My first impression was the sense of oneness that I felt with these beings. It was timeless, with no beginning and no end, a kind of love that always was. It was like a union of spirit or soul with everything that is. The sense of security was indescribable. These beings have a love that can never end. They have transcended self. And because of this transcendence, there is no meaning to the word "death." This kind of love is much more abstract than our electrochemical type of love, and it doesn't have the excitement quality to it and the possessiveness that we feel. It even transcends what we call "unconditional love." Their love is not like ours at all. That's why it felt so secure to me. Their love is *forever*.

This is where human beings have to evolve. If we are to survive as a species, and if our planet is to survive, ultimately we will have to get to a point where we are no longer totally engrossed in self. On that day in my bathroom, this is what I saw: Whether we humans like it or not, *we will evolve* to that stage.

People I talk to about this, including some experiencers, feel that it means we must give up our individuality. And this is not the case at all. Not at all! It is a oneness of spirit, not of the individual mind.

It is hard for humans to see that there is individualism in other species. It is hard for us to comprehend anything but what *we* are. If it's not like us, we think it couldn't exist. Actually, I think this is why some of the beings I'm dealing with are here: to expand the consciousness of humankind. So that we realize that we are part of a *huge* cosmos teeming with life.

We are about to move out into space, we are ready to really explore space. But our spiritual and mental evolution is *so* underdeveloped! It's just not keeping up with our technology.

That is what I think the beings have been doing with me: assisting me in my spiritual and mental evolution, expanding my consciousness with the exposure I've had to other realities. I've seen *so much* in the contact experiences I've had. But it took a lot of prior training and care on the part of these beings, training that started in my childhood, so that I would be able to handle all that I've seen and still stay anchored in this world.

I see it as a kind of training in groundedness. Even though I was having very far-out experiences, I was being trained to stay anchored to *something*. I often wonder why it is that everybody who has had close encounter experiences has not gone through this same training. Unless they have but don't remember it.

Experiencers often have difficulty just *coping* with life. I've seen this in my support group. They find it difficult to hold a job, to try to stay normal, and to be productive. This can result just from having encounter experiences. Until the mental health community can get up to speed and start seeing the bigger picture, we are going to have trouble moving forward in our consciousness expansion.

Personally, I feel so *lucky.* I just feel fortunate to have had these kinds of extraordinary experiences, this kind of contact. And I feel so humbled, I guess by the whole thing. And by the fact that the beings have helped *me,* trained me in these ways.

One fellow in my support group—the same person who was at the contact session with me—relates how one time, when he was on a spacecraft and asked questions of the beings, he was told that "Many seeds are planted, but only a few come to fruition." He thought this meant that many "seeds" were defective, *physically* defective. But I think they were referring to growth and evolution. I think some of the beings help to nurture these "seeds" that they plant, and tend to them throughout their lives. *For some purpose.* And I think that purpose is to broaden and expand the consciousness and awareness of humanity.

CHAPTER 4

Connie Isele: Near-Fatal Accident and the "Rip in Time and Space"

Originally from California, Connie Isele began working on the Sacramento cable television series *UFO Connection* in 1993. That same year, she founded a support group for extraterrestrial encounter experiencers, with meetings held monthly in her home. Since her recovery from a near-fatal automobile accident in 1995, Connie has made some significant changes in her life. At age forty-two, she is now a newlywed and a college student majoring in psychology. She lives quietly in Colorado with her new husband and her teenage daughter by her first marriage.

Connie wrote to me after reading about my book project in a newsletter for experiencers. She included her address, but did not provide a phone number, and then she moved. And moved again. Her letter was intriguing and I felt that her story of celestial healing was an important one, so I spent several weeks attempting to track her down, leaving odd-sounding messages on a long chain of anonymous-sounding phone machines. Connie finally got the message, and our interview was on.

A youthful and high-spirited woman, Connie laughed

readily at the bizarre twists in her life story. She shared openly the pain as well as the humor of her varied experiences with the celestial beings who have so influenced—and possibly *saved*—her life.

Before 1992, I did not recognize the many unusual events of my life as being connected to the extraterrestrial phenomenon. I saw the subject of "beings from outer space" as tabloid hype, sci-fi, or mild madness. However, I did believe in angels and spirit beings because several childhood experiences had opened the door for such possibilities.

When I was around five years old, an angel came into my room one night. Now, I don't know whether the angel was a reality or a memory created by an overactive imagination, but when I was sixteen, I had another angelic experience. I was walking down a steep road at night in such a deep level of despair that I wanted to die. My hopelessness was overwhelming. As a large diesel truck whisked by, I thought, *There goes my chance. It could have hit me and all this pain would be gone.* From a distance, I heard another truck rumbling my way and I walked to the middle of the road.

A voice said, "Run! Run for the lights!" The road I was on led to a little mountain town, the streetlights a blur in the distance. I looked for the source of the voice, which was clearly *not* in my own head. But there was no one around. I looked toward the lit town ahead. "Run! Now!" said the voice. Suddenly, I realized what I was doing and sprinted to the side of the road. The truck whizzed past. I didn't stop running until I was safe beneath the streetlights of the town.

Another time, I heard the voice-not-inside-my-head say, "Love you." I was in bed alone and looked all around for the source of the voice. I even looked under the bed. By then I was totally awake and alert. "She heard us," said the voice, followed by a chorus of giggles.

Thus, my view of the universe had expanded enough to include angels and spirit beings. But my universal view did not include extraterrestrials. I never thought that beings from other planets could interact with humans in the complex, mysterious ways I had experienced for most of my life. So many of my own experiences defied logic, I passed them off as dreams but sometimes questioned my sanity. When the "dreams" began persistently seeping into my waking reality, however, it became increasingly difficult to ignore the oddities. By 1992, I could no longer deny that something truly bizarre was occurring, and not just in my mind. I needed some answers.

I decided to do some research, and began to seriously explore the extraterrestrial phenomenon. The reading material I found at the time was frightening. I was only able to move through the fear of negative possibilities, fear of the unknown, and fear of losing my marbles after I reached out to others who were having similar experiences. My fear finally turned into excitement as I began to look at the grander picture: I was being provided with an opportunity for learning and spiritual growth *through actual experience.* Eventually, I settled into the new reality I found myself in and marveled at the beauty of the mystery.

The ETs are not too pretty to look at, though. One being I see frequently has a hideous head he hides behind a bright glow, and a long thin torso that moves like an insect's body. He reminds me of a praying mantis. This being seems to be an advisor or teacher, whereas the "doctors" are short little beings.

Being examined or operated on by a human doctor is not exactly fun, so being examined or operated on by *nonhuman* doctors with big bald heads and big black eyes can be even more uncomfortable. Yet, I have no complaints. Most of the unpleasant parts of my experiences merely linger in the shadows of my unconscious, within a mental anesthesia of sorts, while the physical results of my experiences have been wondrous. I don't understand the methods behind or reasons for all that the extraterrestrials have done to me, but I certainly appreciate the benefits and comforts that have resulted from the procedures.

For example, in 1989, I received an ET "health checkup," during which they injected me with a clear gel, similar to white grape jelly. I was informed that this was for my benefit, that this was for healing. There were also lights involved in the procedure, but the memory is hazy and dreamlike. The jellylike substance was *very real*, however, and I had to wash it off in the shower when I awoke from the "dream."

I had been experiencing intense uterine cramping and discomfort before this "dream," and had made an appointment with my gynecologist. By the time of my scheduled visit, however, the symptoms had disappeared and the doctor found nothing wrong.

For the next eight years, I never caught a cold or flu.

In 1992, I attended my first UFO conference, a wonderful gathering of experiencers and explorers of the ET phenomenon. The speakers had the effect of taking out the sting and introducing the awe. Meeting others—some four hundred in attendance—who were experiencing the ETs helped me to understand that if I was indeed entering the world of insanity, I was not going alone!

As one of the speakers described something called "ET fingerprints," I glanced down at my knee with its three little bruises, perfectly spaced, just like fingerprints. The knee was arthritic, the result of torn cartilage surgically removed several years earlier. But from the day I spotted those fingerprints, I have not experienced even the *slightest* arthritic pain in that knee.

In November of 1993, my doctor informed me that I had cervical cancer. I reached out to friends from my ET experiencers' support group. Many were knowledgeable about alternative healing methods. One person projected energy from a distance, and I could actually *feel* it. Another flew from Arizona to my home in California to bring me a healing device, which smelled terrible, like ozone.* Someone else suggested that I ask the ETs to "fix" the cancer. I did not do so, however, because I wasn't sure how to ask. After all, the ETs don't just sit down and chat with me over coffee and cookies! But they did seem to be popping in quite often around that time, a few times a week, or so it seemed.

Maybe the ETs "fixed" the cancer, maybe not. Perhaps the love of my friends was enough to fix it. After my hysterectomy, the doctor told me the pathology report indicated that there was no cancer detected.

In November of 1995, I experienced another ET healing. This experience changed me in ways I cannot even explain. The changes were not just physical, but mental and, especially, spiritual.

My friend Dan was driving us home one cold night when our truck began skidding across an icy mountain bridge, spinning from one guardrail to the other. I envisioned us flying over the side of the bridge, but we didn't.

Or did we? I have a distinct memory of the truck flying off the highway bridge, falling toward the cliffs below. In midair, I saw what I understood to be a rip in time and space. A brilliant light coming from within this rip contrasted sharply with the black night sky. I felt myself enter the rip, where I met with light beings, each formed of little sparks of en-

---

*Encounter experiencers and people who see UFOs sometimes note an associated ozonelike odor.—Au.

ergy that glowed together to form a single entity. We communicated wordlessly. I noticed that I, too, was energy, without a body structure. This was oddly familiar to me.

Time and space were nonexistent in this place. It seemed as though I had always been there and would always be there. But I understood that the part of me that entered through the rip in space had to go back out again. I understood that a mistake had occurred and would be corrected. I understood so many things, which I seem to have forgotten. Much of the information I understood then does not pertain to this reality anyway.

Suddenly, I was back in the truck. It was as if no time had passed, but I had been gone for what seemed like an eternity. The truck was stalled near the end of the bridge, parallel to the guardrail. There was barely enough room for me to open the passenger door and squeeze my way out. We were inspecting the smashed truck when we heard another vehicle approaching.

One minute I was stepping toward the door of the truck, the next minute I was falling over the guardrail. The oncoming car had also slid on the ice, smashing into our truck, which then dragged me some eight feet before knocking me off the bridge. I fell about six feet onto a cliff below, landing next to a safety fence that saved me from rolling farther down the cliffside. If I had fallen off the bridge any sooner than I did, I would have dropped at least *four hundred feet.*

At the hospital, I was informed that my right leg would have to be removed in order to save my life. The chaplain spoke with me as if I were about to die. But I couldn't die, my daughter still needed me, with or without my leg! For the first time, I requested the aid of the ETs, adding, "If at all possible, I'd like to keep my leg."

It was an extraordinary feeling to wake up, alive. Out of the corner of my eye, I saw an ET, a very tall being with whom I was familiar. When I turned to look at him directly, he was no longer there. But I felt that he was watching over me, and that *he had done something inside my head.*

The nurse immediately reassured me that my leg was still there, pulling the covers aside so that I could see for myself. As grossly mangled and painful as it was, it was mine. My leg, my experience.

During my month-long stay at the hospital, the doctors called me their "little miracle" or "miracle legs."

A few months after the accident, I awoke for the first time without pain. My room smelled terrible, like ozone. Within a few hours, the aches and pain I was living with at the time returned.

As I recovered from the accident, I had a lot of time for deep thinking. I reevaluated my life. I learned to discipline my mind, to accept each day as it came, to appreciate the little things in life as gifts. I put my life in the hands of God. And I discovered that I had a new way of sensing, a new way of experiencing. Somehow I felt released from an emotional and spiritual prison. I became more tolerant, mellow, compassionate, intuitive. My previous life was shattered, a new one had begun.

Now, several years later, I walk without a limp. If not for the scars and occasional back pain, I could pass off the accident as a long, vivid dream.

Dan remembers seeing the rip in time and space, but he does not recall passing through it.

My daughter Cassie was fifteen at the time of the accident. She became a wonderful source of comfort for me, her hands better than pain pills. Cassie has healing hands. She also has vivid memories of ET encounters and UFO dreams, physical markings, 3:00 A.M. wake-ups, and other typical signs of ET experiences. [See Appendix.] A year ago, a female ET walked into Cassie's bedroom (*through* the wall and stereo) and my daughter was paralyzed with fear. But when the ET hugged her, my daughter says her fear eased. Cassie recalls meeting her red-haired ET sister with big "alien" eyes during the experience. When she was eleven years old, Cassie had a dream about being in a classroom where an ET was instructing the group of children on the structure of the universe and, she recalled, "many, many numbers."

The unusual experiences associated with extraterrestrial encounters have touched most of my family. My mother has conscious, vivid recall of ET experiences. My sister recalls some very disturbing experiences, but has been complaining recently of feeling "abandoned" because the ETs have not been around. My eight-year-old niece has been sharing her ET experiences since she was two and the "bunnies without ears" began taking her for rides in the "planes without wings." At age two, my niece was discovered floating facedown in the backyard pool. There was no water in her lungs. The little girl said that an "angel" was holding her up in the water, helping her to breathe.

Right now, I am pursuing a degree in psychology. My interest lies in emotional and spiritual healing, which plays a large role in physical healing. The body, mind, and soul are all intertwined, creating the perfect changes necessary. I have learned the healing power of touch. I have always believed in the power of prayer, but my understanding of how it works has changed. It is *the intention that moves energy*. The feeling of love is the energy that heals.

One time, I was waiting in the doctor's office with a fellow who had also been in an auto accident. He told me he was not doing well, and since several operations had failed, he would have to lose a leg. Naturally, I felt much empathy. Pretending to read a magazine, I sent him healing energy, praying for spiritual assistance. I could feel him rejecting the energy. He even got up from his chair to sit on the opposite side of the room. Later, I overheard two doctors trying to convince him that there were other options available other than amputating his leg.

Lately, I have noticed that ET communication often comes through to my consciousness in the form of my own thoughts. With everything mingled together, I am not sure which thoughts are truly my own. I believe that all my thoughts are *mine*, but may be formed due to previous discussions and agreements that I am not aware of consciously.

Occasionally, I find myself feeling very odd. I call this condition "la-la land," which may last for only an hour or for days. I find it difficult to function in la-la land, requiring much more concentration than normal. I may feel dizzy, my own voice sounding odd and distorted. Everything feels slower, my surroundings sharper and brighter, yet somehow distorted. *Reality* seems distorted, in sense and shape. I feel as if I am inside a fish bowl, looking out at a world I don't quite understand.

I believe that la-la land exists when I have each foot in two different dimensions at the same time, when there is so much ET activity that I slip back and forth too easily between worlds. I have learned to pay attention to random thoughts at such times as they often turn out to be premonitions. I am much more intuitive when I'm "gone," that is, in la-la land.

The frequency and intensity of this particular type of experience has mellowed lately to a slow hum. Now, when it occurs, I feel more like a simple airhead than like a stranger in my own environment.

More recently, I have been experiencing what I call "waking dreams," which occur suddenly, lasting for no more than fifteen minutes. During these experiences, it seems as if the veil that separates my waking memories from my dream memories drops away, creating a very different perspective on reality. New information floods in, too quickly for my brain to sort and file. I cannot create this "waking dream" state, but I am able to just let it happen whenever it does catch me by surprise.

So, am I glad that all of this has happened to me? That's like asking if I'm glad to be alive. At times, I still question the sanity of it all. But would I have it any other way? Not a chance. Through my ET experiences, I have gained many tools that continue to add new dimensions to the way I think, feel, and live. I am quite content.

Since recovering from the car accident, I find myself living as a normal human being. The contrast between my life before the accident and my current life is immense. Before, the ET phenomenon was my total focus, the business of being an ET experiencer was my full-time job. I traveled all over to meetings, organized annual picnics for experiencers, ran a support group, on and on. After the accident, I had no choice but to focus on my own healing. And I met a very normal, very grounded guy, now my husband, who helps me to stay grounded. Going to college, too, means that there is not much time left over for anything else.

But I am not so sure how long this quiet time in my life will last. During my experience in the rip in time and space, I understood that I would no longer need to struggle for survival, that all of my material and physical needs would be taken care of so that I could get on with what I came here to do. This has proven to be the case. But honestly, I still don't know exactly what it is that I am supposed to be doing.

One time, I received a very important message: "Everyone's got to go." I argued with this voice, saying out loud, "There's no way! Too many people are clueless!" Again, I heard the message, "Everyone's got to go."

I cannot even begin to explain all that I have learned because of this simple message. It is a very tall order, but I believe that it is the job of many of us to help the clueless get clued in. Hopefully, sharing my own healing ET experiences will be of some help in this regard.

CHAPTER 5

Ron Blevins:
Recovery from Depression
and Nightmares

Ron Blevins is of Native American descent and, at one time, resided on an Eastern Cherokee reservation in the Smoky Mountains of North Carolina. He now lives in northern Virginia, within ten miles of where he was born. Ron has been in the security business for some twenty years and currently works for a biomedical research firm in metropolitan Washington. He is forty-eight years old.

Ron agreed to an interview after hearing about the book project from his friend and fellow experiencer, Melanie Green [see Chapter 6]. A somewhat reserved person, Ron never seemed to fully relax during the course of our discussions, yet provided a detailed and richly revealing account in his orderly, precise, and matter-of-fact style.

I have been trained in the Native American traditional beliefs for most of my life. I have also had interactions with these "beings" for as far back as I can remember, beings who have communicated that their place of origin is the Alpha Centauri star system (which is some 4.3 light-years away, a close neighbor).* But I was not comfortable with them for years and years. And, even during times when I was not having one-on-one interactions with these beings, there were insistent periods of telepathic communication in which they were *trying* to communicate. This occurred, to different degrees, all of my life. Then, on September 14, 1989, a healing took place that was kind of remarkable.

I had served in the U.S. Army in the late 1960s, and spent 1970 in Vietnam. Like many others, I came back from Vietnam with some "adjustment problems," which developed into a fairly severe case of post-traumatic stress disorder. As a result of that and of the shift work I was doing at the time, I developed a very acute sleep disorder. I reached the point where I had not had a full night's sleep in over fifteen years: I could not sleep for more than a couple of hours without awakening from really horrific nightmares concerning events that had taken place in Vietnam.

Eventually, I was treated for this condition as an outpatient at the Veterans' Administration (VA) medical facility in Washington, D.C. I also had a severe skin disorder that I had picked up in Vietnam that was diagnosed as *tinear versicolor*.† This condition resulted in large red patches of skin that resembled burns on my torso, particularly on the chest and back, and in the neck area. Although they could not explain why I still had this condition so many years

---

*Alpha Centauri is a triple star, the closest star to us (next to our own sun).—Au.

†*Tinear versicolor* is a chronic fungal infection of the skin.—Au.

after returning from the tropics, the VA diagnosed it and prescribed several medications for it. None of them had an effect, and it continued to get worse.

The VA had just about given up on both counts, and the sleep problem had become so acute that it was definitely having an effect on my daily life. Acute sleep deprivation is a very serious thing, in that it begins to manifest various *other* symptoms during the day. I began to have uncontrolled blackouts for periods of time.

Now, this had gone on and become worse over a period of several years. It had affected my personal relationships. I was living with someone at the time who, between the nightmares and the other things, found it all rather overwhelming and moved out. So the whole situation had deteriorated up until September of 1989 to the point where I was very depressed, had not slept for extended periods of time, and was just at my wits' end.

Prior to this, I had not had a great deal of interaction with the beings for some time. This made the event that unfolded even more surprising.

One night, I found myself alone in my apartment with the lights out. I was sitting in the dark in a chair, trying to figure out where things were going to go from there. Things were falling apart around me, and I was trying to figure out something I could *do* to address these problems.

It is difficult to describe exactly what happened, but I thought perhaps I had passed out. At this point, I was using alcohol as a sedative and I had been drinking that evening, although I was not intoxicated. (After this experience, I immediately quit using alcohol as a sedative because it was no longer necessary.)

Suddenly, a light appeared in the room. I was amazed. It took me completely by surprise. And I was somewhat horrified to see in this light, standing in the room, one of the beings—a being I had seen off and on during my life, one of the *very tall extraterrestrial beings*.

These beings are not your typical four-foot "grays."* They are very tall, between six and seven feet. They are humanoid, but certainly not human in appearance. They are not thin. They are robust individuals with a very stocky or muscular build. Their appearance is almost intimidating; they have an *overwhelming* aura about them, they look somewhat fearsome. But this is because of their size and inhuman features, counteracted by a very solemn, *benign* approach in their interactions.

Their skin coloring tends to be a beige or light tan. They *do* have the typical large black eyes. Very, very *intense*, large, dark eyes. And they have a very distinctive, almost scaly appearance with raised ridges above the eyebrows and around the very small mouth opening. They have a hand that is not dissimilar to our own, but the fingers tend to be *much* longer. And the hand is much larger. They do have

---

*The "grays" are the extraterrestrial beings most often illustrated in the media: small, thin, four to five feet tall, grayish-skinned creatures with large heads and very large black eyes.—Au.

an opposable thumb. As I said, they're humanoid but not human.

To say the least, I was kind of shocked to see this being. And not a little bit terrified.

The being communicated telepathically with me. And it was as if I began to be shown a holographic screen or a holographic image, almost as though they were pointing a film projector at the wall. On this screen, I saw a series of images depicting the various nightmares I had been having. And the being was saying to me, "You know, this can be addressed. This need not happen."

At that point, I must have passed out (this is the only way I can describe it). Or perhaps I entered into a state of altered consciousness, because something occurred so that the nightmare images that were being shown on the wall changed, and it was as though *I was having the nightmare.* It was as though I was asleep and beginning to have one of the recurring nightmares.

I found myself in a dark alley, a blind alley that led to a dead end. I was looking out to the open end of the alley, the end that opened onto the street. It was night, and it was raining. I could see this crowd of people, the people from my nightmares all crowding into the open end of the alley.

The people in my nightmares were usually friends of mine who had died in Vietnam, or enemy soldiers who had been killed, all torn and mutilated as a result of their injuries. They would be walking in a very stiff way toward me. This is the nightmare that had been repeated, over and over again for years and years.

I realized instantly that there was no escape this time. I was obviously trapped.

At this point, I felt a presence behind me in the closed-off end of the alley. I turned and looked over my shoulder. It was this same being. And he said, "This need not occur any longer. We can address this." And then he said, "In order for you to address this problem, you must look to the real source of the problem. The real source of the problem is that *you have a distorted view of reality*. These people are not pursuing you. And *we* are not pursuing you. You have fled from them, and from us all your life. And you have reacted in fear to us all of your life. You must acknowledge the reality of what occurred there [in Vietnam]. And you must acknowledge our reality in order for us to assist you."

They use a very stilted, formal, telepathic type of language. The nature of their telepathic communications is very odd, very distinctive. The communications themselves are almost archaic. They use many expressions and structures of speech that relate more to Old English or the Middle Ages than to our present way of communicating ideas. They use a great many symbolic illustrations or parablelike expressions. [See example, Note 1, page 310.]

So, I was saying to myself, "There is no escape from this place. There is no escape from any of this. I've got the two greatest fears of my life here, hemming me in, in this alley!"

In desperation, I made a decision. I said, "What do I have to do to set things straight?"

The being replied, "You have to acknowledge our reality before we can assist you."

I said, "How do I do that?"

And he replied, "Human beings acknowledge what is real to them when it is real *to the touch*. Very simply, you have to touch one of us."

I'll be perfectly honest: These beings are *very* imposing in appearance. I hesitate to use the word "reptilian" because of the negative connotations, but this is the way *they* put it: They say that they have more physiological characteristics in common with a species similar to reptilian origin than mammalian origin. They do not call themselves reptilian. They seem to have features of both, reptiles *and* mammals, or they are related to what *we* would assign to these life forms. "Similar to" is the expression they use.

The being reached out his hand toward me, showing me that it was real. And he said, "If you would acknowledge our reality, then touch the reality that we are." This didn't particularly appeal to me. But it was more appealing and less fearful than what I was faced with: In a situation with no escape, it was the better of the two options. So I did it; I touched this being's hand. I turned around and touched the hand, very carefully avoiding the being's eyes.

The instant I touched this being's hand, there was a brilliant burst of light. And I "woke up," in the living room of my apartment. There was no one there, no sign of anything. It was dark.

I got up and turned on the light. I felt different. It struck me immediately: *I felt absolutely different.* It took me a few minutes to realize in what way: I felt different because I was no longer depressed, *I was no longer afraid.*

I went to bed almost immediately. And I slept for a full night for the first time in over fifteen years, a full night's sleep with no nightmares.

That was on September 14, 1989. I have not had a nightmare since. And, oddly enough, the severe case of *tinear versicolor* began to recede almost immediately, and disappeared within a week. It has not recurred since.

This was followed by another change: It was as though *I had crossed the threshold of fear.* Things took on a totally different orientation. The experience basically altered my whole perspective. In terms of fear, my whole outlook became different.

I began to have interactions with these beings on a fairly regular basis. The nature of my previous interactions had always been fearful, something I had resented and felt was an intrusion into my life. They had challenged my worldview, in that I could find no place for these beings in the reality that I knew. I now took on a whole different perspective, and the nature of the interactions began to change.

The beings began to instruct me in various abilities that they themselves had. They would describe how there were many innate abilities in human beings that were generally untapped. They would describe and demonstrate these abilities, including such things as psychic abilities, out-of-body travel, and healing. They actually began to describe their technology, and how that could be applied to the healing of individuals.

Since that time, I have experienced an enormous increase in psychic abilities. This is due to the fact that I was curious enough to try what they were instructing me in. It was all so detailed. It made so much *sense*. And it has *worked*. For example, there have been healings of individuals with the methods that the beings have described to me. Also, another example is that I've been awakened several times in the middle of the night with images to be drawn. One time, I was awakened at 2:00 or 3:00 A.M. with the insistent image in my mind of the face of one of the beings. And I was being told, "You need to draw this image." Well, I'm not an artist, but it was *so insistent* that I finally got up and attempted it. And at the end of an hour or so, I was totally aghast. Because *there it was*! So my artistic ability is another thing that seems to have been enhanced since the encounter.

Most of the technology and the methods the beings have described is based on energy work, and on the use of the energy fields of various crystalline forms. The beings say that the majority of their technology is based on the manipulation of natural energetic fields of crystalline forms.

Odd as it may sound, within the next year I was led to a deposit of quartz crystals. I was shown the location of these crystals in northern Virginia, given the location telepathically. Then I went to the location and literally had to dig into the bank of a dry stream, where I found this deposit of quartz crystals numbering in the hundreds, several of which were fairly large.

I've lived in northern Virginia almost all my life and I've collected rocks, but I found this quartz deposit totally strange. They were not so much embedded in rock as they were loose in a "vein": They were embedded in this blue-green marine-type clay-like substance.

So, I recovered these crystals, probably in excess of five hundred of them. And I began to have "dreams." I call them dreams, but I doubt very seriously that's what they are. These "dreams" would occur in an altered state, in which the beings would describe the technology connected with crystalline forms. They even went so far as to inform me that they had interacted with Native American populations for several millennia before the Europeans arrived. And that they had taught some of this technology in its basic forms to the Native Americans. The beings always offer "documentation," so they told me, "If you will research in your traditions and in some of the early documents of European explorers, you will find examples or evidence of the fact that they were using this technology." I did some historical research and I found examples of the recovery of abnormally large skeletal remains buried with large quartz crystals in the mounds in the eastern U.S. [See references in Note 2, page 310.]

I was told that I would be instructed as to how to use these crystals for the purpose of "energy transfer," for healing and that sort of thing. But I was also told not to keep the crystals, but to give them away to individuals who would want them and need them. They did not say, "Now, here's a list." They said, "The individuals will request them." And they have. All I'm doing is giving them away, through a sort of networking effect.

So far, several hundred have been given away all over the country. I tell each individual who receives one how the crystals were found, and I describe the uses that have been explained to me by the beings, and how the crystals might best be utilized. I do take pains to explain that they are not a magical amulet or anything of that nature. And that these crystals are, more than anything else, an *amplification device.* By interfacing one's own energy field and correlating that with the energy field in the quartz crystal, a person can amplify their own natural abilities to do certain things. Such as out-of-body travel. Such as telepathic communication. Such as healing, the transfer of energy for healing purposes.

I use one particular crystal for healing purposes. And I have used it to a great extent with individuals who have expressed needs in that regard. There have been definite healings in people who have requested assistance. I have used the crystal in order to *transfer energy* to these individuals, to augment their own energy.

Melanie Green, for example [see Chapter 6], is a

close friend of mine. Melanie has had various physical problems that she has requested assistance for, if there was anything that could be done. She suffers from migraine headaches, and there have been times when she has been completely out of energy. And energy was transferred. Also, she was scheduled for surgery for a gallbladder problem. I said I would see what could be done. She woke up in the middle of the night, *knowing* that the situation had been corrected. She still hasn't needed the surgery.

I hesitate to say that *I* did something. All *I* did was to use the methods the beings described, in order to transfer energy to the individual in need. I believe that the beings who brought the information in the first place, *they* have something to do with the healings. I believe that they are *aware* and that they *assist*.

I spent a good many years trying to "write off" all the encounter experiences that occurred. But a lot of the experiences early in my life occurred in a conscious state. They were not recovered memories, the result of regression or anything of that nature. So I did not have the luxury of being able to *completely* write off these experiences.

In one case, I had been told during an encounter with the beings that they would come that night to take me somewhere. That very night in a fully awake state, my three brothers and I observed this *spacecraft* outside our house. I was, of course, scared to death, and hid inside the house.

This was in 1964, when I was about fifteen. My brothers didn't know what I knew, because I did not tell them about my encounters. But the spacecraft was real enough because all three of them stood and watched it for about half an hour. They even reported it to the police and to a local radio station. And there were other reports by individuals in the area who saw the object.

So, I had had these sorts of incidents. I had had many conscious experiences that verified the reality of the situation. But nevertheless, I was very resistant to it. And there was a time in my life when I wouldn't have breathed a word about *any* of these experiences to *anyone*.

I don't want to give the impression that I came to a point where I said, "Okay, I'll blindly accept and believe whatever happens from here on out." That's not *me*. I am *not* a person who accepts something just because somebody says it. I look upon myself as a realist. I was very skeptical for a very long time.

After the event in 1989, when the most intense torment I can describe and the years of living in terror were removed almost instantaneously *by whatever source*, I was put into a position where I HAD to acknowledge the reality of what had occurred. But, to be perfectly honest, I have tried every way possible to disprove what the beings have told me since. Yet, I cannot argue with the results. The results seem to assist *so many people* that I would feel I was doing a disservice by NOT sharing the information with others at this point.

From the very beginning, the beings were very insistent that they wanted me to communicate to other people, both the knowledge of their existence and the information they seem to want to pass on for the benefit of humankind. These beings seem to be benign. They do not seem to want to create fear. But the beings readily acknowledge that direct, physical contact is not feasible. They know what our reactions will be, since we all live in a state of fear.

If I have a "mission," I think it can be summed up in this way: Humankind in general is reaching the point in development where we are getting ready to come into contact with other civilizations, and I believe that many individuals (who are commonly called "abductees")* are being prepared for this contact in certain ways by being given certain information and experiencing interaction with these other beings. The purpose is to *help humankind as a whole to understand* what is happening. It is like we are slowly being exposed to this other advanced civilization or civilizations through a measured approach.

I, for one, can certainly understand why these beings haven't just jumped onto the stage. It would be overwhelming for the human population. So I can see a rhyme and a reason in the way the beings are doing the things they are doing.

For example, one of the purposes of the crystals—as described by the beings—is to enhance telepathic communications between themselves and the indi-

*Extraterrestrial encounter experiences are often referred to as "abductees," implying that the experience is an involuntary kidnapping. None of the experiencers I talked to see their encounters as victimization, although many do.—Au.

viduals who use these crystals. I cannot tell you how many people who have received these crystals have reported afterward that they have had very lucid, vivid "dreams" of the beings. So that seems to be part of their purpose, that is, initiating interactions. And these beings have also communicated the *need for change*—not only to myself, but to *many* other individuals. This information is something that is common to the experience of *many* "abductees." I think that the beings are here for the purpose of assisting us in making these changes, a transition.

I think I have gone through this transition. It was a long process, but I have come to the point where I see the validity of what they have attempted to communicate to me over the years: The primary impediment to more open communication is the huge reservoir of *fear* that humans retain within themselves. *Fear of anything that is unknown, unusual, or unfamiliar.* If we can overcome this threshold of fear, a fear that so many of our perspectives are based on, we will have an entirely different sort of interaction with these beings.

I would like to add that even the beings themselves have indicated that there exist those civilizations that are "negatively aligned." The beings do acknowledge that all is not peace and love in the universe. Just as there are human beings who are evil and human beings who are not, the same is true for other, extraterrestrial civilizations. All beings "with soul" (as the beings call it) have free will, and the ability to exercise that free will.

The communications of the beings on the subject of free will have been interesting. They have emphasized that one must be *aware* of one's free will in order to exercise it. If one pictures oneself as a helpless victim, if one operates within fear, one will predispose oneself to being taken advantage of by those beings in those energies that are negatively aligned. It is *vital* to exercise one's free will if one has an experience with negative entities or energies. It is a *universal law* that free will cannot be overridden. But one *may* default on one's free will: A "helpless victim" has no choices, no free will. So, their experiences will be imposed on them.

That was the whole point of what the beings did for me in terms of the nightmares. Their whole point in eliminating them for me was an object lesson: You can never outrun fear. You must confront the fear, you must cross the fear threshold. Once you do this, the fear no longer has power over you. I have learned this lesson in a very real way.

I know that there are individuals who have negative experiences, fearful experiences with extraterrestrials of one type or another. I know this occurs. But a lot of the experiences that are fearful in nature perhaps arise from *our own inability to understand what is happening*.

At least, that has been my experience. I cannot presume to speak for others' experiences. All I *can* say is, what I have come to understand is the result of a long and arduous process. And it has certainly transformed my perspective, my outlook, my life.

*   *   *

Curious, I asked Ron for one of his crystals. A tiny purplish shard, the crystal he gave me looked nothing like the commercial kind sold in New Age shops. I slipped the little crystal into a Ziploc plastic bag, tucked it under my bed pillows, and promptly forgot all about it.

For the next several weeks, my dreams were unusually vivid, what I would call "realer than real." I interacted with some very strange-looking "people" in some of these dreams, at one point climbing a big banyan tree with a group of homeless men before realizing my raggedy companions were actually from "out there"—another planet, another dimension, another world. Eventually, I remembered Ron's crystal and moved it to a shelf in my office. The "realer than real" dreams immediately stopped, and they have not reoccurred. Since I passed on the crystal to a sick friend, I have not used it again in an attempt to reexperience these special dreams.

CHAPTER 6

Melanie Green:
Gallbladder "Fixed"

A registered nurse and former sales representative, Melanie Green is active in the experiencers' support group network. She is thirty-nine years old, and is currently pursuing a master's degree in counseling. She lives in northern Virginia with her husband and two young children.

A vivacious and outgoing person, Melanie was so busy with her studies, mothering duties, and volunteer work with fellow experiencers that it was difficult to find the time we needed for discussing her celestial healing experiences. Because of her professional medical background, however, she was able to relate in some very specific detail her personal encounters with the ETs who she believes healed her. I found her professionalism to be impressive, her healing accounts even more so.

Winter can be a difficult time of year for me because I suffer from seasonal affective disorder, a temporary depression thought to be brought on by a lack of sunlight. Because of a string of migraines, I have been unable to use my special full-spectrum light to help combat the depression. So I have been sleeping a lot. Quite a health report from someone who believes the aliens have healed her of various conditions, eh? But I have had some remarkable experiences that seem to indicate that my ET visitors have taken more than a casual interest in my health.

My life has been like a long walk in two worlds. I have spent the last eight years trying to bring these two worlds together, trying to merge the two paths and learn where I have been, where I am going.

This other world lay dormant, like a forgotten dream, until my children began to share little pieces of it with me. In 1986, my son was only two when he first told me about the "guy" who came into his room through the window, out of the dark night sky. I trembled inside, listening to the recurring dream of my own childhood. My daughter shared more stories about her visitors and, gradually, her curiosity and fearlessness gave me the courage to examine my own memories. By 1990, I had the strength to call them memories instead of dreams.

Living in two worlds is something like trying to put together a puzzle when half of the pieces are painted over and you must guess at the picture. As I turn over each piece, I strive to see it all in the best possible light, to bring healing out of the fear, light to the darkness. I believe I have found the silver lining to my ET contact experiences in the people who have shared these experiences with me.

The profound connection between ET experiencers is as fascinating as the experiences themselves. The exchange of energy, "creative energy" as the ETs call it, has great potential. My friend Ron [Ron Blevins, see Chapter 5] has taught me to apply this energy as a healing force, which he learned how to do from communications with a group of tall ETs I have encountered as well. Ron has also used this "creative energy" to bring about the resolution, or healing, of some of my medical conditions. I have come to believe that Ron was instrumental in the ET intervention into a very painful gallbladder condition I was suffering from a few years ago.

In early 1996, I began to consistently experience severe pain in the right upper quadrant of my abdomen every time I ate. During both of my pregnancies, I had experienced gallbladder trouble that had subsided after my children were born. I had been free of any gallbladder problems for seven years. When the pain began again that winter, it was intermittent. But by early spring, the pain was constant and severe. Even fat-free foods, which should not bother the gallbladder, would cause several hours of pain. I began avoiding food and losing weight.

In April of that year, I went to the doctor and began a series of tests to determine the source of the pain. A sonogram of the gallbladder revealed no stones, so gallstones were not the problem. The doctor informed me that they would need to do more tests, however, because the sonogram *had* revealed a tumor—on my liver.

I was scared to death, and in pain all the time. I next underwent a scan with radioactive contrast so that the doctors could study the flow of blood through my liver. For this test, they injected into my arm a solution that was tagged with a radioactive isotope. Then they took a series of pictures of the blood supply to the tumor.

The tumor turned out to be a benign vascular hemangioma* requiring no treatment. But I was still in pain every time I ate even a *bite* of food. Sometimes a drink of water would set it off. I was at the end of my rope, exhausted from the constant discomfort.

The gastroenterologist I had seen for tests informed me that I probably had what they called a "nonfunctional gallbladder," and that it would have to be removed even though there were no stones. He suspected that the gallbladder was filled with "sludge" that would not show up on the sonogram, and ordered yet another complicated, expensive, and uncomfortable test to be conducted the week after the liver scan. After that, I would be off to the surgeon and the OR.

I had been planning to travel to South Carolina the first weekend in May to attend a UFO abduction research conference. My family was very worried about me, with the constant pain and talk of a liver tumor, so no one wanted me to go. But I figured my abdomen would hurt just as much if I stayed home, and at least if I went to the conference, I would be distracted. I was especially determined to make the

*Vascular hemangioma is a noncancerous tumor composed of a cluster of newly formed blood vessels that can be present at birth in various parts of the body, including the bones and liver.—Au.

trip because I was traveling with Ron, and his birthday was that very weekend. I wanted to help him celebrate.

When my condition threatened to interfere with our travel plans, Ron said that he would talk to the ETs about it. I remember giving him a quizzical look.

Once my family was reassured that I did not have liver cancer, they gave up their protest. The night before I was to begin the drive south, I packed a suitcase and went to bed early, hoping that the abdominal pain would subside so that I could get some sleep before my trip.

Abductees joke with one another about the mysterious hour of 3:00 A.M. because, for some reason, many of us will awaken inexplicably between 3:15 and 3:30. Oddly enough, abductees on both coasts and in all time zones report waking at this particular time. Most of us believe that we are returned from abductions at this hour.

In the early morning hours of May 3, 1996, I awakened with a start. I said to myself, out loud, "Oh, good, now I don't have to have my gallbladder removed." I laughed, wondering why on earth I would make such an absurd statement, and I went back to sleep. The clock next to the bed read 3:25.

Since it was a five-hundred-mile drive to the conference, we left early that morning. I had adopted a habit of avoiding breakfast and lunch so that the morning and early afternoon hours could be pain-free and productive. By midafternoon I was hungry, so I reluctantly pulled off the interstate to get something to eat, knowing that the remainder of the day would be marred by the familiar gnawing pain in my abdomen.

It was not until several hours later, when I was unpacking my suitcase in the hotel room where the conference was being held, that it dawned on me: *I was not in pain.* I suddenly recalled my 3:25 awakening and the accompanying thought that I would not have to undergo surgery after all. I was incredulous, but began to consider the idea that my gallbladder had somehow been "fixed" the previous night.

Excited by this possibility, I recruited a few of my fellow conference-goers to accompany me to the Waffle House next door. I ordered a bacon cheeseburger with onion rings, the greasiest item on the menu, and ate the whole thing. Still no pain!

Suddenly and for no apparent reason, a painful condition that had plagued me for more than six months had been completely alleviated.

When I returned from the conference, I canceled the remaining diagnostic test and my appointment with the surgeon. I encountered some resistance, but I simply explained to the doctor that my pain was gone and I saw no need for further tests at that time. I wish I'd had the guts to tell him what I believe happened to me: *There is no doubt in my mind that the ETs repaired whatever was wrong with my gallbladder.*

Now, why would the ETs heal me, and why at that particular point in time, after so many months of pain? I have no conscious recall of an abduction experience taking place on the night before my trip.

But I *think* that my gallbladder problem finally came to their attention as a result of the radiation left in my body from the radio isotope study conducted earlier in the week. During a routine abduction, they probably detected the low-level radiation and, in asking me about it, learned of the upcoming surgery. So they fixed it. And it is very possible they fixed it because of Ron's intervention. Whether they fixed it out of a sense of goodwill, or to prevent someone else from messing with their "laboratory specimen," is unknown. It appears the ETs have their own reasons for keeping me well. Whatever their reasons, you will not be hearing any complaints from me!

At times, I wonder whether some of my minor, chronic health problems are the result of my abduction experiences. I have chronic headaches, fatigue, and my memory is not what it should be for someone not yet forty. Just the stress of repeated abductions could be enough to impact my health in an undesirable way. Still, it does seem that many interventions have been made *on my behalf.* The motive behind such interventions cannot be known. Are the ETs intervening in order to enhance my quality of life? Or are they simply protecting their own investment in me?

In the spring of 1991, I was in a car accident while driving a car full of children to school. We were rearended at a stoplight by a driver who failed to brake. Fortunately, the kids all had their seat belts on and were unharmed. I was not seriously injured because I was also wearing my seat belt, but I did end up with a very sore neck and bruised knees where they hit the steering column. The other driver's insurance paid for a few chiropractic visits, after which I thought I was fine. We settled the claim.

A few months later, I was extremely dismayed when I began to experience pain in my right knee. The knee would "click" when I climbed stairs, and sometimes it locked up, making it very uncomfortable, if not impossible, to walk.

The impact from the car accident had resulted in loose cartilage in the knee, which would require surgery. Since I had already settled the accident claim, it would be no simple matter to get the insurance companies to agree on who would pay for my surgery. But before I could even make an appointment with the orthopedic surgeon, the click and pain in my knee suddenly disappeared. All that was left behind was a scar: a new, perfect, one-quarter inch in diameter, circular scar on the bottom of my knee.

In another case of ET healing, I actually have conscious recall of the alien involvement. This was a *conscious healing experience*, not a dream, not recalled under hypnosis. I also have physical evidence that was witnessed by others at the time. I was never diagnosed by doctors for the problem that the aliens healed, but I am actually quite grateful for that.

In the fall of 1993, the tall shimmery beings I often interact with took me once again. These are the ETs who sometimes abduct me, beings I can never see clearly, aliens who appear as shimmering density in the atmosphere. They tower over me at about seven feet in height. They are kind but stern, formal. I think they are the same beings Ron describes. I know that they will not hurt me, so I am not afraid when I am with them. But I do feel disgruntled as I often find myself in circumstances that are not of my own design.

In this particular instance, I found myself sitting on a table, watching two of the ETs discuss me as doctors on rounds discuss their patients. There was no spoken dialogue, but I could clearly understand what they were saying telepathically. Just like doctors, they were talking about me as if I were not there, even though they must have known that I could "hear" them.

One of the ETs turned toward me, gesturing at my chest with his hand. A vertical plane of light appeared out of nowhere, intersecting my body at chest level. There was no discomfort, no sensation at all, but I jumped with surprise. The ET gestured toward me again, this time with a slightly different motion. A horizontal plane of light appeared, intersecting my body in a cross section with the first light plane.

The light planes looked like floating sheets of glass, brightly lit from within, and with a prismatic quality, glimmering with a rainbowlike effect when viewed at an angle. I felt both fascinated and terrified at the same time.

Suddenly, a transparent, highly detailed, three-dimensional cross section of one of my breasts floated away from my body and into the air in front of me. I gasped loudly. Floating there before me was a holographic model of my breast! *My* breast! A tiny dot of light glowed in the middle of the holographic image. One of the tall beings said to the other, "It is still very small. She doesn't even know that it is there."

The conscious memory ends there. It seems that whenever I become agitated or disagreeable during an abduction, the ETs "switch" me off, putting me into a more passive state—for their protection and my own. But what I did remember was disturbing, as it seemed obvious to me that the ETs had detected an early breast tumor.

I was only thirty-four at the time, and knew that it would be unlikely that my doctor would order a mammogram since I did not have a discernible lump in my breast. I certainly did *not* want to tell him that aliens had informed me I had a small, undetectable breast tumor! So I did not take action, I did not take the logical, immediate step most women would take in such a situation. Instead, I lost a good amount of sleep over the next few weeks, wondering what I *should* do.

Meanwhile, a very curious thing began to happen: Marks began to appear on my body. Even though I had no conscious memory of ongoing abductions, almost daily a new mark would appear on my breast. About three-eights of an inch in diameter, the marks resembled minor burns, raised red circles like insect bites, always in the vicinity of my right breast. Sometimes there would be a puncture wound, too, in the center of one of the red circles, almost like a needle mark. One morning, I awoke to find needlelike punctures on my left eyelid just below the brow. Another time, I found a needle mark on the inside of one of my arms, as if blood had been drawn.

I was excited, frightened, and, in a way, relieved. Although I did not know who was actually doing what to me, it certainly *seemed* as if the tall, shimmery ETs might be treating the condition they had discovered during the hologram experience. I had never heard about even a *similar* experience from other abductees, so I was beside myself. But the marks on my body were proof enough that it was not my imagination. I became quite the exhibitionist that month, ensuring myself of a few witnesses to the marks that kept appearing on my right breast.

When I turned thirty-five, I had a mammogram. The results were normal.

This year I will turn forty, and I will go for a second mammogram. I am anxious to receive another clean bill of health, as my aunt died of breast cancer last year, and my mother had a lumpectomy in 1997 as well. In 1993, I had no idea that my family history for breast cancer would be so strong. Knowing what I know now, I am grateful that someone was looking out for me. And *I have no trouble at all believing that the tall ETs diagnosed and treated an early cancer in my right breast.*

In 1994, I had the opportunity to discuss my hologram experience with a prominent UFO researcher. He told me that other abductees had reported being shown holograms, and that many abductees held the belief that their illnesses were diagnosed and treated by aliens. I also find it interesting that in the last few years holograms have begun to be used by the medical community in certain diagnostic and surgical procedures.

The abduction phenomenon is deep and complex. The physical aspects of the abduction experience are only the tip of the iceberg. There is a profound, yet unknown purpose behind what is going on here. By definition, it is likely to be beyond our understanding: Their purpose is *alien* to us.

For me, the ETs' interest in our emotions, our hearts and souls, holds a more compelling question. Because the most profound change I have experienced is an extraordinary increase in my empathic abilities. When I sit and listen to someone, I hear their words with my ears *and I feel their feelings*. Their feelings seem to jump inside me so that I actually feel what they feel, positive or negative.

As my personal history of ET encounters came into consciousness, I abandoned a successful career in sales to pursue a degree in counseling. I have an unwavering sense of mission, the exact nature of which has yet to be revealed. Each facet of my life seems to be another step, in preparation for some eventuality. I am compulsively studying alternative healing and mind-body medicine these days, not knowing why, but knowing that the reason will be revealed someday soon. I don't know whether to hope for or dread the coming of that day.

My sense of hope for the future comes from the

community of experiencers. While the motives of the ETs still remain to be seen, encounter experiencers know that our intentions toward one another are good and true. Once we set aside our disagreements about whether ET contact is "good" or "bad," we find a rich and fertile ground for building community. Rather than imposing our views on one another, we learn to accept the validity of individual experience and embrace our differences.

People who have extraterrestrial encounters often experience great isolation. I have spoken to hundreds of experiencers and it is the isolation that is the toughest part of the lives of most experiencers, including those of us who view our experiences as positive. Experiencers feel as if they have "come home" when they finally find others to talk to about their encounters.

Those of us with a history of ET contact have experienced the loss of a world, the world we grew up believing to be true. When you realize that your life has been, in actuality, *two completely separate lives*, there is an existential crisis of profound proportions. You are then forced to synthesize *a new worldview*.

For encounter experiencers and abductees, the isolation ends when we come together. With the support we bring to each other, we can help one another to heal, *blending the two worlds*, healing the split. This is the magic that occurs when experiencers come together.

CHAPTER 7

Nan Cooper:
Healed by the Arcturians

Nan Cooper lives in Pine, Arizona, where she and her husband have a New Age/spiritual literary and music publishing company called Planetary Heart Publications. She is in her late forties.

When she heard about my book in process, Nan wrote me a long letter detailing her own healing experiences with extraterrestrials. Unlike many experiencers, Nan has *specific ETs* she seeks out for help in healing herself of various physical problems. I found her stories quite fascinating, and her particular approach rather unique. We conducted our interviews during the early morning hours, before her busy day at her publishing business began.

I have been extremely interested in the topic of healing in relation to extraterrestrial contact, and I believe that I have had several experiences myself.

First, let me offer a general overview of my personal health problems and concerns. In 1980, I had a Pap smear that was abnormal, indicating cervical dysplasia. I was retested several times within six months, each result indicating the abnormality had worsened, advancing another stage. Finally, my gynecologist suggested that if I let it go untreated, I would have full-blown cancer within several years. So I underwent conization of the cervix to remove any abnormal cervical cells. I felt fine, but my doctor was not satisfied. He pushed for partial hysterectomy.

Meanwhile, I went to a channeler, a young lady who did a channeled health reading in an Edgar Cayce style, that is, in a sleep state, lying prone. (Edgar Cayce was a great American psychic who conducted many medical readings in a sleep-trance state.) The reading claimed that I didn't have a cancer cell in my body, nor would I. Consequently, I refused the partial hysterectomy and continued to have checkups on a frequent basis. This experience caused me to reevaluate a great number of things in my life.

My second health concern has been a chronic case of sinus problems, which began in 1972 when I broke my nose in a minor accident. Although my eye was bruised and blackened underneath, I had no idea that my nose was broken. However, I was to discover years later that the injury resulted in a significant deviation of the septum. A constantly runny nose, headaches, and swelling of the sinuses forced me to use antihistamines. I could barely function on the medication. I then chose to receive biweekly electronic acupuncture treatments instead, which helped me to recuperate. I was not bothered very much by the sinus problems for a number of years.

In 1990, a dentist in Columbus, Ohio, showed me some X rays that indicated that my sinuses were totally blocked and that I did indeed have a deviation of the septum. My husband and I then spent the fall and winter of 1993/1994 in Munds Park in between Flagstaff and Sedona, Arizona, where we were learning the publishing business. A wood-burning stove was our primary heat source. Because I breathed ashes all the time, my nose ran profusely for five straight months.

However, it was during this time that I began to have some subtle visionary experiences with ETs, notably the Arcturians.* So I read everything I could get my hands on regarding extraterrestrials, but mostly the material that was more spiritual in nature. I was not very interested in the hard-core evidence of UFO researchers, even though our neighbors (a very reclusive couple) were, in fact, UFO researchers.

Sedona has a reputation as a "hotbed" for all kinds of UFO activity. There are people in Sedona (and elsewhere) who experience things that are seen as

---

*Arcturians are the extraterrestrials from Arcturus, the brightest star in the constellation Boötes, approximately thirty-six light-years away. These "light-body" beings are believed to assist humans in changing the self through conscious awareness of the unconscious mind, to evolve and ascend spiritually.[1] A channeled message from the Arcturians explains: "We are not here to rescue you. We are here to help you enhance or amplify your healing energies."[2] Nan recently informed me she has learned that one of the more powerful ET healers she has worked with is actually Arcturian/Andromedan, that is, "the offspring of an Arcturian and an Andromedan union." The Andromeda Galaxy is the nearest galaxy to our own, some 2.2 million light-years from Earth.—Au.

being on the darker side. I know that these experiences do exist, but I do not consider them to be my own reality. Since multiple realities do exist simultaneously, I believe my reality to be quite different than the reality of those who choose to view ETs as "evil." I choose to view most extraterrestrials as benign, loving, loyal, technologically advanced, and quite capable of establishing wonderful interactions with willing humans in order to assist them with healing of the body, mind, emotions, and spirit. I also believe that those ETs who have engaged in abductions have done so for the express purpose of genetically creating a separate race of heartier beings in order to allow their own race to survive. Although I do not agree with their approach, I do have compassion for these ETs and I understand their plight.

Because my reality is of a *higher nature* of living in light and love, and because I choose to look on the ETs as benign, I believe that the ETs without higher motives will not bother me. Only fear attracts negative experiences, including negative ET experiences.

During that five-month period of breathing ashes, I believe the Arcturians were helping me. I feel that during this period I was being adjusted and operated on in a sleep and/or meditative state—with my conscious permission, of course. I had a sore on the inside of the end of my nose that would not heal up, no matter what I did. It truly felt as if an object had been inserted there, but I could never see anything. Since my nose and head were being worked on a lot during sleep and meditation states, I just continued to believe in my very benign, loving connection to the Arcturians, whom I felt had only my best intentions and good health in mind.

When my husband and I returned to Ohio in the spring of 1994, my sinuses began to clear up. The sore at the end of my nose seemed to magically disappear. I have always suspected that a benign implant was placed in my nasal area to facilitate my healing. However, this has never been confirmed by an X ray.

In early 1996, another Pap smear came out slightly abnormal. I knew in my heart of hearts that this situation needed my attention, that my dysfunctional female health problem was raising its ugly head again. It was a distinct message to me that it was time to clear this area of my body. However, this time the emotional and mental imprints had to be released as well.

Between Pap tests, I did some intense visualizing and healing work with the Arcturians, focusing on the cervical area of my body. I released much repressed emotion around the manifestation of this unhealthy condition. Intuitively, I knew when the healing work was complete. I also knew that I was completely well and did not have to experience this health problem again.

I went for a retest two weeks later, and this time the Pap smear was normal. My Pap tests have been normal ever since, and I believe I have been completely healed in this area, with the help of the Arcturians. They are incredible doctors and healers.

In April of 1996, I made an appointment to see an ear, nose, and throat specialist. My sinuses had been acting up again for several months, and I was so uncomfortable that I was ready to consider a surgical procedure. The night before I went to see the doctor, I had a dream that he would tell me there was nothing wrong with me.

During the appointment, the doctor poked and prodded my nasal passages, all to no avail. He said he wouldn't even waste his time giving me an X ray because he could find no appreciable deviation. He said he suspected that my nasal problems were due to allergies.

This was amazing to me. No more deviation? At the time, I had been introduced in my meditation state to a powerful ET healer. I had been receiving healing treatments and adjustments in my nasal area, again while in sleep and in meditation. I feel that this ET healer may have helped to facilitate the healing of my deviated septum, and I am truly grateful to him.

In August of 1996, I accepted the position of librarian at a brand-new elementary school in central Ohio. We moved outside of the town where my job was, out in the middle of farm country. This meant we were constantly breathing in chemical pesticides. At the school, all of the library books were new. So were the carpets. I was informed that the books and carpets were saturated with formaldehyde. By this time in my spiritual journey, I had become ultrasensitive to many toxins because I had been raising my vibration and becoming clearer. I couldn't even perm my hair anymore because the chemicals brought on all sorts of ill effects.

As you open up spiritually, I believe you become more sensitive and receptive to higher vibrations and energies. You become *ultrasensitive.* Your psychic senses, sight, and hearing seem more sensitive. However, you also become more sensitive to lower vibrational and toxic substances, to chemical toxins and pollutants and negative energies. As you are transmuting, changing and finding that certain things in your environment become bothersome, the Arcturians can offer invaluable help.

By that October, I had reached a crisis point. My eyes burned, itched, ached, and carried a red-yellowish tint most of the time. The skin beneath my eyes became very dry, red, and wrinkled. When I was not in the school building and when I was away from the farmlands around my home, my condition would clear up almost completely.

I tried the conventional route: I was tested for allergies, and tried three different allergy medications. Every test was negative and nothing worked. By springtime, I had requested some healing help from the Arcturians. I soon began to improve, and I realized that their healing work was being done during my sleep time. This was later confirmed during a group meditation. I credit a female Arcturian healer for assisting me in curing my eye problem that stemmed from the toxic substances in my environment.

These days, I believe that I just have to follow my

own internal feelings and intuitions. And I believe that I *always* get imprinted with the right information—if I choose to listen to it. I am doing as much healing in altered states, in dream states, and in meditations as I would ever do in a conscious, waking state. And this work is much more long-lasting, effective, and powerful. At times, I feel that these higher dimensional states are more real than our conscious, waking reality.

Healing has a lot to do with what we are willing to believe. If you know that something is not going to affect you anymore, if you are not going to make it a part of your reality, then illness has no reason to persist. The body is pretty amazing. It will respond and heal, according to the beliefs you allow for in your reality.

In fact, one of my friends even has a pet who was healed in this way, with extraterrestrial assistance. Her cat wasn't doing well. She was disoriented, she was limping, she would not eat. My friend got a strong message from an Arcturian: "If you would visualize sending your cat up through the corridor to our ship, we'll go ahead and work on the cat from here." So my friend did this visualization, and by 4:00 A.M., the cat was jumping all over her bed, acting as if nothing had ever been wrong.

My husband and I have long desired to serve as emissaries for the extraterrestrials who are here on Earth helping humans. I consider my relationship with the ETs to be deep, sacred, and always accepting. They are truly some of the most important members of my "spiritual family," and I am keenly aware of and very comfortable with my origin in the stars.

My spiritual code of ethics includes living simple spiritual principles. The Arcturians are one example of those ET groups that emphasize simple spiritual principles in order to assist in personal and planetary transformations. I believe that everyone on the planet is, in their own way, trying to transmute and to change. It is a much slower and more difficult process, however, for people who do not realize their own healing powers. But I believe that many different extraterrestrial groups are working with us to facilitate our natural healing processes and help us regain our personal power as spiritual human beings.

When we returned to Arizona in October of 1997, this time to live there permanently and set up our publishing company, I was apprehensive because of my previous sinus experiences. Fortunately, I have experienced only minor sinus-related problems and very little negative reaction to anything in my new Arizona environment.

I am truly grateful to the Arcturians for all they have done for me personally. They are a loving, selfless group of extraterrestrials who only wish to see us evolve, raise our vibrations, and ascend spiritually. I look forward to the day when I encounter them with full visual presence.

CHAPTER 8

J. Dean Fagerstrom: On Angels and Extraterrestrials

At age sixty-six, J. Dean Fagerstrom has explored numerous career paths and avenues of study including music, mathematics, theology, poetry, and photography. After eleven years in the U.S. Army, including time spent in Germany where he met his wife Helga, Dean left the service to work as a writer in New York. Since he had been in the Intelligence field while serving his country, he eventually established a sideline career in corporate security. He recently retired, and now devotes all of his time to writing a numerical science provided to him by the spiritual society he refers to as "Anglion."

A widower, Dean lives in Putnam Lake, New York, and has three grown children. He has enjoyed a lifetime rich with angelic/extraterrestrial contact. I was quite pleased that he was willing to share his encounter experiences with me, and to come to my home during a visit to his son who, at the time, was living in South Florida. Over strong coffee on my sun-washed patio, Dean, a gentle, ethereal-looking man, talked of his love for his family, his writing, and his celestial guide, Maxine.

It all started for me at a very, very young age. On the fifteenth of December, 1924, a child was born into our family. She lived for less than fifteen minutes due to a respiratory ailment. She had been named Maxine.

At this time, my parents lived in Oregon. They were nominally called Christians, but were still searching for a greater kind of spirituality. (Eventually, my mother would become an ordained minister and establish her own ministry in Tennessee.) But the loss of Maxine caused my parents to become estranged, and although they did not separate, there was not any "closeness" for almost eight years. Then, I was conceived.

My mother told me the following story: "When you were born, your father and I were so happy that we reconciled. I always told everyone that you were my 'child of reconciliation.' When you were about three weeks old, I bundled you up in a blanket and walked to the local church. There was no one there but ourselves. I walked you down to the front of the little church and placed you on the low table before the altar. And I prayed this prayer: 'Oh Lord of Heaven, You have taken one child from us. And now I give You back the one that You gave me after eight long years. He is Yours from this day forward. Do with him what You will.' "

I happen to firmly believe that Maxine was assigned to me on that day. When a mother prays like that over a child, and virtually says to God, "My child is Yours, he is no longer mine," I think the spiritual realm responds in a very decided way. I don't have any other explanation for the fact that, by the age of five, I was beginning to see things that existed in another dimension. I had all kinds of other-worldly experiences in my young years, experiences that have continued to this day.

Whatever my destiny in life was to be, it came in random bursts. But it always reverted back to that commitment my mother had made. There was always the *feeling* that "You represent something, Dean. Now, fulfill it."

Maxine is an Emissary. She has access to the two spiritual societies that I communicate with: Anglion and Aphax. She has always told me this: "You have to think differently. You have to be able to communicate with me on my terms, the terms that come from the Divine Source." My conjunctions—Maxine uses the term "conjunction," she does not use the term "relationship"—are with those whom Maxine sends to me.

In March of 1953, I was in a terrible state of clinical depression while at a theological seminary in Missouri. I left there after what I have described as an "encounter," which resulted in a very dramatic enlightenment.

My brother was the public relations director at the seminary, and had coerced me into becoming a seminarian. This was not what my heart wanted to do. I was disgusted and frustrated with what I felt was a bigoted, dogmatic atmosphere. I knew that there had to be something different.

I began to fast, pray, and meditate. I cut myself off from everything and everyone. Finally, I prayed this prayer: "Dear God in Heaven, You must do something in my behalf. I cannot take this any longer. You have *got* to intervene."

At 2:00 on the morning of the fifteenth of March, I went to the music theory classroom. (In high school, I had received university scholarships in music and had wanted to become a choir director.) As I sat in the seminary music room, I opened my copy of the Bible. The book happened to open to John, and I looked down casually at these words: "I am the resurrection and the life."

All of a sudden, the words on the page turned completely red. They lifted off the page and moved around, so that I was reading them as if on a page held in front of me. And then I heard a voice, the voice that had *originally* uttered these very words. I fell forward onto my face, onto the floor. And I passed completely out of my body and into this other world.

From that moment on, my life was completely transformed. *Every single molecular particle in my system changed.* All of my atoms underwent a total change, all of my particles completely realigned. This was *not* a religious experience. It was a *spiritual* and a *celestial* experience.

When I walked out of that music room at daybreak, I was filled with an ecstatic sense of wellbeing, of knowledge and understanding, of total peace. I gathered up my belongings and I fled the realm of institutionalized religion forever.

Now, this is not an historical anecdote. *It is a present reality.* It had nothing to do with time, nothing to do with space. So I don't look at this encounter as "history." I look at the experience as being the *exact same reality* from which I speak at this point.

I have had so-called extraterrestrial contact. But I really don't spend a lot of time on extraterrestrial or terrestrial matters. I'm much more interested in communicating with the Kingdom of God. This is where *all* reality has its origin. The Earth is just an effect, an effect of a Divine Creation. The so-called extraterrestrials were made by the Divine Creator, too, just like any terrestrial.

Over the years, I have had contact with an extraterrestrial being called Donestra, from a planet *tentatively* called Solarian. (I don't want to be dogmatic about this.) Through Donestra, I was given a picture of what it was like to live as an extraterrestrial being. But he was not located in the time and space at the particular moment when he was speaking to me. And I understood that. He had lived during an earlier time, and had progressed to the spiritual world.

In 1962, I was stationed in Germany. My wife and I had been fortunate enough to secure a lovely apartment six or seven minutes away from the base. On the nineteenth of July, at 3:00 A.M., I was working with numerical complexes on a pad of graph paper at an easel. Suddenly, the paper became like a TV screen and I could see on it this gentleman. He was dressed in a blue bodysuit with a cape. He had a belt with an insignia, and a necklace with a medallion on it. He just smiled and spoke to me.

He told me his name: Donestra. He told me that there were many other civilizations throughout the universe that had progressed on a spiritual plane such that their science was not contaminated with the faulty principles and concepts that we are accustomed to. These other civilizations were therefore able to go about visiting *other* planetary civilizations.

Donestra was, at that time, with the spiritual world. And he began, over time, to acquaint me with what he represented. Later, I wrote *The Book of Anglion,* and then a second volume, *The Book of Aphax.*

It was one of Donestra's contemporaries, I believe, who gave me the drawings. At 2:00 on the morning of the twentieth of January, 1968, I woke up from a sound sleep. Looking up at one corner of the bedroom ceiling, I saw what resembled an old-fashioned microphone. Protruding from the center of this instrument was a kind of needle or "feeler." The instrument approached me, coming closer and closer. I realized I was in a state in which I could not move: I was fixated. The instrument put the feeler right in the center of my forehead above my eyes. It did not penetrate but stopped there, and I felt (and heard) a high frequency. This intense vibration passed clear through me. I continued to lie there until the instrument receded and disappeared.

At around 6:00 A.M., I got up and made coffee. Then I sat at the dining-room table. At around 8:30

or so, I felt someone with me. They said, "Get in your car and go down to the stationery store. We'll show you what to buy." And I did. I bought some graph pads, certain kind of pens, some triangles, and other drafting instruments. Then I went home, and I began to draw. I drew *under the influence* of someone. It was like I was programmed.

I completed thirty-two pages of diagrams over a three-day period. I was instructed to name each diagram, but I do not claim to understand the meanings and functions of all of these instruments. I do not even know their purpose.

In 1981, Phil Imbrogno* came to see me. I was instructed by Donestra to give him all of the drawings. I said to Phil, "I was just instructed to give you these. I don't know why."

*Philip J. Imbrogno, a science educator and astronomer, writes about Dean's drawings in his book, *Contact of the Fifth Kind* [*see References, page 317*]: "The diagrams are a marvel to behold. They are in vivid color, drawn with extreme precision. They have been examined by professional people from many different fields . . . A professional draftsman said that a person would need at least twenty years [of] experience in drawing technical diagrams to produce them. He also said that a top-notch professional would need at least six hours to complete each diagram. Many of the diagrams show devices that were unknown in 1968, but are being experimented with today . . . Scientists at Princeton, Northwestern, and M.I.T. have also looked at the diagrams and agreed that they are accurate in design, although there is not enough information to tell you exactly what each device is, how it works, or how to build it." One design was of a three-dimensional viewing screen, some showed a variety of optical test equipment, and one device, a "Helical Coil," was actually constructed. According to Imbrogno, "It produced an electromagnetic flux much greater than can be produced by any similar coils available today," before it burned out.[1]—Au.

In January of 1988, I was called by a friend and invited to a party where I was expected to play a new Korg electric piano. I had agreed to the invitation, but did not know how to play the piano. I'd always had a great love for the piano, but had never learned how to play it.

At the party, I requested that the piano be turned around to face the gathering. I turned it on, and started playing. I did not understand what was happening. The music was somewhat crude, yet quite *beautiful*.

On the way home, Maxine made her presence known. She said, "You are going to buy a piano exactly like that one." I said *"What? I don't have that kind of money!"* Maxine said, "It will be provided for you."

Within ten days, there was a brand-new Korg electric piano in my house.

I sat down and simply started playing. *Under the influence* of someone else. Later, using an internal recorder, I recorded many, many tapes. And every professional who has ever listened to my tapes says, "This is Franz Liszt.* Undoubtedly."

And I think it is Franz Liszt all right.

I never did practice, and I was playing music of a

*Phil Imbrogno took a copy of one of Dean's music tapes to an expert pianist, who recognized the style of Franz Liszt, a famous Austrian composer who lived in the 1800s. The expert said that the music was a Liszt piece, but one he had never heard before. According to Imbrogno, Dean has recorded some two hundred tapes channeled by Liszt, "all astounding."[2]—Au.

complexity that would be impossible for anyone who had not been taught piano. Yet, I had never taken lessons. The music comes in a spontaneous influx, as *I let someone take over*. But I am not in a trance. I watch my fingers flying up and down the keyboard. The scientific explanation would create a new science.

One night in the fall of 1973, I woke up at 3:00 A.M. to see two little beings in hoods entering the bedroom. They were very diminutive, less than five feet in height, dressed all in black. They just marched *through* the closed door, then walked up to and *through* the large German bed my wife and I occupied.

A separation occurred so that it seemed as though I were suddenly *above* my body, hovering over it. From this vantage point, I observed the surgical operation the two beings conducted.

The one on my right side opened up a stiff black packet that resembled the fold-up packages one uses to store silverware. The lining inside was a red velvet, and there were straps to hold each surgical instrument in place. He removed something that resembled tweezers, while the other being, the one to my left, held an illuminated object shaped like a boomerang. Giving the boomerang a kind of flourish over my head, the one on my left actually laid back my skull from cerebrum to cerebellum. The other then took out a vial from the surgical pack, poured out what appeared to be sapphires and rubies, and used the tweezers to implant these gems in certain locations in my brain.

When they were done, one folded back into place the flap of my skull. The other used the boomerang instrument to heal it up. Then they walked back to the bedroom door, turned to one another, and bowed respectfully. As if to say, "Mission accomplished!"

I was never afraid. I knew it was all part of the program. These individuals were not terrestrial beings. When these individuals came, I knew that they were representing something *spiritual.*

For several days afterward, there was a strange sensation around the top of my head, as if I had been wearing a tight sweatband. And I began to see blue pinpricks of light: When I read, or stared at something, I'd see these blue globes, lights that moved like comets, then hovered. It continues to this day.

This experience sounds so bizarre. But it was not a *physical* operation. It was done on a *spiritual* plane. It represents a kind of "cleansing," so that when messages are transferred from the spiritual world, they are no longer distorted by my brain.

I've had my brain "cleansed" for most of my life. They've cleaned up my brain, so that it can function as an organic adjunct to the mind. The brain is just a series of references, like the Library of Congress. It is the *mind*, however, that is free.

I've been involved in every field that you can imagine. But none of it is meaningful in itself. What *is* meaningful is that I have attempted to *open myself up to every propensity that God gave me*. So that I can express all of it, for His sake, and for the sake of men and women everywhere. There is only one purpose in life, and that is to instigate love in the hearts of men and women. Everything in my life reverts back to this.

I've never known an illness, I've never had an organic illness affect me in my whole life. I only had one childhood disease: chicken pox. Other than that, there hasn't been a single bad day. I don't *have* bad days. I have no complaints.

I must admit, however, I am a smoker. Now, this is not a promotion for cigarettes. But there are individuals who die of lung cancer who never smoked a cigarette in their life. The point is, there is only *one* cause of cancer. To flatly say that *cigarettes cause cancer* is nothing but an outright fallacy.

Years ago, under the influence of Donestra, I was taken on a visionary experience. I was flying over some islands where there was no foliage to be seen. These islands were totally barren. They resembled a highly enlarged picture of human cells. And they looked like oysters, out of the shell, in their mucuslike broth.

I asked my hosts, "What does this mean?" They said, "This is how carcinoma of every kind has its beginning." Then they explained it to me, but purely as an *organic* situation. Since the human being has three aspects—body, mind, and soul—the cancer is conjoined to these other two aspects. So the following cannot be taken as a remedy for the disease itself.

What they showed me during that visionary experience was this: When protein is not properly rendered for its purpose and is not flushed out of the body, it can reside in the system and become crystalline. It then has the ability to send or receive a signal. When these residuals are in the body cells in their crystalline form, the cells can send and receive the *wrong* signals. This results in chaos, and the breakdown of the cell. Once the tissue breaks down, the cancer results.

The incidentals regarding the protein were not made clear to me at that time. But I think that, with some reasonable research, the particulars could be determined.

This information does not mean that anyone who overindulges in meat will experience such a buildup of protein residue and contract cancer. The incidence of cancer is integral to one's *state of mind*. Emotional perturbation, impacted feelings, and changes on the *soul* level can cause a reaction in the organic system so that the cells' signals become chaotic.

I think that this information was given to me to provide me with a greater understanding of the human being. Cancer is one part of the larger picture: body, mind, and soul. The body itself is only an effect. It is the mind and soul that are actually in control, because the body is only an outgrowth of *who we really are*. When there is a serenity, a peacefulness, a *oneness*, then there is no room for an intrusion such as illness or disease. This is the information as it was explained to me by Maxine.

Trying to condense a lifetime of spiritual experience is very difficult. But it all reverts back to Maxine. Those who have no appreciable time on Earth often will choose to have vicarious experience through others living on this planet. I am Maxine's surrogate. She can see down through my eyes and thereby understand what a human being experiences. And she allows *me* to express my soul.

I believe that my conjunction with Maxine is *a state of evolutionary progress.* It is a mutual effort, part of a course to render spiritual truth through the material. God does not preempt our understanding, but allows us to understand what we are *willing* to understand. From my experiences with both the spiritual realm and extraterrestrial civilizations, I know that there exists a rational basis for everything in life.

PART II

We *Make* It Happen

"*The vital force is not enclosed in man, but radiates around him like a luminous sphere, and it may be made to act at a distance. In these semimaterial rays the imagination of a man may produce healthy or morbid effects.*"

—PARACELSUS,
sixteenth-century alchemist
and physician

CHAPTER 9

Bev Marcotte:
Remote Viewer and
Healer

Bev Marcotte was born and raised in Connecticut. For many years, she worked as a graphic artist and graphic designer. In 1996, at the age of fifty-four, she changed careers: Bev attended the Farsight Institute in Atlanta for training as a "remote viewer." Currently, she works as a professional viewer of forensic targets for TransDimensional Systems in Atlanta. She is also the cofounder and coordinator of Lightkeepers Remote Viewing/Remote Healing Network, a national group of psychics trained to do healing work at a distance.

Bev currently lives in Ohio with her husband, an engineer in fluid aerodynamics. They have six grown children.

Before talking to Bev about her experiences as a healer (and someone who has also received celestial healing), I was only slightly familiar with the paranormal technique she practices: Remote viewing or scientific remote viewing (SRV) is similar to meditation and psychic skills in that the practitioner accesses a part of the mind that is typically not used during normal waking consciousness, making this highly intuitive function dominant in their awareness. The difference between meditators, psychics, and remote viewers is that *SRV practitioners are trained* through highly structured programs. They learn how to utilize the paraconscious mind and to *record the results in a specific, scientifically reproducible manner.*

Based on ancient practices of various indigenous peoples and their "shamans" or spiritual healers, remote viewing was developed into a scientific protocol by the U.S. military for the purpose of the collection of intelligence information. Government-trained SRV officers planned, conducted, and reported on long-distance intelligence missions accomplished completely *in their own minds.* The government program was apparently successful enough that the SRV training for "psychic spies" established sometime in the 1970s existed for several decades—and may still be in operation as a protected (top secret) program.

Bev is one of a growing number of privately trained remote viewers who utilize their special skills both for communicating with extraterrestrial/extradimensional beings and for conducting healing sessions at a distance. How she became such an extraordinary sort of healer is a fascinating story. Throughout Part II, you will read some remarkable case reports of healers who, like Bev, utilize celestial energies in order to help others achieve an improved state of physical and emotional health and spiritual well-being.

The oldest of five children, I was always considered the oddball in the family. I saw and felt things differently, and was called "eccentric" and "strange" by my parents. At age eleven, my eyes began to change color from brown to hazel, then to green, the color they are today. At about this same time, I began to experience premonitions. I would tell my mother in advance of unannounced company that would be arriving, and one time I informed her of the death of a distant relative, confirmed later in the day by my uncle.

Shortly after my twenty-first birthday, I got married. At age twenty-seven, I had a near-death experience when I was hospitalized for surgery to remove an ovarian cyst. During the operation, which did not go well, I "woke up" and watched the procedure from *above* my body. And during the recovery period, I began to experience brief episodes where I again found myself out-of-body, sometimes feeling as if I had access to all of the answers for all of life's questions.

After this, my psychic ability expanded markedly. I began to experience spontaneous "astral projection," my conscious mind leaving my body to travel to distant places and gather information. I also began to have prophetic dreams and to recall details of my past lives. I kept most of this to myself. When I did disclose the details of one of my experiences to my husband at the time, he replied, "I could have you committed, you know." I decided that silence was a better idea.

In 1980, I divorced my first husband, and in 1986, I remarried. My second husband and I are happily married. However, after only nine months of adjusting to our new partnership, I began to realize that something strange was going on, something I had been experiencing all my life but had not been aware of *consciously.*

One beautiful, sunny day in July of 1987, I got out of bed and went into the bathroom. Gazing into the mirror, I noticed something odd: I had a small cut, a hairline slice nearly an inch long, which ran horizontally across my top lip. It nearly blended into the red of my lip and would have been easy to miss. Except that I knew *I was supposed to see it.* Suddenly, a recognition moved from my subconscious mind into my consciousness: *I am an experiencer,* an extraterrestrial encounter experiencer.

Within a few weeks, the "baby dreams" began. These dreams (or "trips," as I sometimes prefer to call them) involved a small, sickly newborn. Although there were no genitalia, I knew the baby was a boy. He was gray in color, with such thin skin he seemed to be almost transparent. He was so listless he looked as if he must be dying. But when I held the baby, his skin began to change color. His complexion gradually went from gray to pink, and he opened his eyes to look at me. He had no eyebrows or eyelashes, and his eyes were oval-shaped and slanted. His eyes were blue, with only a little bit of white on either side of the iris.

In the first baby dream, I was also introduced to the short little gray beings commonly called the "grays." (I prefer to call them the gray people.) I realized at once that in some as yet unclear way the gray people had played a very important role in my life ever since my own babyhood. I was only mildly shocked by this realization.

One morning after waking up from a baby dream, I fell into a very light sleep state. "Who is the baby's father?" I asked. A nonhuman male appeared, tall and very slim with long, wavy blond hair, and blue eyes identical to the baby's. He was striding toward me in the vision, and he seemed angry. Just as he reached me, I bolted awake.

As fall turned to winter, the "trips" continued. There were nights I awoke from these trips to the realization that nothing in my life would ever be normal again. Nothing would ever be the same because *both my husband and I were being abducted*, we were experiencing regular, frequent extraterrestrial encounters. Fortunately, we could ask one another, "Honey, do you think I'm crazy?" and know that the response would be, "Of course not, dear."

My husband and I have been poked, probed, and injected, tissue samples taken, our body fluids withdrawn. Eggs and sperm have been removed, tests have been conducted, our bodies scanned. What an amazing thing it is to get out of bed on a winter's morning in the snowy, cold Northeast, to discover that your face and neck look *sunburned*. Try explaining *that* to the people you work with every day, the people who know you haven't been to the Virgin Islands recently or even out of town.

There were weeks when physical markings on our bodies would appear again and again. I began taking photographs of these rashes, bruises, and other strange markings. I now have quite a collection of photos.

One summer night when my husband was away on a business trip, I let the dog outside at about 10:00 P.M. As soon as I let the dog in, the cat, determined to have equal time, meowed to go out. He jumped up on my shoulder and we strolled slowly down the length of the driveway, enjoying the warm night air. At the end of the driveway, I turned and looked up at the star-studded sky above the house. A telepathic voice said, "You are connected to us." I *felt* connected to something, and this released in me simultaneous feelings of love, hate, fear, and anticipation. I returned to the house, knowing that I would be visited that night by extraterrestrials.

This was my first *conscious* close encounter (as opposed to the many dreams and night visions, or "trips"). When the three gray people entered my bedroom later on that night, around 1:00 A.M., I was *fully conscious*, wide awake.

An eerie, cold, white light was flooding the room as the three little gray people approached the bed. I found I couldn't move. But I could hear the low, even hum of something moving up and down the length of my body. Nothing actually touched me, yet I felt a subtle sense of some kind of radiating energy. It did not hurt, and I had no feelings of fear.

When I felt their energy receding, the white light disappeared. Suddenly, the sounds of night resumed. It had been abnormally silent during the visit: no highway noise, no crickets chirping, total silence. I looked at the clock: Only seven minutes had passed. It was as if time had stood still.

Later, I took the cat outdoors again, this time to see if there was any sign of the visitors. There was nothing, not even a star in the sky, which by then had clouded over.

As a veteran of many such visits now, I can honestly say that I believe what the extraterrestrial visitors are doing to us is in no way experimental. *They know exactly what they are doing to us* as a species, and have been doing it quite knowingly for a long time. There is an exchange occurring between the two species. Some would say that the exchange is not balanced, not in our favor. The visitors do invade our homes, render us helpless, and take what they feel they are entitled to: eggs, sperm, blood, tissue, DNA, whatever they want or need *to enhance their own species.*

We must acknowledge the fact that the gray people have been coming to the Earth for hundreds, perhaps thousands of years or longer. They have been interacting with humans for generations and, I believe, *there is a positive aspect to the relationship:* Over time, they have aided *us* in our evolution as a species.

The body scans, which occur on a very regular basis in the lives of most abductees, serve to keep the visitors informed regarding our health status. The "medical examinations" inform them about the levels of toxins in our bodies, thus tracking the amounts of pesticides and pollution in our environment. (Could this be one reason why so many abductees report that the visitors have strongly advised them to clean up the environment?) I believe they are working on our body energy as well, keeping everything in balance.

For me, these "checkups" typically occur several times a year. It is almost as if they have me on a regular schedule of visits, balancing my body's energies and testing me for toxic buildup. Both my husband and I are, by the way, in excellent health.

At times when illness has threatened, I have called upon the visitors to "please, take care of it." I feel that since they have the freedom to use our bodies for their own purposes, it is their responsibility to keep us healthy.

One Christmas season, my husband and I began to feel ill with stuffy noses and the onset of flulike symptoms. As we sat watching television one evening, I noticed a ball of blue light float through the air across the room. Later that night, I saw the ball of blue light again, this time floating across the bedroom ceiling. When my husband climbed into bed beside me, we held hands while I asked the Creator to minister to us through the angels as we slept.

Despite our discomfort, aches, and pains, we both fell asleep immediately. In the middle of the night, my husband felt so restless he decided to sleep in the guest bedroom. Later on, I awoke to the sensation of something touching the right side of my head above my temple. It was a tickly, electric feeling. Suddenly, and even though my eyes were closed, I saw the ball of blue light again. This time, the energy ball entered the right side of my head and floated across to the left side. The left side of my body began to shake. Then I felt my nasal passages begin to clear. My eyes stopped burning, my headache went away, the symptoms I had been suffering just disappeared. I knew I was being healed.

"Thank you," I said. "Please go to my husband now." Then I sat up and, for some unknown reason, turned to examine the wall behind my head. Just above the pillow, a pattern of light about seven inches high lit up the wall. The light image looked exactly like an angel, an angel with its wings folded. I couldn't believe it. I kept opening my eyes wider and wider, trying to get a closer look. The light did not come from the bedroom windows. There was no explanation for it. And I have not seen it again.

The next morning, both my husband and I felt fine. Our symptoms were gone. We knew that *something* had connected with us the night before, something that was angelic or extraterrestrial in nature.

There seems to be a much larger picture than I had originally thought in regards to the "whos" and "whys" of these experiences in my life because I also have had these types of experiences with what seems to be angelic contact. Yet, I wonder: *Are* these beings angels? Or are they *extraterrestrials*, operating in the form of beneficent messengers, the form traditionally ascribed to angels?

The most beautiful encounter experience I've had to date was with a being I thought was an angel. But this experience, too, left me with questions.

My husband was away on business when I awoke in the middle of the night to see the most beautiful being standing beside my bed. I could *feel* his love. (The being looked androgynous, but there was an element of masculinity present.) He had wavy blond hair that fell to his shoulders, and wore a long white robe. His arms were folded, his hands tucked into the deep sleeves of the robe. He did not have wings. He stood by my bed in an attitude of protection, his *black* eyes steadily watching, looking in my direction without looking directly at me. It was as if he were guarding me. Suddenly, he began to disintegrate into millions of tiny, sparkling fragments. It looked like fireworks, and then he was gone.

For almost a year afterward, I was unable to relate this incident to anyone without crying because the effect on me was so profound. Still, I had questions: What exactly *was* this being with black eyes, this being without wings? Could angels actually be *aliens*? Might the gray people be capable of shape-shifting, changing themselves to look like angels, somehow manifesting in *any form acceptable to the mind* of the human being?

There is, I am convinced, an alien-angel connection. How tightly bound that connection may be, however, is something I am not sure of.

There was a particular angel/ET entity who showed up regularly to offer me advice and guidance. I could never remember much of what she told me, however, once I returned to the waking state. One night, finding myself in her presence, I asked,

"Why is all this happening to me?" This time, her answer was imprinted on my *soul*: "You are being adjusted in order that you may offer others the choice of staying or leaving in times of crisis."

Soon enough, I learned what the entity meant by this statement.

During the summer of 1990, I had an unusual dream in which I found myself at the dentist's office. I was seated in one of those low-slung chairs you would find in any dentist's office, except that there were two or three of the very short, bald, *gray* people walking around. They each looked busy, focused on his own individual responsibilities. Then the "dentist" came into the room. He was of average height, but dressed completely in black (black crew neck sweater, black slacks) and his eyes were slightly slanted. He approached the chair on one side and asked me to open my mouth. He didn't touch my teeth as one would expect, but put something inside my mouth. I could feel a kind of warm assurance that seemed to be radiating from his clothing.

Whatever he put into my mouth did not hurt initially. Then it was shoved up into my soft palate and I could feel it moving up into place between my eyes, and possibly into my brain. There was a very odd sensation between my eyes that felt erotic as well as uncomfortable, then painful. "It's uncomfortable, stop, stop," I cried.

My head hurt upon awakening the next morning. When I got up, I realized that I was seeing light in front of my eyes. It was almost as if the light was coming *from* my eyes. My bedroom was bathed in light! As I moved about, my headache went away and my vision gradually returned to normal.

I now realize that the dentist "dream" was actually the insertion of an implant.* This implant was placed in my head, possibly in my brain, by extraterrestrials—or someone *not* "from here." This implant was inserted in order to enhance my awareness and psychic ability. Now, years later, I look at the experience objectively, knowing that, because of the implant, my abilities as a psychic and eventually as a remote viewer/remote healer were purposefully enhanced. I was "being adjusted" so that, sometime in the future, I would be capable of offering others "the choice of staying or leaving in times of crisis."

In the fall of 1990, three gray people led me into a white room to witness the implant insertion procedure on another human. The abductee was a white male with short brown hair. His eyes were closed and he as reclining in the same kind of "dentist chair" I had found myself in during my own experience. One of the gray people came up behind the chair with two small squares of light, one in each hand. The squares were laid against the man's head, one behind each of his ears, and I watched as the light was absorbed into his skull.

*Many experiencers report the insertion of a small, BB-sized object typically in the sinus area, tear ducts, or ears. Theories regarding the purpose of extraterrestrial implants vary, including the possibility that they are tracking devices and/or communications technology.—Au.

About six months later, I met this man. In *this* physical reality. We are now the very best of friends. We feel that the gray people introduced us, in a rather strange way, for a reason.

One day in 1996, this same friend called to recommend that I read *Cosmic Voyage* by Dr. Courtney Brown [see References, page 316], a book about scientific remote viewing. Since my friend tends to be more skeptical than I about these things, his opinion is, I believe, quite reliable. I knew nothing about remote viewing, but I read the book. Almost immediately, I announced to my husband that I very much wanted to attend Dr. Brown's Farsight Institute to train to become a remote viewer. And the following autumn, I flew to Atlanta for my first week of training at the Farsight Institute.

A *skill* that must be taught by trained professionals, remote viewing is the ability to accurately perceive information at great distances across space and time. Anyone can be taught the techniques, and the reliability of individuals trained in remote viewing is thought to be much greater than that of the best untrained psychics. It is not only a fascinating adventure, but a scientific exploration into the workings of the conscious/unconscious, or the "subspace" mind or soul. Remote viewing allows the participant's unconscious mind to communicate with his or her conscious mind. Training then allows the participant to accurately record information gleaned from the subspace mind or soul.

I've seen the past and I've peeked into the future.

Using remote viewing techniques, I have "targeted" places, events, and people from times distant in the past and way ahead in the future. I've traveled "off planet" to other worlds, other dimensions.

The remote viewing experience is both fulfilling and inspiring. It provides a grand overview of who we are and where we stand in the universe(s). Remote viewing is unlimited in its potential and has been used to locate missing persons, to diagnose illness, even to heal. Remote viewing is also one way to initiate contact with extraterrestrials.

At the Farsight Institute, one of the first things most of the students in my group noticed was the enormous amount of ET contact we were experiencing at night during the week we were there. Almost all of the Institute students in my group were abductees/experiencers. In fact, I would estimate that ninety percent of the trainees (to date there have been over a hundred Farsight Institute graduates) are close encounter experiencers. So none of us were frightened. Instead, we would gather around the breakfast table each morning and discuss the previous night's encounters. During these discussions, some students would recall encounter time spent in otherworldly classrooms. Sometimes we would remember encounter time spent *together*. One night, two of the instructors were taken up into a spacecraft above the hotel where we all stayed during our week of training. Later on, the event was remote viewed, confirming it in our minds.

By the time my plane left Atlanta for home, I had

decided to change careers. At the very least, I was determined to spend the next year training and developing my skills as a remote viewer.

After advancing through the second level of training, in which fifty targets were remote viewed (with a mentor monitoring me by telephone), I returned to Atlanta for the advanced training course. Advanced level remote viewing results in a keener detection of target information, and may lead to more conscious ET contact for many students. During the week of advanced training, we received complex protocols on extraterrestrial targets and targeted the Galactic Federation, which is like a United Nations for many extraterrestrial species throughout the universe(s). As I had been warned, the week at Farsight Institute was one of the most intense and exciting experiences of my life, with a lot of ET contact.

One significant physical event that occurred during this time was the disappearance of a rather large benign cyst from my back. I had been thinking how convenient it would be if the visitors were to remove it for me, since my doctor had told me that if a surgeon were to excise it, I would be left with a hole in my back. So one day while in my hotel room, I thought, *You've had so much control over my body all of my life, couldn't you at least remove the cyst? Please?*

The next day, I wore a lightweight but slightly itchy mohair sweater to the training sessions. Reaching up to scratch my back, my hand brushed the cyst: It felt softer, *different.* Suddenly, it broke apart. The cyst drained over a period of two days. Then it simply healed up, leaving no trace of scar tissue or any other indication that a cyst of that size had been embedded in my back.

Several months after advanced training, I began to use my remote viewing skills in a new way: *remote healing*. The healing potential of remote viewing has become my full-time job, and I am currently the founder of a network of remote healers from all over the country.

My first remote healing, however, was spontaneous. My youngest sister called one night in early August of 1997 to inform me that our sister Jane required outpatient surgery to unblock severely clogged neck arteries. She had been scheduled for two separate surgeries after an angiography* had revealed arterial blockage on the left side of seventy-five percent, with eighty percent blockage on the right side.

That evening, I began to meditate as usual. An image of Jane appeared before me, and in that moment, I *knew* that I could help her with her physical problem. I imagined myself shrinking, getting smaller and smaller until I was small enough to move into her left neck artery. (I was probably there *astrally*.) I moved to her collarbone and entered the artery. It was dark, so I created a tool for myself made from white light, a scraper that also radiated light. I held this tool out in front of me and moved

*Angiography is an X ray of the vessels of the body, in this case to determine the degree of obstruction due to cholesterol plaques.—Au.

it in an arc, swinging it back and forth, scraping off the cholesterol lining her artery. As the tool touched the plaques—which looked a lot like Brie cheese—the cholesterol melted like wax, dripping into the artery. I instructed the cholesterol to pass into the waste system and leave Jane's body by the normal elimination process.

I repeated this meditation several more times. Each time I entered my sister's left neck artery, the opening was larger, cleaner, obviously healthier. I knew that something was happening.

On August 19, Jane underwent the first scheduled surgery. The surgeon noticed that, to his surprise, the blockage had already been reduced by fifteen to twenty-five percent. He completed the procedure without incident.

The following evening, I called Jane's house and her husband informed me that she was still in the hospital, experiencing some complications. I immediately began a remote viewing meditation, in which I traveled to my sister's bedside. There, I pictured a blood pressure monitor with the indicator gradually falling from an elevated to a normal reading. I pictured rich, oxygenated blood circulating throughout her system, relieving her of headache pain.

The next afternoon, I called Jane's home once again. My sister answered the phone. She was in the middle of making dinner! "Since my headache went away and my blood pressure dropped last night, they let me come home this morning," my sister announced. When I asked her what time her symptoms

had cleared, she said, "Sometime before midnight."
I conducted the remote viewing session at 11:00 P.M.

A week or so later, my sister went to see her doctor. When she informed him that "My sister did this: She went into my artery with a scraper and cleaned it out," he appeared nonchalant. "Tell her that *whatever* she's doing, keep it up," he said, "because we have to operate soon on the other side."

I continued to use the remote viewing technique, this time to work on her right neck artery. I was able to conduct six to eight sessions before Jane's ultrasound in September. The scan revealed that the cholesterol level had dropped by forty percent. No further treatment was required. The second surgery was canceled.

This was, for me, an overwhelming, humbling, and *empowering* experience. I realized how readily this type of healing technique could be incorporated into remote viewing protocols. And I knew that anyone with training in remote viewing could utilize these techniques in order to *heal people at a distance*. It was an incredible discovery. But certainly not a new discovery.

This technique is, I soon discovered, very similar to certain ancient shamanic healing rituals. Military remote viewers, I was told, had also stumbled across the healing potential of remote viewing. And, once I began to network, contacting other remote viewers regarding healing techniques, I was amazed to discover that others, too, were exploring the idea of remote healing.

By the end of the year, I had organized a team of a dozen remote healers. Some viewers had been trained at the Farsight Institute. Others had attended the Monroe Institute in Virginia or had completed Silva Mind Control training workshops. [See Chapter 18.] We all felt very strongly that we had been guided by other, *higher* powers to join forces as remote healers. We called ourselves the Lightkeepers Remote Viewing/Remote Healing Network.

All members of the Lightkeepers have noted an increase in extraterrestrial contact since forming the Network. We feel that we are being guided, assisted in the development of our remote viewing and remote healing skills. Several mornings, I have awakened to the sound of a voice instructing me in the use of specific remote healing techniques. One night just recently, I had an encounter experience with a group of extraterrestrials I believe are directing us in our remote healing endeavors. Unlike the gray people, these ETs are very tall, over six feet. They are muscular, rugged, masculine-looking beings with golden tan-colored skin. They *look* intimidating, but are very gentle beings. I found myself feeling very grateful to be with them, yet afraid to look the beings in the eye. Other members of the Lightkeepers Network report encounters with these same beings.

Sometimes it is difficult to consciously recall the exact healing techniques and procedures taught to us during encounter experiences. But I feel that these beings are here now for a reason, and that the information they are sharing will become more and more conscious as time goes on. I also believe that as we pursue the study of remote viewing, we will naturally move to higher levels of awareness. Many of us are experiencing extraterrestrial encounters that are on a more conscious level than we've experienced in the past. So, for us, the extraterrestrial experience is now becoming more and more a part of *this* physical reality.

This has brought some of us to another level of awareness, one in which we experience interdimensional bleedthrough in the form of smells, sounds, even visions. For example, many experiencers recognize distinctive odors they associate with an interdimensional overlap and the "presence" of a specific ET species (e.g., the gray people are said to smell spicy sweet or smoky). This is one aspect of our evolution toward *an existence in integrated dimensional realities*.

Strange smells, balls of light, glimpses of other life forms . . . The bleedthrough of interdimensional experience requires a shifting of one's perception of reality to a more multileveled concept of what is "real." This requires a truly flexible attitude, something that evolves with much self-acceptance and self-validation. One must really learn to "go with the flow" in order to be able to integrate the anomalies into one's daily life.

I have now completed over 150 hours of training as a remote viewer. I teach remote viewing to students across the U.S., and I coordinate the Lightkeepers Network. There are not many days when I'm not up for remote viewing, ET contact, and the tweaking of my conscious mind. There are times, however, when I realize that "the good old days" of mundane concerns and everyday routine are over for me. Remote viewers learn one fact very quickly: The soul that travels, the person who bilocates, cannot stop the drive to seek the Truth. We must travel until the subspace ride comes to a complete halt, and no one can be sure (consciously) of exactly where their soul ride will end.

Seeing and healing at a distance is a gift. It is an inherent gift, as old as humankind, a gift we've forgotten how to use, a gift we forgot we even had. We can all access higher consciousness *if we so desire.*

Our bodies have been explored and explained to us by science. Our brains and minds have been mapped out by psychologists. But our *subspace mind or soul remains a place of mystery.* We can each choose to seek the truth of ourselves, using meditation, using remote viewing to discover a more complete picture of who we really are.

What might life on this planet be like if many of us were able to see and heal at a distance? What if millions of us could do so? Governments, businesses, medicine would be forced to change drastically. Honesty, ethics, and a serving of the people would be required. A relaxed, open society would probably result. Eventually, as we evolved into this new paradigm, we would trust ourselves to live by instinct. We would learn to solve our problems by creative, never destructive means. We would become a self-realized, nonviolent species.

The shaman has always known of the Spirit within. In our quest to become civilized, we've forgotten who we really are, created in God's image, connected to all that is. As we evolve, we will reintegrate with the God within each of us, to become all that we are meant to be.

CHAPTER 10

Peter Faust:
On Energy Work and
Extraterrestrial Healing

In 1992, Peter Faust went public with his ET encounter experiences, and has since become a leading voice for experiencers. Originally from Pennsylvania, where he became a licensed professional chef and teacher of the culinary arts, Peter moved to Boston in 1990 to change his career and to attend the New England School of Acupuncture. He currently has a private practice, Healing Arts of Belmont, and teaches at the Barbara Brennan School of Healing in New York. He is forty years old and is married to Jamy, a psychotherapist and energy healer.

Peter is a member of a small but growing segment of the alternative healer population, an energy healer who helps clients to *self-heal using extraterrestrial energy,* that is, energetic forces that come from elsewhere—other planets, other dimensions, other worlds. How he is able to assist his clients in utilizing this otherworldly energy for the purpose of healing their bodies and psyches is quite amazing.

All healers channel energy. But because of my abduction experiences, I have the ability to channel *extraterrestrial* energy. A lot of other healers do, too. I'm not unique in this regard. And I think a lot of other healers could be *trained* to channel extraterrestrial energies for their clients by going through certain "initiations." I use this term loosely because most healing schools are schools of initiation into healing energies of one form or another.

I have no experience of being healed by the aliens myself, except on a spiritual level. These experiences are *very* spiritual.

I was managing a hotel in the British Virgin Islands in the mid- to late 1980s when I began to have conscious extraterrestrial experiences. Around that time, my wife and I started to get interested in the metaphysical—crystals, channeling, things of that nature. Eventually, we left the hotel business to study energy healing. We attended the Barbara Brennan School of Healing in New York, one of the premier energy healing schools in the United States.

In 1989, I became conscious of my extraterrestrial experiences. Then, in 1992, I met Dr. John Mack* and began exploring my memories. (You can read about this in Dr. Mack's book, *Abduction*; my story is Chapter 13.) [See References, page 318.] It is unclear as to whether I had my extraterrestrial experiences and then the aliens somehow steered me to leave the hotel business and get into energy healing; or that,

---

*John Mack, M.D., is a Harvard psychiatrist who has worked with many ET experiencers. He is the founder of PEER, a national educational, research, and support group for experiencers. [See Appendix.]—Au.

because I got into energy healing, I was open to recover the memories of my extraterrestrial experiences. Regardless, what has happened since I
remembered my ET experiences is this: I have gone
from being a professional chef/hotel manager to
being a full-time energy healer and a licensed acupuncturist. I have a full-time practice now, which
combines acupuncture with energy healing.

Most healers are channels of energy. They don't
necessarily use their own energy for healings, but use
the life force, or the earth energy, or energy from the
Divine or from the Universe. A good healer really
has to get their ego out of the way, becoming egoless,
to let Divinity or God work through them. I utilize
this approach, too. I am the *instrument* for energy
running *through* me. And there are specific times
when I feel quite strongly that the quality of this
energy is *directly related to my extraterrestrial experiences* and to my willingness to open up to them.

Currently, I see twenty to twenty-five people a
week for acupuncture and energy healing, and I
probably work with one or two people each week
specifically around their abduction experiences. What
I do in these cases is to channel the extraterrestrial
energy, or the energy that is closest to the vibration
of their abduction experiences. This is a way for them
to *reexperience* those energies that they have during
contact or during an abduction, but in a gentler fashion. Most of the time, these people have a *positive*
experience in feeling the ET contact again. It feels
familiar to them. It feels like the aliens to them; it

feels like the quality of energy they've experienced when going through an abduction. Only safer, gentler.

I am not a hypnotherapist. But there *is* an aspect of regression work, kind of like what John Mack does, in that I'll help my client to go back and relieve their ET memories. But where I seem to be different from hypnotherapists is that it is my intention as a *healer* to invite the extraterrestrial beings—on an energetic level—into my healing space, and to work with me and through me in order to help the client. That is, I am able to help those clients who come to me and want to work on their abduction experiences by *bringing that extraterrestrial energy into the healing session.*

So, as a healer, I am consciously choosing to channel extraterrestrial energies. Whatever that means. I don't even *know* what that means, but that's what I do when I am not choosing to channel other types of energies. And there is no question that the channeling of extraterrestrial energies is very specific. I have a number of clients for whom it is *very clear* that this specific quality of energy comes through for them, particularly around their extraterrestrial issues.

Most times, my clients have a positive experience. Very often, they first go through the traumatic experience of reliving the abduction. I believe that they are essentially experiencing the psychological breakthrough of an existential experience, an otherworldly experience. In the regression, the trauma that is experienced is the shattering of their psychological boundaries. What I've seen is that, most times, when people break through that, when they get to the other side and the extraterrestrial energy is being channeled into the healing session, they begin to get very calm. Then they feel that ET contact again. And there is actually a longing and a missing of that connection they had with the extraterrestrials.

The more I do this work, the more I believe that the abduction experience is nothing more than contact or *reestablishing contact* with the beings that you have some kind of agreement with. Others might disagree, but everybody that I have worked with and everybody that I have known who has worked through their emotional biases has gotten to a place of positive experience with what is commonly called the "abduction experience." I see "abduction experience" as a fear-based label. The word "abduction" in and of itself has a negative connotation. I would prefer to see it called, more accurately, "contact" and "reestablishing contact."

In working with clients on their contacts with extraterrestrials, or on their own feelings of extraterrestrial energy, what has become very clear to me is that there are three levels of energy. That is, there exist three levels of energy a client will feel in order to reestablish contact with the extraterrestrials. These three energy levels are experienced when the client reestablishes contact through something called "cord connection."

Let me explain: There is a concept in energy healing called "healing cords" or "relationship cords."

Most esoteric teachings recognize that there exist energetic cords or strings that connect two people in a relationship. In other words, you are connected to your family, your friends through energetic streamers. These are the "cords which bind us together." Now, these cords exist on the etheric level, not the physical level. They're on the energetic level. As for our relationships to extraterrestrials, the cords are connected to our temples, primarily on the right side of the head. Also on the left, but mostly the right temple.

So, what I will very often see in my work is these relationship cords, strings that lead from the right side of the head out of the client's energy field, out of the auric field of the body, up into space. These strings lead *literally* back to the beings the client is connected to, the beings the client has had abduction experiences with or had a pre-incarnation relationship with.

It's kind of hard for me to say whether the strings lead up to a *planet* or to the beings. This gets a little fuzzy for me. I'm not real clear as to whether it's another dimension the cords are connected to, or whether it's an actual physical location. I think that beyond the Earth plane and the spiritual plane attached to the Earth plane, beyond all this lie the other dimensions, which is where the *extraterrestrial* dimensions may be. What is *very* clear to me is that the cords lead up, out of the energy field, and to the beings that the individual has a relationship with.

When clients come to me because they are confused about their abduction experiences or they want to remember and understand ET contact they might have experienced as a child, very often what I will do is reestablish their cord connections. How I do this is by holding a neutral space between the individual client on a human level and the extraterrestrials on an extraterrestrial level. I do this by splitting my consciousness, allowing myself to inhabit both worlds and to be a bridge for the client.

Now, this is not such a big deal in this context because most healers do this all the time when working on relationships. A healer will make a deep connection with their client, and they will energetically and psychically make a deep connection *long distance* with the other person in the relationship. Healers do this to try to bridge the relationship and try to clear it, so that the client can have an opportunity to reestablish the relationship on a clearer level—without all of the history, the psychology involved, and the trauma that goes along with all that. When I am working with clients to reestablish their relationships with extraterrestrials, I'm doing the same thing.

What allows me to do this work is my own abduction experiences. The other healers I have trained to do this work have had to work through either their own abduction experiences or their *fears* of extraterrestrials in order to be able to do it. The UFO field is very loaded. *Everybody* has an opinion: The aliens are good guys, they're bad guys, they're gray or they're blue. Are they Arcturians? Where *are* they from? My opinion is that a healer needs to work through their own projections around abduction experiences. A healer needs to be able to hold a space of *neutrality*, before being able to hold the space for someone who comes to them for a healing around extraterrestrial experiences.

My role as a healer is to hold that space, to make deep human contact with the client and help them to feel safe, and then to reestablish the relationship with the extraterrestrials. I invite the ETs into the healing space, into the room. I invite them in just the same way I would invite a client's ancestors or guides.

As I reestablish these cords with the extraterrestrials, *waves of energy* will begin to pass through the client. People often experience the first wave of energy as slow, heavy, a "molasses" type of feeling. This first wave may last for a few minutes, or for thirty or forty minutes. This is the first level of energy.

The second wave of energy is faster and deeper in the body. This energy level is a much higher vibration and has a finer quality than the first.

The third wave of energy comes through on an even deeper level. This wave feels *much* deeper in the body, and has a much higher or faster vibration than the previous two.

Now, if you understand the concept of past lives, you are aware that healing will often bring up past lives. I think there is another aspect to healing: *parallel lives*. I think that our consciousness is able to have relationships with beings that are not part of our past lives, but are part of our *present* life—only *on a different dimension*. Past lives connotes a linear progression of time and consciousness. Parallel lives connotes holding simultaneous consciousness with other beings. *Extraterrestrial healing* connotes holding this simultaneous consciousness with other beings.

If the person has a positive experience during the healing, then the trauma is somehow released from their body. That way, they can come to peace with the past life or the abduction experience. And I think a lot of the trauma people are experiencing is the trauma of *different energetic vibrations,* the trauma that comes from the difference in vibrations that exists between ourselves and the extraterrestrial beings.

When we first meet someone from a different race or culture, there is a "getting used to," a trying to feel a resonance with the other person. When we begin to establish a relationship with someone who is foreign to us in any way, there is this energetic give-and-take that happens as we achieve a sense of comfortableness with one another. With extraterrestrials, it is no different. Except that they are *extremely* different than us *energetically* because they are nonhuman.

Now, some clients come to me who have not had ET contact but want to go through the healing process. I believe that this healing technique then establishes an energetic connection for the client with beings that will, in our lifetime, make contact with us. (And this information came through in my own abduction experiences: There are going to be Earth changes, planetary changes, and contact with extraterrestrials because of it.) When these beings come here and we interact with them, there will be an energetic connection. So, my clients will have already established the energetic connection. And there will exist a familiarity there. These clients may not go through the trauma that others will when the ETs show up.

By channeling the extraterrestrials' vibrations in a very specific manner, I am helping my clients to *encode the vibration.* That way, they will be able to feel comfortable in the presence of ETs much more quickly than people who have not experienced the extraterrestrial healing techniques.

I have used this extraterrestrial healing technique both with people who are having trouble integrating their abduction experiences and with people who do not have any conscious memory of abduction experiences or ET contact. And they all feel the vibrations, the three waves of energy. But there is no perceivable change in their bodies afterward. In other words, the extraterrestrial healing technique that I use has not healed cancer or any other illness to my knowledge.

But sometimes when people come to me with a physical problem, I will tap into what I consider extraterrestrial energy and channel that. I have seen that with certain physical problems *it works.* I think this is due to the fact that the beings seem to be very *exact* in their energy. So, if I go into a trance state and invite in the extraterrestrials as I know them and have experienced them, there is a certain energy that will work through me. It inhabits my body, and then

I get very focused and very nonemotional, almost robotic and laserlike. I seem to be able to really focus energy out my fingertips and out my palms. And with a different quality to it that is really *exact*, really laser beamlike, very sharp. Primarily, I've seen the technique help on simple stuff, and I'm not sure if this is because the beings are just showing me how to use this energy. But it sure seems to help backaches, knee problems, and things of that nature.

There is a specific way to access and use extraterrestrial energy. What I do is, first, I get grounded. Then I feel my own connection to the extraterrestrials by feeling my own relationship cords, and allowing the connection to work as a two-way street. I allow the extraterrestrial energy to then move through my body, and to fill the whole room. I bring that quality or that vibration of energy around myself, my client, the healing space we are in, so that I am creating a sacred healing space.

Next, I help the client to feel *their* connection to the beings. Then I begin to work energetically, allowing the energies to come through. At this point, it might be enough. But very often, the next step is to begin to run the energy very specifically, into parts of the client's body. I run the energy through my hands, through my fingertips, into specific parts of the client's body.

Just as in the typical healing session in which spirits show up—angels or guides or ancestors—in these healings what I would perceive to be extraterrestrials show up. Sometimes they take the form of little gray beings, the "grays" most people are familiar with from the media. Sometimes they take the form of other beings that have a different quality to them, a non-Earthlike quality.

Healers often see implants in the energy fields of the clients they are working with, so a lot of healers have opinions about ET implants. My personal opinion is that an implant, like anything else in a client's energy field, has a *reason* to be there. I have yet to see an implant in a client's *physical* body.* But to work with the implants I see on the astral field, I will bring my consciousness to the implant and help the client bring their consciousness to the area of the body where they feel the implant. Instead of just removing the implant, I will then ask the client to focus in on it and on why it is in their energy field at this time.

Nine times out of ten, whenever I begin to feel around for an implant, an extraterrestrial guide shows up. The guide is always in the form of an etheric being, but *distinctly extraterrestrial*. Very often, I will then receive information from the ET as to why the implant is there, and the client will also receive this information simultaneously. I think it is impor-

---

*A number of implants have now been removed surgically and examined in scientific laboratories. A report on the results of such research published in *MUFON Journal* in 1998 indicated that laboratory analysis of six implants revealed a complex structure that included crystals. Some researchers have speculated that such implants may be fragments of meteorites. The implications of recovering crystalline pieces of meteorite embedded in the human body are unknown.[1]—Au.

tant for the client to receive their own information. It is not right for me, as the healer, to tell the client why the implant is there. The client needs to begin to understand their own relationship with the ETs, and their own relationship with the implant.

After this, sometimes an implant is removed and returned to the ETs. More often, the implant will be activated, or reactivated in some fashion, in order to change the vibration in the energy field of the client. I've seen this happen over and over again! So I will not simply remove the implant unless I receive instructions to do so from the ET guides *and* the client, instructions that are in sync.

It's been almost six years now since I began my regression work with Dr. John Mack. And I am *very* glad that I have had the extraterrestrial experience. It's changed my life in every way I can imagine and *cannot* imagine. It's changed *me*—on a cellular level. I am not the same person I was six years ago.

When I was first uncovering all of my extraterrestrial experiences, it flipped out everybody in my family. I lost friends because of it. I thought I would never get a license as an acupuncturist, I thought I would be laughed out of my hometown, I thought my wife would leave me. And I thought I was losing my mind. Which I was, because you *do* lose the boundaries of your mind when you go through this experience. But *it expands your consciousness.*

So, back in 1992, when I was sitting on my back porch smoking cigarettes and drinking whiskey and wondering if I could hold it together, wondering if I was losing my mind and if I had made the whole thing up, back then I would have said *no*, I did *not* want the extraterrestrial experience. Even three and a half years ago, I would have said, "I don't know." It put a lot of strain on my marriage; it put a lot of strain on *all* of my relationships. I wasn't sure *how* I felt about it.

But today, I can say that I am grateful for the experience. It's made me feel "different" and separate. But it's also made me feel closer to my wife, to my family, and to God.

When I say "God," I do not mean God in a religious sense, but in a global, universal sense. Because of my ET experiences, now I *know* that we are not alone in the universe. I know now that God created a *lot* of things in His or Her likeness, not just us. I know that when I die, there's another world, another life. But I am certainly going to have a lot of questions when I die!

My experiences have made me more convinced that there is a lot more to life than a house in the suburbs and money in the bank, all of that materialistic b.s. that I'm caught up in just like everybody else. I have a glimmer that there is more to life than this. It has made me appreciate life on a much deeper level.

I have also had the opportunity, because of my extraterrestrial experience, to help other people. And that has been a gift to *me* as well. I am very grateful for that, too.

CHAPTER 11

Nancy Leggett:
Celestial Healer

Nancy Leggett grew up in South America and Haiti, the daughter of an American diplomat. She is fifty-one years old and works as a billing administrator in a major metropolitan hospital in South Florida, where she has lived for over twenty-five years. Nancy is the woman on the bench at the cancer center, the healer who used blue light to scan my thyroid, the person who told me that she is from another world, here for the purpose of healing others.

Nancy is one of a small subgroup of medical practitioners who hold what I consider to be the most radical beliefs in medicine today. Healers like Nancy offer a *radical alternative* to all of the more popular alternatives to Western medicine currently available. In order to work with celestial healers like Nancy, one must stretch oneself to what may be the furthest reaches of believability. Believe *me,* I know what it takes to do just that.

The cutting edge of biomedical understanding today includes vibrational or energy medicine, that is, recognition of the unseen energy fields around the physical body and the influence of these fields on health. These energy fields are regarded as part of a unified field that exists as vibratory bands, possibly electromagnetic in nature, occurring in a spectrum of varying vibratory frequencies. In energy medicine, all healing is regarded as a change in the body's vibration, and any illness is viewed as a manifestation of disturbances in the body's normal vibrations. To simplify, if one regards the body as a kind of human radio, good physical health exists when you are "tuned in" to the right "station," while illness results if you are not properly tuned in but slightly off, between stations for example. Energy healers tap into the unseen energy forces to change their clients' internal vibrations, aligning the ill person with the proper "station" for health.

If this sounds far out, it is. Especially when one recognizes the fact that celestial healers like Nancy—and Ingrid Parnell, and Peter Faust, and Bev Marcotte, and others— tap into the *extraterrestrial realms* for the energy they utilize to help their clients heal.

I was born a healer. It's a gift. Even when I was young, I knew I was a healer. Then, in my thirties, I started searching. I studied the American Native Indian tradition, and this led to extraterrestrial contact.* I've always had contact, but I never could pin down what it was before that. It's funny because I feel very comfortable with ETs. I feel like I'm a part

*For many generations, Native Americans and other indigenous peoples have experienced contact with nonhuman beings they may refer to as "star people," accepting such extraterrestrial relationships as a part of their worldview.—Au.

of them. I *am* part of them. I'm not even from this planet.

Growing up, I always felt that I was weird, not your usual person. I felt I was an oddball. Even now, I don't connect with people. I find it difficult to relate to people on a third dimensional level. There are only a few close friends that I'm able to talk to on a different level, on my level.

I believe I had contact with extraterrestrials when I was young. I had imaginary friends, and I used to play with them a lot of the time. My parents sent me to a psychologist because, I guess, I wasn't the way other kids were. Yet, with the ETs, I always felt at home. I could talk and be understood, because I was with my *real* family then.

After my father's death, I had hypnotherapy. Then I got into self-hypnosis and meditation, and I began working with crystals. Overnight, my life changed. It was like a bomb: The energy was such that it just *had* to explode. And when I began living by myself, I began having a lot of contact with the ETs. But, like I said, they've *always* been there.

In 1987, I came into contact with other people who were "walk-ins," that is, souls from other planets in human bodies. I learned about the Arcturians and the Pleiadians.* And I started doing their technologies. What I do is called vibrational medicine or energy medicine. People call me to speak to me because

---

*Pleiades is a star cluster in the constellation Taurus consisting of several hundred stars.—Au.

they experience certain changes in energy, and it helps to lift their vibration. In order to raise their vibration, I advise people to use Tachyon* and Etherium Gold. [See Resources, Products list, page 321.] Tachyon raises the body's vibration and gold holds the highest vibration so if you take it, it raises your body's vibration. The higher your vibration, the better it is when we—as a planet—go through energy shifts. We're all raising up into another vibration right now because the planet is rising to the fifth dimension. It *is* happening! We're *right there*. Everything is crumbling, paradigms are cracking. It's inevitable.

All the technology that I have researched—Tachyon, Etherium Gold, and whatever comes next—the ETs guide me to these things. For example, the Pleiadians encourage us to take gold. It works like a cleansing, helping you to get rid of the baggage you're holding on to, emotional baggage. You *have* to let it go. And, I would have to say, the Arcturians were guiding me to Tachyon. I started doing research on Tachyon, and eventually started working as a distributor. I also got involved in the Ascension technologies. But the Arcturians work with Tachyon energy, so that's what I use now.

I definitely think I'm guided by the Arcturians. And I feel I've done this before, in other lifetimes. Plus, a lot of work has been done on *me* by the Arcturians, which is like an initiation.

*Tachyon products are comprised of tachyon energy, a faster-than-light, free energy form.—Au.

I also work with implants and remove blockages. But I form my own modalities. I have developed a combination of different modalites, including reflexology, but I am not limited to just working on the feet. I'm at the point now where I'm receiving information from the ETs about reflexology, as the newest in the mix of modalities I work with for healing.

I always work with the blue light, because I hold the blue ray. (Everybody has a color. I was told I hold the blue ray.) I work with a lot of cobalt. I direct this cobalt blue light while in a meditative or semitrance state, bringing it into the client's body to heal the affected area.* I also use other colors but blue is the primary color I use. Now I even see in that color: If I'm looking at something, I'll see a cobalt sheen. So I know I'm raising my vibration.

The first healing I did, my friend wanted me to take a look at this girl who had throat cancer. So I did psychic surgery. Whenever I do a healing, I'm in a state of semitrance. When I go into this trance state, I feel like I'm completely guided. It's like I'm being guided as to what to remove and what not to remove. That's where the psychic surgery comes in: removing and sealing, removing and sealing.

Afterward, the girl went to the doctor and he couldn't find anything. He couldn't even find the adhesions from the radiation they'd given her. He told

*According to the Arcturian teachings, the vibrational frequency of an individual who is being healed must be accelerated with a crystalline field of light.—Au.

her, "I don't know what you did. And I'm not going to ask you. I'm going to call this a miracle."

That was five years ago. Since then, there have been a selective few people that I've done healings for. I don't do it all the time. I guess I've held back. I think sometimes, "What am I *doing*?" You know? But that's my struggle: not having the faith.

If you really want to be healed, I'd say your main healing will come from *learning not to fear*. Fear sets limitations. You see, people of the light are out there. And they—we—have cut the path for the rest. So you've got to have trust. The people of the light, we're here to say that sometimes you don't have to go through all the physical pain, the medical "cures." Instead, people must look at themselves mentally and spiritually *first*. And *then* physically. Often, what people are going through is actually very spiritual, or mental, or emotional.

I tell many, many people this because I work in the system: *Medicine is a business.* Usually, the spirituality of healing is just not there.

Today I was standing with a doctor and an accountant. (As the billing administrator for a hospital department, I manage its accounts.) And they were talking about percentages. Percentages! To me, it was intense. I'm saying, "This is not a *factory*." But the reality is that people are railroaded like cows. *Some* people are going to need surgery. But how many are being railroaded because of percentages? I have to stand there and look at this every day.

But there is one doctor I'm working with on

Tachyon. You see, I don't take on the multitude. I just take on one at a time. And if I change his vibration, then I'll be changing everyone he works with. Then that can make a change all the way around.

Maybe I'm at the hospital to make changes in a very subtle way. I take my healing tools in to work. When a coworker has a headache, I'll do some healing work. I also sell Tachyon to some of my coworkers. I take my samples with me and I start to work with them. And the interest is growing.

One coworker used to go to "happy hours," things like that. Then I started her on Tachyon and the Gold. She told another coworker that it turned her whole life around. I was happy to hear that. But I can't reach everyone. I help one person at a time.

So, I've been aware of the ET presence for a long time. And there's tons of them here. Tons! It looks like a parking lot upstairs. Over the Earth? It's like a parking lot. You've got the Andromedans; you've got the Arcturians, the Pleiadians, the Orions; the ones that do the abductions, the "grays," the Zetas from Zeta Reticuli . . . Meanwhile, abductees are *still* trying to convince people that they've been abducted! And they're angry. They feel like they've been victimized, that they're being stopped from telling what has happened to them and they're being looked at as abnormal.

More and more people are going to have to become aware of the fact that *the ETs are here.* If people deny it, it's because they fear that extraterrestrial beings must want to take over the planet. That's the concept presented to us in the movies, the media. But it's not true. They're *not* here to take over. They can't deal with this vibration, the Earth vibration. It's too dense, it's like Jell-O to them. So why are they here? Because *we* are rising, moving into the fifth dimension. And they have come here to help with that.

Public awareness is on the rise. The light is really coming in. And it's inevitable that we're all going to experience seeing these extraterrestrial beings because, as I said, the planet is rising to the fifth dimension. And as Mother Earth rises, the veil is going to drop.

CHAPTER 12

Ingrid Parnell: ''Healer of Love''

Born in Trinidad of Swedish/Scottish ancestry, Ingrid Parnell moved to the U.S. in 1978, becoming a citizen in 1984. For more than a dozen years, she has worked for two obstetricians as an insurance secretary. She is sixty-five years old and a grandmother.

An exceedingly warm person, Ingrid immediately charms with her melodious Trinidadian accent. I interviewed Ingrid after discovering that she had worked with Nancy Leggett to conduct a celestial healing on *me* [see Chapter 17].

I really don't know, but I think I'm a healer of love more than anything else. I teach people to love themselves, to accept life as it comes and to rise above it, and to strengthen themselves as they move along in this world. Obstacles or bad situations that come into our lives are just there to make us stronger.

I've always had people telling me things, ever since I was a little girl. Eventually, I got into healing. I have no idea what drew me to it except that I felt it was something I *had* to do and I had no control over it. So here I am.

I was born in Trinidad. People here are fascinated when they meet me because of my accent. It was great growing up there, among so many races and creeds. Island people are a happy kind of people, tolerant and accepting of others.

From an early age, I was very attuned to the earth, stars, planets, animals, and, above all, people. I also have long felt very connected to Native Americans. But my mother was not very open to anything other than traditional religion with its rules, beliefs, and fears. So it was not until I came to the U.S. that I began to allow myself to open up to what was inside my soul center.

Today, I am a certified hypnotherapist and a practitioner of touch-type natural healing.* With a group of others, I work very closely with the Arcturians. The Arcturians are extraterrestrials who are helping the Earth and her people to once again honor all living things and to understand and know the immense God-given power we have within us.

I studied hypnotherapy and was trained in the touch-type of natural healing, in which you learn to open yourself up like a channel to God and the Universe. You are like a conduit. You trust, and open yourself up to the healing energies, or the healing life forces, that are available to you. And you trust that whatever the person you are healing needs will move through

---

*Also known as Light Touch healing, the "hands-on" healing methods rely on the practitioner's hands for energy transfer/healing work.—Au.

you and into them. Whoever comes to you for healing has to have the faith that what you're bringing into them is not something that will harm them, but is something they may need. And it doesn't matter whether it's physical, mental, or spiritual.

This type of healing work is a very beautiful experience. Every time I do it, I feel as if I myself receive a lot from it. It's something that I really love to do. I hope that someday I'll be doing healing full time. I'd like to work with a doctor who is willing to let me help with patients diagnosed with cancer. I would like to help them to work through the illness, whether the result is to heal or to accept that it is time to leave this life.

The healing energy I work with comes from whatever you want to call Source, or God, or the Universe. It's a universal energy that I feel is beyond anything we can name or put into a category. To me, this force that comes through me is so huge and so beyond anything we know, it must be the God Source.

When I'm doing a healing, I can feel myself guided to put my hands on different areas of the body. Sometimes, I find I might put my hands in one particular area for most of the session because I feel within myself that's what the person needs. It's almost like if you let go and allow your hands to be moved, you will move yourself to wherever the energy is needed. I sometimes find that I have to consciously make myself let go. If somebody comes to me for a session and I'm a little bit nervous, all of a sudden, I'll feel an incredible energy envelop me. And I'll be relieved of that doubt, and just trust.

Healing is very difficult. But we *can* do it, especially if one believes that there are other energies all around us. That God is all around us, and angels, and whatever you want to call "them." It doesn't matter what your religion is. They're all the same. And they're here to help us.

I love working with Nancy [Leggett] because that's another kind of healing: We open ourselves up to different energies from different planets. These energies can move through us and help us to see things. And then we can help others to heal themselves.

My first ET experience was strange and amusing and wonderful. I had gone to a psychic fair where I bought a book about extraterrestrials, the Pleiadians. I didn't know anything about them at the time, but I was drawn to it and brought the book home. The next day was a Sunday, and I lay down on my bed and began to read this book. It was *fascinating*.

Now, I'm not a person who sleeps during the day. But the next thing I knew . . . Well, I *thought* I was dreaming, and then I realized I was *not* dreaming. It was an amazing experience: I saw a being, I felt this wonderful being right next to me. And he (I say "he" because the energy *felt* male; it wasn't that I could *see* he was male), he held my head very gently between his hands. Then he took a beautiful sort of crystal and pressed it against my right temple very, very forcefully. He drew it down the right side of my face, right down to my jawline. As he drew it down, the pressure got more and more intense until I felt that I was going to scream. I couldn't stand the pressure any longer! And when it got to that point, all of a sudden something gushed out of my nose. It was a big relief: Something had moved through me, and at the same time, he released the pressure and moved his hands away, gently letting go of my head.

So, what I had felt was this extreme pressure and this very powerful gush of whatever it was that came right through my nose. It felt as if it were being drawn down from my brain. It was liquid, but almost solid, strange. It was from my brain, and it was removed through my nose. It was really incredible. You know when you uncork something and then release it? It felt like that.

The most amazing thing about this experience was that I was not in the least bit frightened. Afterward, I was in amazement as to what had happened. I thought to myself, *What was that?* But I wasn't afraid. I was never scared. And I was very aware that it was *not* a dream. I was *sure* within myself that it was not a dream.

I also felt *very* strongly that it was some force from somewhere else, maybe another planet, another world, or some*one* who knows a lot more than we do. I felt that they were removing something from me that was like a blockage, and that they were doing a clearing, so that I could see things differently, maybe work differently. It was a very powerful force. I was in awe of it.

This happened four or five years ago. Since then I've catapulted forward in my healings, in my awareness, in my intuition, in my inner strength, and in my knowingness that what I need to do is this healing work. So the experience did change a lot in my life.

I had another experience, something very similar. It was maybe two years ago and was also pretty exciting and wonderful. Nancy [Leggett] does psychic healings sometimes. The first time she asked me to assist her, we went to a friend's house to help her because she was having a lot of back pain. All I needed to do was to stand at her feet and, putting my hands there, allow the energy of the universe to move through me. I was to help her keep calm and accepting during the healing session while Nancy healed her. It took about an hour.

All of a sudden, I saw and felt Nancy differently: She was like a being from somewhere else. *It wasn't Nancy anymore.* The being turned *his* face and looked straight at me and smiled. I felt as if he were saying to me telepathically that we had done this many times before. And then he gave me the strangest smile. It was like a smile of recognition. Yet, it was not only of recognition but of "Don't be concerned, you've done this already." Like a confirmation. And then it was back to Nancy again. The being was gone.

If you are interested in this kind of healing work and you trust that there are products you can use to help you be more centered, to feel more connected to the energies around us, and to clear your system, then Tachyon is something that I would recommend you try. Tachyon has helped me a lot. [See Resources, Products list, page 321.]

I also recommend to people that they learn to visualize. I keep telling people all the time that *there is energy available to us.* If you meditate, and allow a beautiful light to come into you (a white light, or whatever colors you like), you can renew and rejuvenate *all* the cells in your body.

To do this, visualize a light. Bring the light inside yourself, and move it to every area of your body. Fill yourself up with it. You can do this in five seconds, or lie down and enjoy it, or sit with your spine straight and let it flow through you. You can put the light into an area of your body that is bothering you, or hurting you, or that you have concern about. You can visualize the light there. You will see it getting bigger and brighter, and healing the area.

It's also nice to teach your children to do this. Teach them that all these energies are available to them to keep them healthy. I do meditations with my grandchildren. I tell them that there is a beautiful, huge, blue star that is above their heads. I let it come right down onto them, and then I tell them, "Okay, now the star is going to burst into millions and millions of tiny little blue stars. And they're all going to enter into you until your whole body is tingling with these little blue stars. Your fingers, and your toes, and your knees . . . *everything* is tingling and healing, helping you to stay healthy."

So they do this visualization. One is seven and one is ten. They love it! I have a nice table that I do my healings on. And they can't *wait* to get up there!

I am sixty-five now. And my life has turned into an adventure of the soul.

CHAPTER 13

David Miller: Channeler of ETs and Celestial Beings

David Miller is a trance medium, a "conscious channeler" who channels celestial beings and extraterrestrials, including the Arcturians, often for healing purposes. His meditation project, "Group of Forty," involves people from all over the world who meditate simultaneously while he channels the Arcturian energies. Group meditations are aimed at lifting the Earth's vibrations, and typically include healing experiences for members.

David's channeled book, *Connecting With the Arcturians*, was published in 1998. He is fifty-two, and lives in Prescott, Arizona. You can read a transcript of the channeled healing he conducted for me in Chapter 17. Since I had been a client, David agreed to share his insights on the origin and practice of the type of celestial channeling and healing he effects.

Around six years ago, I went on a camping trip with my wife to the Grand Canyon. We took a four-wheel drive trip on a dirt road to this place called Sublime Point, one of those very beautiful overlooks on the North Rim. When we got there, we were sitting, meditating, and I started to spontaneously talk about my wife's past lives. Then I started doing what I would call automatic speaking, which is another name for channeling. For the next day or two of the vacation, I continued to spontaneously channel.

Now, I had studied Jewish mysticism for sixteen years before this happened. I'd had a long metaphysical interest. But it was only after I started studying about channeling, after this happened, that I realized that many of the ancient rabbis were trance channels as well.

I started by channeling a rabbi teacher, that was the first entity I channeled. He worked with me for around a year, helping me in my studies. I also began attending lectures about channelers, and I frequently attended channeling sessions in Sedona [Arizona] to see what other mediums were doing.

Then a friend gave me a copy of the book *We, the Arcturians.*[1] I read about three chapters. When I put the book down, I started channeling the Arcturians. I was very moved by the book. The Arcturians were the first extraterrestrial entities that I channeled.

After listening to some of the other channelers, after being with them for several hours, I was able to pick up the energy and channel the entities *they* were channeling. It seems that I was stimulated by these other channelers, but I can't channel *everybody* who is being channeled. Only if I feel a very strong resonance with them, like I felt with the Arcturians.

The Arcturians are fifth dimensional beings, so they are actually *extradimensionals.* They are in charge of a very high energy point called the Stargate. I have channeled several lectures about the Stargate, and I have also seen references to it in Edgar Cayce's writings. He stated that when we are finished with our lifetime here on Earth, we can go through a central clearing place (these are not his terms, these are my terms). This central gateway is guarded or overseen by the Arcturians. They are helping us in ways that would foster our moving into our fifth dimensional experiences.

The fifth dimension is higher than this dimension. It's beyond the Earth experiences, so when you are in the fifth dimension, you are no longer in an incarnation here. There is an energy field around the Earth, and when you die, you go into that energy field; then you incarnate and come back. But when you go to the fifth dimension, you are beyond that. The fifth dimension has no dualities like we have here, so the fifth dimensional beings have no concepts of life and death, good and bad, etc. Also, *there is no fear.* In order to enter into this kind of realm, you have to be of a very heightened energy. You cannot be in hatred or violence or fear.

The Arcturians are living in this type of dimension, and part of their mission is to assist those of us who want to come onto that level. (Now, they are not the only beings who are on the fifth dimension. The Pleiadians, for example, are also on the fifth dimension.) The Arcturians are not human figures, they have a different form. They have given many lectures to humans, and not just through me. There are several other people in the United States who channel the Arcturians.

The Arcturians have what they call "healing chambers," areas that are in their spaceships. Their ships are in "corridors," areas that are between dimensions. So they have these ships that are in corridors, and in these ships they have these healing chambers where they can take us (if we want to) in our meditations. When we go up to that place, we can experience the Arcturians' special vibrations, special tones, special sounds, and special crystals that they use to work with us.

We go up to their healing places in what is called the "etheric body." It is my understanding that they can help us heal the etheric. The etheric is the *other* body, the energy field that is invisible around the body. It could also be viewed as a type of mental energy. It can travel, "astral travel," without the physical body. If we take that etheric or astral body and go to the Arcturians' healing chambers where they can work with us, then, when that etheric body returns to our physical body, we can experience a physical healing. Also, because we are living in a lower density where there is lots of fear and hatred, anything we can do to get ourselves out of this type of energy field is very healing. But it's hard to do.

The healings that occur with channeling the Arcturians also have to do with the tones. I've had to become more skilled with using sounds and tones.

The healings with the Arcturians (and the other beings that I channel) are not only in words, but also via channeled *energy*. This is an interesting concept because we are so geared to words, but there is also a channeling of actual *energy*. So the channel is not only a conduit for telepathic thoughts, but also a channel of energy. The channel can bring down different energies for people that can be very healing. Or the channel can bring down certain tones, those tones that can change a person's energy field.

One time I was doing a channeling in a group and we were bringing in what was called the "Divine Light from the Creator." After the session, a woman in the group discovered burns on the back of her legs, blisters from the energy generated by the Light! She wasn't freaked out by it, but she said that she felt she was in *so much of the higher energy* that it burned her legs. She said that this was the first time she had been able to experience this heightened energy. Later, she wrote me a letter saying how good she felt, that she'd been able to find a kind of harmony or peace.*

One woman I worked with had Bell's Palsy.† Her

*From the letter to David Miller: "The areas behind my knees actually blistered with a large burned patch on each leg from upper thigh to middle of my calf. The burn was very cold and seemed to be caused by extreme cold instead of heat. I am happy to report that the burns healed quickly and I am back to normal. Has anyone else ever experienced anything like this.?"[2]—Au.

†Bell's Palsy is a neurological disorder with paralysis of facial muscles, causing an inability to close the mouth and one eye. The cause is typically unknown, unless a tumor is present or a physical trauma to the facial nerve has been identified. Facial deformity may be temporary or reduced with plastic surgery.—Au.

doctor told her that it might or might *not* heal. We did a channeled healing session, translating energy into her energy field. Within a few weeks, she experienced almost total recovery. Now, this raises the issue of whether she had the recovery because she *felt* that something had happened during our session, or whether she was going to recover anyway. You can go through a list of all the possibilities. But *it doesn't matter to her.* It would have been devastating to her, at age forty-one, to be suffering from Bell's Palsy.

One of the things that I've found in doing this kind of healing work is that when energy is released from the person I'm working with, I have to be careful that I don't absorb that negative energy. Released negative energy can be floating around for a while. I'm learning to protect myself with grounding and by putting energy protection around my body. I don't want to end up absorbing this negative energy and falling ill. This can happen to psychotherapists, too. I'm going to New York where I'll be channeling in front of five or six hundred people. So I think this is something I have to learn, how to protect myself from the negative energy.

My understanding is that beings like the Arcturians will use you as an instrument, but only for what you can tolerate. People may ask a channeler, "If you're channeling, why can't you do surgery and remove a tumor?" or "Why don't you have knowledge of everything when you channel?" But people have to understand that we are *instruments*. The beings we channel are not going to interfere in our karma. And part of the channeler's karma is to be telepathically in touch with higher beings. But the beings are not going to turn us into supermen (or superwomen)! Channeling is an interaction, helping the channeler to use his or her higher skills, and perhaps to stay on the cutting edge.

So, sometimes I can do extraordinary things when I'm channeling. Other times, I work with people who are very stuck and it is really hard to move them. And sometimes, I'll start channeling things that I don't want to channel. Recently, the first words that came to me during a session were, "My condolences." And I thought, *I'm not sure I want to transmit* that *message.* But, obviously, such information needs to come through. I, too, have to remember that the channeler is just a channel.

It takes lot of maturity as a psychic to work with these types of issues. For example, if someone is dying: You have to be clear that you do not interfere in their karma, and that you do not take on their karma. Unless it was their karma to come to you and you are *supposed* to heal them.

All healers have to consider these issues. I know I don't have all the answers yet.

PART III

More Celestial Healings

"Penetrating so many secrets, we cease to believe in the unknowable. But there it sits, nevertheless, calmly licking its chops."
—H. L. MENCKEN

CHAPTER 14

Preston Dennett: Ufologist

A field investigator for the Mutual UFO Network (MUFON), one of the largest UFO organizations in the world, Preston Dennett has been researching UFO incidents for over ten years. He is the leading authority on extraterrestrial healings, listing over a hundred cases in his first book, *UFO Healings.* Dennett lives in southern California, and lectures nationally on unusual UFO phenomena.

When I first began researching this book, I received a very friendly letter with an open offer of assistance from Preston Dennett. So I took him up on his generous proposal: I telephoned him at once, and he referred me to a number of individuals who were willing to speak of their celestial healing experiences. A bright and funny young man, Preston also entertained and enlightened me by sharing some of his own experiences and insights into the celestial healing phenomenon.

Part III features interviews with two professionals who work extensively with cases of celestial healing. In addition to Dennett, Barbara Lamb, a therapist who conducts hypnotherapeutic regression sessions with experiencers, provides her professional insights on the phenomenon. A brief historical overview of some of the most interesting cases of celestial healing follows. This section concludes with my own case and reflections on the extraordinary extraterrestrial healing experience.

I used to be a skeptic. I didn't believe *any* of the UFO stories and I was really *not* into it at all. I was kind of repulsed by the topic, actually. I would think, *They're all kooks,* or *It's just misperceptions.* The usual skeptic's reasoning.

Then, in 1986, I heard about a UFO sighting over Alaska. It was on the news. Again I assumed, "Oh, this guy, the airline pilot, he's lying. Or he saw a reflection over the ice cap, or something like that." But the story interested me enough to start asking people what they thought about UFOs.

That's when I found out that members of my own extended family had seen UFOs and had had encounters with aliens. And when I asked people at the accounting office where I work about UFOs, one lady had experienced a missing-time encounter, another lady had a close-up UFO sighting. And then a friend told me about a missing-time UFO sighting.*

I wasn't skeptical anymore. These were people I

---

*In "missing-time" encounters, experiencers realize that a gap in time has occurred (of usually an hour or more) of which they have no conscious memory. The missing time may encompass the entire experience or, commonly, what took place just after the ETs appeared and just before they left the witness.

trusted. They just hadn't told me their experiences before for fear of ridicule.

That got me started. I began reading all the UFO books, and then interviewing people and writing articles. Initially, it was just my family, coworkers, and friends who confided in me. Then it was *their* friends, which adds up to quite a number of people. When I started speaking at the local UFO meetings, people would come up to me with their stories, their experiences. And now that I have two books out [see References, page 317], more people are contacting me. The oddest thing is—and I *swear* this is true—even strangers will come up to me now and start talking about their UFO experiences! I must have a sign over my head that says, "Tell me your UFO story."

The office where I work has twenty employees and a high turnover rate, and that's where I've heard a lot of the UFO stories, from my coworkers and their friends. Some of the contacts I make, however, seem really coincidental in a very bizarre way: To "run into" a UFO abductee should be a pretty rare experience, but it isn't. I hate to say this, but it sure does seem like sometimes we're being led together by a higher force. I'm not saying it's true, but it *seems* that way. Coincidences pile up to a point where it really blows my mind sometimes.

After researching a number of UFO experiences, I began to feel that the aliens were not evil. I would hear a lot about UFO abductions, and how horrible and traumatizing the experience was. But part of me intuitively felt that the experience wasn't necessarily *bad.* Sure, I know that it's traumatizing. I know that from the people I've talked to. But the aliens haven't taken over the world—and they would seem to be able to, given their technology. I began to believe that there was a positive aspect to the UFO abduction experience, and I was leaning in that direction when I began to hear about UFO healings.

At first, I was skeptical because healing cases are kind of "out there." You don't hear a lot about them. The whole contactee phenomenon is ridiculed, even within the UFO research community. Some of the researchers believe that anyone who thinks that UFOs are positive are deluding themselves. I find this more than a little offensive. I've read plenty of objective research. And I really do try to be objective myself. *But it is only the people who are traumatized by their UFO experiences who seek help.* They are the ones who seek out the therapists. People who are not traumatized don't seek help. *They don't necessarily tell anybody.* So the healing experiences are almost undercover. We don't tend to hear about them.

But as I researched, I kept hearing about UFO healings. I heard about five, maybe ten cases before I thought, *I'll write an article about this.* I'm always looking for new ideas. I started doing research specifically on healings, and in just looking through the UFO literature, I found around fifty different healing cases. I thought, *Wow! This is much more than I thought.* Then I really did some heavy-duty research, and after a couple of years, I had found over a hundred cases.

At my local MUFON meetings, I give updates of

recent sightings in the area. Lately, I've been giving a lot of lectures on UFO healings at meetings, and at bookstores, UFO conventions, places like that. I had thought that UFO healings were quite rare. And, of course, in the beginning I had thought that they were unheard of. But whenever I speak to groups about healings, even small groups of ten or so, literally *every time somebody comes up out of the crowd afterward and shares their own healing story.* Sometimes they're a little embarrassed. Many people say, "I've never told *anyone* about this." But one after another, I've heard healing accounts. All different types of healings from many different illnesses.

After a person tells me their healing account, I usually ask if they would agree to being interviewed. A lot of the time, they don't want to. Even people in my family told me they hadn't told *anyone* else about their UFO experiences. And that's one of the first things people say when I interview them: "Well, you know, I've never told *anyone* about this." So I think a lot of people are having the UFO experience, and they're just not telling anyone. I think a lot of people are having healings, too, but they aren't talking about it. Or they're in a state of denial about their own UFO experiences. Or maybe they're not even aware of it. Some people may be healed by aliens, and they never even know it. They experience a miraculous healing, but they attribute it to God, or to alternative healing or whatever. I think there's a possibility that some spontaneous remissions are actually UFO healings. You hear about somebody who has cancer, and then they don't. And you wonder.

Also, people have a hard time categorizing a UFO healing experience. Some people feel like it is a religious experience. The whole room will fill with light and then they're cured, so people might think it must be angels that healed them. I'm not so sure that it is.

One lady I interviewed had chronic back pain that she thought had been cured by "the grim reaper." Because in walked this figure—tall, hooded, its face hidden—holding a cylindrical instrument that was glowing. But she was also taken through a closed window, up a beam of light; and she had missing time, and other UFO-related experiences.

Recently, I read of a case, a healing done by "fairies." A lot of these types of cases are probably aliens. It is just a different way of categorizing the experience. I think there is a wide variety of mystical experiences that people are having. And I think that the UFO experience, for one, is happening more often.

Back in the 1930s, not much was happening regarding UFOs. But then, after the atomic bombs were released, waves of UFO sightings occurred. I don't think it's slowed down much since 1947, since the Roswell crash.* If anything, UFO experiences have increased.

In the fifties, you didn't hear a lot about humanoid

*In July of 1947, the crash of a UFO was reported in the desert near Roswell, New Mexico, by the U.S. military. The report was soon retracted, and the issue remains controversial to this day.—Au.

sightings or UFO landings. There were lots of UFO sightings, radar cases. Then, in the sixties and seventies, UFOs started landing and you started to hear about aliens coming out of the UFOs. And in the seventies and eighties, there were more and more abduction accounts.

Now, in the nineties, we're hearing about more UFO *waves*, like the Belgian wave [1989–93] or Mexico City [1991] or Phoenix [1997]. I think the phenomenon has moved to a whole new level where UFOs are becoming more brazen. It's escalated. I think they're trying to change our consciousness. Eventually, I think, there will be open, official contact.

There are a lot of stories circulating, reports on how the U.S. government has already had contact with the aliens. A lot of these rumors, I think, are true. I've interviewed some "whistle blowers" for the government or the secret government, so I think our government knows very well what is going on in the UFO field. For *years*, people have been saying, "There is going to be an official disclosure by the government, and UFOs are going to land on the White House lawn." And UFOs did fly *over* the White House. Twice.* I think one of these days, we're all going to be really surprised when a UFO hovers over a major city and *just does not leave*.

Obviously, *somebody* in the government thinks

*Two waves of UFO sightings over Washington, D.C, in the summer of 1952, created massive global interest in UFOs, and led to a rash of UFO movies including *Earth Versus the Flying Saucers* (1955).

UFOs are really important because they are controlling the information that comes out. But in the long run, I don't think they will be successful. *So many people are having these experiences*, and the truth has a way of taking care of itself.

I joined a group called CSETI [Center for the Search for Extraterrestrial Intelligence; see Chapter 18], and we go out into the field and try to contact UFOs. We use meditation, lights, and tones recorded from UFOs. The very first night I went out, we saw a UFO. I was just amazed. It was a very distant sighting, a blob of light way up high in the sky. But I've taken a lot of astronomy courses and done a lot of reading, and I *know* what we saw was not just a satellite. It was much too big. And it wasn't a shooting star or a plane. I could go through the whole list because I know what it *wasn't*, but I don't know what it *was*.

Last spring, I woke up in the middle of the night. I live alone, in a condominium. I woke up in my bedroom and I felt what I thought was a cat walking across the foot of my bed. And I don't have a cat. So I opened my eyes. It was early morning, not even light yet. But I thought I saw a figure—very, *very* thin. I didn't see much detail, but what I did see scared me. I really got alarmed! And it zipped out of the room *really* fast.

Now, I have wanted to have an experience, a UFO experience. But then, when I thought I *was* having one, I got really scared. My heart was beating really fast! But I rolled over and went back to sleep. Instead of getting up to check the house! And I kind of convinced myself afterward that it was a dream. I was laughing at myself, saying, "Hey, isn't this what *all* witnesses say?"

To this day, I feel like it could have been a dream. But it woke me up. I not only *felt* something, I *saw* something. It wasn't clear, and it was extremely brief. But I *was* awake. You *know* when you're awake, there's no doubt in your mind.

People who have contact experiences tell me that their intuition becomes more pronounced as a result of their experiences. Over and over again, I hear this. And not only their intuitive abilities, but also their healing abilities. I hear this *so* often. And I think that there's a reason why people who have contact experiences are becoming adept at healing.

One of the strongest themes in UFO accounts these days is that there are a lot of upcoming Earth changes. One researcher told me that one of her clients was instructed by the aliens on how to do healings, and they told her that the reason for teaching her this was the upcoming Earth changes. The ETs said that she was going to need to know how to heal people. This may be true in a lot of contact cases, although it may not be made clear to a lot of contactees. But many *are* given this ability to do hands-on healing or remote healing or alternative healing.

I think we're already seeing some of the Earth changes. I don't want to sound like a "doom and gloomer," and I'm not sure there's going to be an apocalypse or a second coming or anything like that. (On the other hand, I wouldn't be too surprised either.) I think it might be more of a *change of consciousness*, rather than the death of humanity. It may be the death of the way we *think*, the way we *live*.

Supposedly, a lot of extraterrestrials are saying that we are moving into the fifth dimension. I don't have any idea what that means, but it's interesting at the very least. When I'm speaking at a convention or a meeting, people come up to my table to tell me that we have to "increase our vibrations," that by doing this we can rid ourselves of all disease and disharmony. Supposedly, we should all be thinking good thoughts, doing meditation exercises, and practicing right behavior in order to raise our vibrations. I *have* noticed that the people who are getting healed by their extraterrestrial contact experiences are people who are doing good work for humanity. This became real clear to me after a while. Also, people who lead unconventional lifestyles in some respect will often have UFO experiences, healing experiences.

There is a *lot* to learn from the UFO healing cases. For example, a human disease may be labeled as "chronic," but then the aliens come and cure it. Obviously, the disease need not be chronic if it can be healed. I think these healings have a lot to teach us about what disease is. And what *we* can do. This should inspire people—especially doctors—that we may be healed of supposedly chronic (or even terminal) conditions. The healing cases alone tell us to never give up hope because a healing *could* occur at any time.

Also, there are techniques the aliens are using to heal people, techniques that we should take advantage of. In particular, most of the healings seem to be done with light or beams of light. There is medical technology coming out now using light, like the particle beam laser that is being used on tumors.* This is a noninvasive surgery technique—which is exactly what the aliens are doing. I have heard from many sources that some of our medical technology is actually back-engineered from the aliens. I don't know if this is true, but it does seem possible. Technology-wise, there is a lot to be learned from the aliens.

Now, I'm not recommending to *anyone* to pray to the aliens to cure them. But I do know of two cases where people have asked the aliens for a healing and received it. So maybe there *is* some hope there. But I think the aliens don't want us to depend on them. I don't think this would help us that much anyway. We have to learn our own lessons. And I think they

*"Phytodynamic therapy" (PDT) uses light to treat malignant tumors and viruses with photosensitive chemical agents and laser beams that destroy the diseased cells. A relatively new treatment, PDT is regarded as experimental and noninvasive with fewer risks than surgery or chemotherapy. The Food and Drug Administration recently approved PDT to treat advanced esophageal cancer and early lung cancer, and it is being tested for use in treating other types of cancer and other diseases including macular degeneration, a leading cause of blindness, and endrometriosis, a common cause of infertility.—Au.

want us to learn our own lessons. I think they want us to be able to *heal ourselves.* That is what I keep hearing now, in case after case. And that is what I believe is most important, that *we learn how to do the healing.*

One of the strongest messages from the UFO healing cases of late is that there are alternative methods of healing. In some of the accounts, the aliens heal not with technology, but with mind power. This is a hands-on healing type of experience. I think we need to be studying these types of alternative healing methods now, too.

All of the UFO healing accounts demonstrate the positive side of the alien contact experience. Some people who have been healed still do not like the aliens. They feel they're being manipulated and maintained by the aliens like some sort of farm animal. Maybe this is true, maybe it's not. But in some healing cases, the experiencers feel as if the aliens are their friends. And they may feel a great love for these beings.

The classification of an experience—"abduction" or "positive contact"—is more in the mind of the witness than it is in the actual experience. An "abductee" is simply someone who doesn't *want* to be with the aliens. But I've seen people evolve throughout their UFO experiences: They start out as abductees, they get past the fear barrier, then they start having a lot of positive experiences. They may go on tours, perhaps to other planets. They may be given scientific information, healing or intuitive abilities. And they may experience healings.

You hear so much about the negative aspects of the UFO abduction experience. But it can be a positive experience, a *very* positive healing experience.

CHAPTER 15

Barbara Lamb:
Regression Therapist

A licensed marriage, family, and child counselor and certified hypnotherapist and regression therapist, Barbara Lamb has a private practice in Claremont, California. A therapist since 1976, Barbara has been doing regression therapy since 1984. Since 1990, she has regressed more than two hundred clients to their experiences with extraterrestrial beings, conducting a few hundred regressions that focus on ET encounters. Her documentary film, *Into the Mist,* is available for educational purposes. She is currently writing a book on the wide range of ET experiences her clients have recalled during regression therapy.*

Originally from New York, Barbara has lived on the West Coast for many years. She is sixty-three, the mother of three grown children and grandmother of three. When I telephoned her to discuss the possibility of an interview, Barbara sounded a bit out of breath. She had rushed in to

---

*Regression therapy is used in psychotherapy to assist the client in reverting to an earlier pattern of feeling or behavior through the use of hypnosis.—Au.

answer the phone from tending to her beloved garden. I was pleased when Barbara agreed to share the insights she has gleaned after nearly a decade of work with celestial experiencers.

In the early years of my regression therapy work, I would take people back to the source of their problems using hypnosis. Often, clients would go back to past life experiences as the source of their current problems, past life experiences that seemed to carry over into the present day. But in 1990, I began to realize that sometimes the source of a client's trauma or fear or dysfunction was that they had been having experiences with extraterrestrial beings.

Actually, my interest in this began in 1986 or 1987, when I was taking some advanced, intensive training for my past life regression therapy work. The trainer, who is a therapist I admire very much, told us to be aware that one source of some clients' distress was that they had been experiencing abductions by extraterrestrial beings. I was really startled at the time because it was the first I had ever heard of the idea of extraterrestrial contact. But I was even more startled by what I call "the big voice of my soul," which said (silently, inside my head, but very loudly in my awareness): "Pay attention to this. You will be doing this."

I started to research the topic, going to lectures about UFOs and extraterrestrial contact, trying to find out what other researchers had been finding out: Are UFOs *real*? Do they *really* come here? Are there *really* extraterrestrial beings who interact with people?

Then, in 1990, a client came to me presenting symptoms and clues that maybe something like that was actually happening. We explored the idea in regression and realized that, yes indeed, this particular young woman had been visited in her bedroom by extraterrestrial beings.

Since then, many different cases involving extraterrestrial contact have come to my practice. I really rejoice whenever I can work with one experiencer for quit a number of times. With my second client who turned out to be an experience, for example, I have done at least fifty regressions. With certain other experiencers who live within an hour's drive, I have been able to do ten, twenty, or thirty regressions. This is wonderful, because we can look at a big *span* of their experiences to see what is *really* going on with the experiencers and the extraterrestrial beings.

Often, people will come to see me when they have had certain experiences that they wonder about, but can only remember a teeny little bit about. Or people will come because they feel a lot of fear about a specific thing, like going to sleep at night. They might be afraid that someone is watching them, or that someone is going to come and intervene and take them away somewhere. They might be afraid to drive alone at night. Or maybe they are afraid of certain types of public places like airports, hospitals, or public facilities where there tends to be a light, shiny floor and it is difficult to see where the lighting is coming from. They have these persistent fears, but they do not know consciously where these fears are coming from.

Sometimes, the first experience that comes up in regression is one of the more fearful ones. Typically, the person will, under hypnosis, find him- or herself lying on a medical-type table with these unusual beings standing all around, looking at him or her and doing various things. There might be the very bright light, and they cannot see exactly where it comes from. There may be procedures being done to them that might hurt or cause fear or concern.

Very typically, my clients will go to an experience like this in a regression. But, if we *continue* the regression, after the physical examination part of the experience there will be an educational part of the very same episode. This happens *very* often. The person may sit up, get dressed, and be ushered into another room of the spaceship, where some kind of education is going on. They may learn about star systems, star routes, or routes of travel in space. They may learn about the ship they are on, how it works. They might be taught about certain things that are occurring on Earth, things these beings want them to pay attention to or educate others about. Or they might be trained in some type of healing work, or in some kind of mental work where they can influence with their minds.

In subsequent regressions, experiencers tend to get the sense that the physical exam and physical procedures are only *part* of a much *larger* picture, which includes education and training. Sometimes experiencers realize that they have a very special mission that they are to carry out here on earth, a mission inspired by these extraterrestrial beings with whom they are having experiences.

These beings seem to have a much clearer overview of the Earth and our dynamics because they are not caught up in it, subjectively living lives here like we are. They are able to objectively see the tendencies human beings have toward violence, toward greed and avarice. And they will choose certain humans to work on these issues, to help educate their fellow human beings and show them a different way of living and treating each other and the Earth.

Even if I have not been abducted in the traditional way, I think it is very possible that I could have been guided by extraterrestrial beings to do the work I am doing. It is very possible that others have been, too. There is good reason to believe that extraterrestrial beings work closely with certain people whom they do not "abduct." Scientists, for example, or people in governments or positions of importance of various kinds, people working on health or technological breakthroughs. In such cases, there may be a kind of mentoring relationship in which *the beings will be influencing these people*, giving them brilliant ideas in their sleep for instance.

Out of my two hundred-plus encounter cases, there have been some fifteen healings. These clients have either *remembered* that they experienced a healing associated with extraterrestrial contact, or it has come out in *regression* that they have been healed of some physical condition. And there have been various kinds of conditions that have been healed.

In one case, a migraine headache problem was reduced in severity and duration, making the problem much easier for the client to handle. It changed from three to four migraines per week, wiping her out for a *whole day and night*, to a few hours maybe every two to three *weeks*. This really has made a difference in the client's life.

In other cases, there have been corrections of reproductive problems. I have seen this in a couple of female clients. And in one case, a little girl about four years old was healed by little beings, whom she called "the little people," following a sexual molestation incident.

In another case, the wife of a man who had a couple of severe medical problems was assisted in their bedroom one night by extraterrestrial beings, who ran special healing energy *through* her to help heal her husband. They instructed her where to place her hands while her husband was in a deep sleep state. This actually helped to heal him of a couple of dangerous, life-threatening conditions. I found this experience to be very striking.

Although this was the only case I have seen in which a client received instructions on how to heal a human being right then and there, on the spot, I do have three clients who made a total switch in their careers from corporate work to healing work. They all happen to be women, each of whom felt a tremendous draw to body work of one kind or another—polarity therapy, deep tissue massage, Reiki healing, reflexology, energy balancing work. They all began to study healing work, taking classes and training, becoming certified, and eventually leaving their regular jobs to concentrate on body work. Each found out in regression that her experiences with extraterrestrial beings had been influencing her unconsciously to do healing work, providing her with a strong imperative or inner drawing toward this kind of work. It was not until they were actually very engaged in doing the body work professionally that they began to realize, through regressions, how there had been a tremendous amount of extraterrestrial influence on them to do this work.

It is very hard to empirically prove what, exactly, is going on with the extraterrestrial encounter experiencers and the beings they are in contact with. But I think there is a *lot* going on. And since there seem to be a wide variety of beings who come here, quite a number of different species of extraterrestrials, each of them may have their own agenda. I do not think there is just *one* "Extraterrestrial Agenda."

The little gray beings, for example, seem to be very intent on reproducing hybrid offspring by interbreeding in various ways with human beings. They have told experiencers that their own species is in grave danger of becoming extinct, and that they are trying to preserve themselves by mixing with some of our genetic material. This is what I would call a more self-serving group of extraterrestrials, perhaps coming here more for their own sake than for ours.

However, I think that a lot of these groups of beings are actually from different dimensions. They are able to *look* like they are three-dimensional, enough so that experiencers can see them and communicate with them. But they actually come from higher, more spiritual dimensions. And some of these beings seem to direct their attention to the *spiritual awakening of humanity*.

In some regressions, clients will find that they have had extraterrestrial contact experiences in former lifetimes. Some people have discovered in their regressions that they have *been* a member of a certain species of extraterrestrial in another lifetime, or in a number of lifetimes. This may explain why certain extraterrestrial groups may work with certain human beings: These individuals were once members of the extraterrestrials' own species, or may still be, but are having a human lifetime at this point.

Any one experiencer is likely to be having a whole *variety* of experiences with extraterrestrial beings, meeting with *different groups* of extraterrestrials, sometimes with the more physically oriented beings, other times with another group more concerned with spiritual enlightenment. So, sometimes experiencers are having definite *physical* experiences, with physical exams. And sometimes it seems as if they are having *astral* experiences, where they have experiences with the extraterrestrial beings *without their physical bodies*.

Yes, a lot *is* going on. And I don't know that we

will ever get it completely pinned down. But every time we listen to yet another experiencer, we can add to this big, ever-growing picture puzzle, this *huge* puzzle for which we can only find little pieces here and there. I love to work with experiencers because they get such relief and such enlightenment from finding out what has been going on for them in their experiences with extraterrestrials. And they are so glad to have someone to talk to who does not think they are crazy.

It is a strange and mysterious thing, the extraterrestrial contact experience. Ever since I have been doing this work, I have had *so* many amazing perceptions about humanity, insights that I am sure I never would have had otherwise. And I feel extremely fortunate that my parameters of thinking keep getting extended, again and again. I really like that. I've always been philosophically inclined. I was always wondering what lay *behind* what we see without having any idea there was so much *life* out there! I had no clue, until I began doing this regression work with extraterrestrial contact experiencers.

I love the work I am doing. And I think it is important for *everyone* to be aware of the amazing range of things that is happening with extraterrestrial beings. The positive aspects of these experiences are very, *very* important for us to recognize.

CHAPTER 16

Additional Cases

The experiencers who have shared their stories in the preceding chapters represent a *cross section* of the numerous cases in existence of extraterrestrial or celestial contact with healing results. These interviews are only a sample, taken from a much larger subgroup of contact experiencers.

In the course of examining the UFO literature, studying dozens of books, piles of articles and reports on UFO sightings, abductions, and encounter experiences, I came across many, *many* cases in which individuals claim a variety of medical cures they attribute to extraterrestrial encounters, to UFOs and/or their occupants. In communicating with hypnotherapists, psychiatrists, and ufologists, additional *unpublished* cases of healing encounters with otherworldly beings continuously popped up. And most of the ET experiencers I talked to had met, or at least heard of, others who had received healing visits from celestial beings.

It appears that celestial healings are not really as rare as we might think. In fact, I have begun to suspect that such otherworldly cures occur quite often, but are rarely *reported*. Sometimes, perhaps even *most* times, such healings are not recognized and understood, and are thereby attributed to other sources—by doctors, therapists, even the experiencers themselves. And when experiencers do understand how, if not why, they have been healed by otherworldly beings, it may be years before they tell anyone about it. It is easy to understand why someone might hesitate to do so. Can you imagine saying to *your* family physician, "Well, Doc, I no longer need that gallbladder operation. It seems that my medical friends from outer space have already completed the surgery—painlessly, and for free!"

Preston Dennett, the ufologist you met in Chapter 14, provides an historical overview of the reported cases of ET healings from 1947 to the present in his book *UFO Healings*. In his collection of 105 cases, Dennett's list of recorded cures directly associated with ET contact ranges from minor ailments to miraculous recoveries, including healings from aneurysms, arthritis, asthma, back pain, blindness, bronchitis, burns, cancer (of the breast, colon, skin, stomach, throat, lung), colitis, common colds, diabetes, fevers, flesh wounds, head injury, heart conditions, infertility, kidney stones, liver disease, multiple sclerosis, pneumonia, polio, tuberculosis, ulcers, warts, and more. Dennett cites cancer as the disease most commonly reported as cured, but he concludes: "No illness is too small or too great to be cured by aliens."[1] Over ten percent of the cases Dennett reports are multiple cures, that is, the individuals experienced healings of more than one disease or disorder.[2] His cases corroborate one another to a remarkable degree, with individuals who have never met reporting stories of ET healings that include very similar details.

Let's look at a few of these cases, some "small," some "great."

"Frederick": A deputy sheriff in Texas, Frederick was driving with another sheriff. Earlier in the day, he had been bitten on the left index finger by his son's pet baby alligator. The day continued to grow stranger. The two sheriffs encountered a UFO, which radiated purple light. They felt heat coming from this weird glow, and quickly sped away. Pulling into a diner to discuss the incident, Frederick immediately noticed that his finger, which had been red and swollen, was no longer sore, so he yanked off the bandage. "Hell, you couldn't tell I had ever been bit," he recalled later, noting that his left arm had been outside the window of the car when the light beam from the UFO struck. The U.S. Air Force investigated the case, which was widely reported in the news. (1965)[3]

"Paul": This New York syndicated columnist saw a UFO in the sky above a park in Brooklyn, along with several other witnesses. When he returned to his apartment, he unwrapped the bandage on a finger he had accidentally slashed earlier in the day. "I discovered much to my amazement that the wound was completely healed, as though absolutely nothing at all had happened," Paul reported. (1974)[4]

"Helen X:" This anonymous woman from Arizona was diagnosed with cancer, which spread from her hipbone to her pancreas and intestines. Treated with chemotherapy, she was told she had only a short time left to live. Weakened from the treatments and a loss of some fifty pounds, Helen awoke one night with an irresistible urge to drive to a certain location, which she did, despite the fact that she could barely walk. A UFO landed and two small creatures helped her aboard, where she was treated with strange instruments and injections of a purple fluid. The ETs, whom Helen perceived as friendly, informed her that she was cured and was not to take any more medication. She drove home and went to bed. The next day, Helen was rushed to the hospital, her family prepared for her imminent death. She refused all medication and recovered within days. "It was like I had never been sick," Helen X stated. As of 1988, she was healthy, busy managing her own business. (1974)[5]

"Ellen": Diagnosed with inoperable colon cancer, this young woman from Los Angles was given three months to live. She had experienced ET contact all her life, and soon underwent another "abduction," this time including an extensive operation: "They said, 'Relax.' And they did a cure." When she returned to her doctor, all traces of cancer were gone. Ellen states that her cure has been verified by a major medical university. (1989)[6]

"May": As a child, she was diagnosed with diphtheria, which went untreated due to her parents' religious practices. The doctor finally informed the parents that May would not live through the night. Abducted by "angels in white robes with silver belts," May was transported to a UFO, where she was "cleansed" and cured with bright blue light. The next morning, her mother found her playing on the floor, completely recovered. (1959)[7]

"Karen": A thirty-nine-year-old day-care center operator in New York, this woman experienced a simultaneous out-of-body near-death experience *and* an extraterrestrial healing. After discovering a golf-ball-size tumor in one breast, Karen found herself in "deep space" with a group of ETs, who eventually operated on her. In the presence of her husband, she was unconscious for two hours, awakening to discover "the lump was gone—totally." She reports that the ETs gave her two messages: It is gone; and follow your husband, with whom she had been experiencing marital difficulties. Ten years later, she was still married and in good health. (1978)[8]

John F. Schuessler is another ufologist who has documented a number of UFO healings from historical reports. In attempting to provide some actual proof of the existence of UFOs by compiling a catalog of the physiological effects reportedly caused by UFO encounters, Schuessler's *UFO-Related Human Physiological Effects* lists both the injuries and the positive physical effects experienced by those who have sighted UFOs and/or had contact with extraterrestrials. Noting that "Most doctors are unaware of the facts about UFOs and UFO-related injuries," Schuessler founded the Medical Committee for the Mutual UFO Network,* organizing medical specialists from such diverse fields as dentistry, gynecology, pediatrics, and psychiatry, to work with ufologists in investigating cases.[9]

In citing nearly four hundred cases of UFO-related physical symptoms and side effects, Schuessler has included only seven healings, but does conclude that UFO cases involving harm to humans "happen in only a small percentage of the reported UFO incidents."[10] One of the healing cases he reports on is of interest.

"Etienne": An ambulance driver from France, Etienne was severely injured in a head-on collision. Declared dead, he was revived after an extraterrestrial appeared in the seat beside him and told him that he would survive. Etienne recovered completely. (1982)[11]

Edith Fiore, Ph.D., worked for many years as a clinical psychologist, managing a busy hypnotherapy practice in Saratoga, California. Before she retired recently, Dr. Fiore counseled numerous clients who recalled extraterrestrial encounters, helping them to recover from any associated traumas by bringing the

*Mutual UFO Network, or MUFON, is the largest organization of ufologists and UFO buffs in the U.S., with over five thousand members, including more than five hundred scientific consultants from every field of science.

repressed experiences to light. She found that "Interestingly, in at least one-half of the cases I've been involved in, the people were greatly helped by their encounters. Operations, usually involving lasers, and other treatments relieved symptoms, even correcting some conditions that were potentially fatal."[12] She collected fourteen case studies in her fascinating book, *Encounters: A Psychologist Reveals Case Studies of Abductions by Extraterrestrials*, including several accounts of healings. Let's look at some of Dr. Fiore's reports of ET cures. (Note that Dr. Fiore does not use her clients' real names in her reports.)

"Mark": Although he originally contacted Dr. Fiore to discuss how his health issues were affecting his mood, this eighteen-year-old talked of recurring UFO dreams and, under hypnosis, provided an account of an extraterrestrial healing that had been performed on him. To treat his diabetes, Mark recalled how the ETs used "a big clamp" that "sends pulses, shock waves into my pancreas . . . I kinda feel that they're just putting this energy in me."[13] The treatment neither helped nor hurt his condition, but Dr. Fiore concluded, "I was very interested in the visitors' efforts to help his diabetes and perhaps his arthritis as well," since Mark's arthritis was in remission.[14]

"Barbara": This client consulted Dr. Fiore for help with severe anxiety attacks, but she also weighed over 350 pounds and suffered from a number of physical ailments. Hypnosis uncovered a medical exam conducted by an extraterrestrial being: "Nothing but kindness flowed from him. He said he didn't like to upset people, but it was his job to check people out," Barbara recalled.[15] Discovering the source of her panic attacks resulted in an immediate cure, plus a gradual, ongoing loss of weight: "No diet. My appetite decreased . . . and I don't feel at all deprived."[16]

"Diane Tai": Although quite active and mobile, this client was afflicted with spinal muscular atrophy, a debilitating genetic disorder. The disease had killed her nine-year-old sister, who had never walked. Under hypnosis, Diane recalled many encounters with extraterrestrial beings, who had once informed her, "The body is not as important as the spirit. Your spirit is already well, and your body will follow." Diane explained that "It's like this contact is made every so often, to give us strength and to see how our bodies are doing physically . . . We're part of this group that comes into the physical body that sometimes has trouble adjusting to the vibration of the physical form." According to Diane, the ETs were training her, along with many other humans, to transcend time and space, to see the past and the future, and to heal others.[17]

Included in Dr. Fiore's book are two other case studies in which clients reported receiving instructions on healing from the ETs who contacted them.

"Linda": A forty-five-year-old artist from a psychic family, Linda uncovered a history of ET contact while under hypnosis with Dr. Fiore. During one encounter, Linda recalled how the ETs "said I had cancer!'' and were "cleaning this black junk out of my stomach region." They had placed small glass objects all over her body, running a sensor-type diagnostic instrument over the glass. Linda also recounted how the ETs taught her to heal others: "It's all this . . . power coming through my hands. It's like electricity. Strong. I can learn to scan, like they do . . . They say there are these portals, where you can gather energy and bring it up through the body, to cleanse and renew each cell." When Linda had asked the extraterrestrials why they did not choose only healthy people to teach their healing methods, she received a response: "They say they are trying to prove a point . . . trying to change the mental concepts of people . . . We will be changed. Our energies will be vibrating at a higher level." The ETs also taught Linda how to use one of their healing instruments, a long silver rod with a rounded crystal tip that would glow and pulsate. She was able to observe a number of healings of other human abductees as conducted by the ETs, including their treatment of ulcers, a tumor, bursitis, and arthritis in a teenage boy. ("A large machine with crystallized light . . . to generate energy to promote new cell growth.") During one contact, Linda was treated for a yeast infection, along with her mother and sister. Linda's treatment ("A jellylike substance that looks like aquamarine blue . . . They say that's to help freeze the bacteria.") worked temporarily, but her sister and mother were permanently cured. Linda's mother had been afflicted with a yeast infection for forty-three years.[18]

"James": A physician in his mid-thirties, James was using innovative healing methods in his practice, including electric acupressure. Under regression with Dr. Fiore, he recalled ET encounters in which he was provided with instructions on how to heal using acupuncture and other energy work. James also remembered a childhood encounter in which he was treated by the extraterrestrials for chronic headaches: "I used to get these horrible headaches when I was a kid. Then they went away . . . Those headaches were terrible! Really heavy duty! Then one day they were just gone. I've never known why. As a physician, I couldn't understand it."[19] During one regression session, James recalled the treatment used to cure his headaches: "It's like an energy transfer . . . the front part of my head is just . . . it feels alive."[20] In explaining what he believes to be the principal healing method used by the ETs, James stated: "What they're doing is speeding up the process that would occur naturally." He also told Dr. Fiore that he believes the ETs are conducting research to determine what is blocking the energy flow in our earthly environment, creating ill health and disease.[21]

John Mack, M.D., is a professor of psychiatry at The Cambridge Hospital, Harvard Medical School, and founding director of the Program for Extraordinary Experience Research, or PEER, a nonprofit organization dedicated to international research, education, and support regarding abduction and ET-related experiences. Dr. Mack is the author of *Abduction: Human Encoun-*

ters with Aliens, the best-selling book that recounts his therapeutic work with ET experiencers. He sees the encounter experience as "both traumatic and transformative," a phenomenon that can serve to "expand our sense of ourselves and our understanding of reality, and awaken our muted potential as explorers of a universe rich in mystery, meaning, and intelligence."[22]

We have already met one of Dr. Mack's clients, Peter Faust [Chapter 10]. Two other experiencers who have worked with Dr. Mack are of some interest here. Again, note the use of pseudonyms by Dr. Mack to protect the privacy of his clients.

"Paul": This twenty-six-year-old client told Dr. Mack how he had learned much about ET technology from his contact experiences, including "a flood of information about how they heal . . . I've got notebooks of this stuff and it's very solid." According to Dr. Mack, others who know Paul outside of the therapeutic setting have attested to his extraordinary healing abilities. He now teaches others how to heal, using the methods he was taught during ET encounters.[23]

"Scott": An actor and filmmaker, twenty-four-year-old Scott received much medical treatment as a child and teenager for what was diagnosed at different times as "seizures," "confusional episodes," "spells," and "visual hallucinations." After working with Dr. Mack and recalling a lifelong series of ET encounters, Scott began to pursue a more spiritual path in life and grew to believe his physical symptoms were actually due to a "post-abduction panic attack" with "flashbacks," or reevoked memories of encounter experiences.[24] He began to challenge the traditional treatment model, resentful of the years he spent undergoing medical tests and taking substantial doses of anticonvulsant medications that had little effect. In his book *Abduction*, Dr. Mack concludes: "There is a poignancy for Scott and his family in the vain and intrusive search that was made during his childhood and adolescence for a conventional medical explanation for his abduction experiences. Countless hours of medical examinations, tests, and procedures resulted in wrong diagnoses and inappropriate treatment. I suspect that even as these words are being written, a child abductee somewhere is being taken by anxious parents to a physician who is steadfastly ignorant of the abduction phenomenon, as Scott's parents were when he was a child."[25]

C.D.B. Bryan, a journalist and novelist, attended the Abduction Study Conference held at M.I.T. in the spring of 1992. Cochaired by John Mack, M.D., and M.I.T. physicist David Pritchard, the invitation-only scientific seminar gathered together more than 150 of the world's top researchers, psychiatrists, professors, and scientists to discuss the ET encounter experience. "Abductees" voluntereed to share their personal experiences in a series of panels over the five-day event. Fascinated by the discussions, Bryan evolved from the typical media skeptic into "a believer in the sincerity and merit of their quest," and wrote a detailed chronicle of the conference, *Close Encounters of the Fourth Kind.*[26]

A number of healing-type encounters were mentioned, more in passing than in any detail, during the M.I.T. conference as recounted by Bryan. Let's briefly examine the cases reported by two of the researchers at the conference.

Yvonne Smith: A hypnotherapist from California, Ms. Smith reported on one of her clients: "I have an HIV-positive abductee who now tests negative." No further details were given at the conference.[27]

John Carpenter: This licensed social worker from Missouri, who uses hypnotherapy in his work with psychiatric patients, discussed his client "Eddie," a twenty-year-old abductee cured of color blindness after ET contact. During an exam by "Beings," Eddie felt his right eye removed and replaced, and believed that they were "fixing" him. Carpenter reported that he has a doctor's statement attesting to the changes in his client's vision from "profound color blindness" to "green color blindness" only.[28]

During one of the abductee panels at the M.I.T. conference, a forty-two-year-old woman explained how she had abruptly changed her career from marketing to massage therapy and adopted the name Star after ET beings told her that Star was a good name for a healer. She began working as a "deep healing" massage therapist, and reported that she could feel her clients' blocked energy vibration and return that vibration to normal, "which is what we call healing."[29]

Scott Mandelker, Ph.D., explores the topic of "dual identity" in his book, *From Elsewhere: Being ET in America.* A California psychologist, Dr. Mandelker lectures internationally on the spiritual dimensions of extraterrestrial contact. He believes that he is "from elsewhere," and sees many clients who also feel that their souls have incarnated here to serve Earth as "ET volunteers." Dr. Mandelker estimates that "There may be as many as 100 million extraterrestrials currently living on Earth," most as yet unaware of their otherworldly origins, and sees human ETs as a "real and vibrant subculture." He theorizes that accounts of benevolent extraterrestrial contacts are "wake-up calls" for those ET volunteers who are not aware that they, too, are "from elsewhere."[30]

Quite a few of Dr. Mandelker's clients have experienced beneficial physical and psychological changes as a result of their "wake-up calls." A thirty-five-year-old architect was cured of a suicidal depression during his college years after many visits from a hovering ball of light, which he saw as intelligent and sentient. He told Dr. Mandelker that he now views the visits as a "soul transfer," after which he became more of a "universal citizen."[31]

Another client, a gay man in his late thirties, was depressed and suicidal upon realizing he exhibited many of the symptoms of HIV infection. Paralyzed and in pain, he was being rushed to a hospital by ambulance when he ceased breathing and felt himself leave his body. Unlike most near-death experiencers, however, he felt as if he had actually died and received "a new spirit," imbued with healing energies "of a seemingly intelligent design." His life changed for the better in every aspect afterward, including his health.[32]

Dr. Mandelker also treated an English woman in her sixties who recalled a childhood near-death experience in which she was pronounced dead by the family doctor. "Oh, she's coming back," her mother had responded at the time. "She's talking to a Being all dressed in white. And I know she's going to decide to come back." The young child recovered, becoming a nurse and, later, a teacher of personal development. She now believes that her near-death experience was actually a "soul transfer," and that she visits her "home planet" in her sleep.[33]

In his entertaining anthology, *Zen in the Art of Close Encounters*, psychologist Paul David Pursglove includes an essay by artist Ron Russell regarding his odd experiences while exploring crop circles in England. A creator of "outer space paintings," Russell became curious about the swathes of gently flattened grain crops found on a regular basis by farmers in fields largely, but not exclusively, in Britain. The theory that an alien intelligence produces these circles and other geometric figures led to Russell's interest in the markings as possible "communication and evidence of intelligence from Other Worlds." He joined a crop circle research tour group [organized by CSETI, see Chapter 18] in 1992, and walked about *inside* several seventy- to eighty-foot circular formations that had suddenly appeared in grain fields around the English countryside: "After walking around a few of the 'pictograms,' I began to notice my own somatic and psychological feelings. I was sure that I was observing subtle physical changes. All my low-grade chronic joint pain was gone. I needed little sleep. I was blissful . . . The forms emanate a vitality and a definite presence that slips past our personal defenses . . ."[34]

In another *Zen* essay, Rima E. Laibow, M.D., a psychiatrist from New York, recounts a post-encounter healing she was able to observe firsthand. The client, a doctor who had suddenly begun to recall past ET encounters, met with Dr. Laibow early one morning after awakening and finding her toe had been "slashed in a radial pattern" sometime during the night. Dr. Laibow reports: ". . . she and I watched together while, within the space of an hour, the wound on her toe went from presenting a series of open gashes to a series of approximated but reddened edges to a series of thin white lines to a totally unmarked skin surface with no palpable or visible evidence of any trauma." Dr. Laibow, founder of TREAT, a center for Treatment and Research of Experienced Anomalous Trauma, stated that this particular healing incident "represents a process which, if it could be understood and reproduced, would have strikingly important implications for surgery and trauma medicine."[35]

As we have seen, in certain encounter cases the methods of healing utilized by the visiting beings *have* been taught and later reproduced, if not fully understood. A remarkable example of the link between extraterrestrial encounter experiences and an ability to heal is presented by the prolific author and parapsychologist Dr. Hans Holzer in his 119th book, *The Secret of Healing*. Dr. Holzer introduces Ze'ev Kolman, a gifted healer who received his otherworldly ability as a thirty-six-year-old businessman and reserve soldier in the Israeli army.

While doing night surveillance duty at a military post in the Sinai Desert, Ze'ev had an urge one morning to climb a nearby mountain. Sitting alone at a lookout post on top of the mountain, Ze'ev saw a "bean-shaped structure, elliptic in shape." The lighted craft moved toward him, enveloping him in a "sugar candy" cloud. Eleven short, hairless, humanlike beings then surrounded him. Although they communicated with him, Ze'ev was unable to understand their language. He awoke to find himself lying on his back at the edge of the mountain, feeling dizzy and confused. It was afternoon, and afraid of becoming a "laughingstock," he resolved to not speak of his encounter to anyone. However, upon returning to the base camp, Ze'ev soon discovered that his touch would cause others to feel an electric shock, curing them of such physical ailments as skin lesions and headache pain.[36]

Ze'ev currently works full-time as a "bioenergetic healer" and treats people all over the world, including members of Europe's royal families and such Hollywood celebrities as Melanie Griffith, Don Johnson, Raquel Welch, and Carly Simon. In the U.S., he has successfully treated individuals suffering from a variety of cancers, multiple sclerosis, heart disease, and other serious ills. In Israel, where he is also well known as a psychic, many doctors now refer their patients to Ze'ev for treatment.

According to Ze'ev, his healing abilities are due to the energy field that was placed around him by the extraterrestrials he encountered in the Sinai Desert. He believes that the ETs changed his bioenergetic potential, so that he can draw on the energy of his own aura and then eject this energy through his hands: "I believe that my body underwent a certain energetic process through the dense fog—the plasma that enveloped me—and through which my body must have absorbed something. Sometimes I feel a kind of thread that passes from my head through the length of my body—a thin silver thread. I remember that days after the event when I looked at the palms of my hands, little silvery flakes appeared that I was able to scrape from my skin."[37]

He now feels "guided by hidden forces to pass my hands at the correct distance" over the bodies of the individuals who come to him for healing treatments, transferring his energy to their bodies in the guiding presence of entities that look like "transparent figures or shadows with faces."[38] Ze'ev sees his role as one of a "utensil," simply a means to hasten the natural course of healing for "those who are meant to be helped."[39]

Dr. Holzer refers to Ze'ev's gift as "part of an experiment in terrestrial medicine jumpstarted by extra-terrestrial biotechnology," and does not regard Ze'ev's experience as unique: "I don't think that in 1995 properly reported incidents involving human-oids can be dismissed as fantasies or hallucinations. We are indeed not alone. Regrettably, it appears to me that a powerful technique of healing known to the strangers cannot as yet be shared fully and regu-larly with us and pops up only now and again in situations like Ze'ev's encounter in the Sinai Desert."[40]

As I write these words in the final days of 1998, it appears that powerful encounters with celestial be-ings who seem to impart the ability to heal and be healed are "popping up" in ever-increasing numbers. In considering just the people who say that they have been healed and those who have become healers in-cluded in this book, one might conclude that an oth-erworldly source of healing power is being made available to us far more often than is commonly believed.

CHAPTER 17

My Case and Conclusions

Although I would not refer to myself as an "abductee" or a confirmed extraterrestrial encounter experiencer, I *have* opened myself up to the possibility of a relationship with celestial beings. I have experimented with celestial healing in several forms, including consults with individuals who use extraterrestrial energies for healing purposes. And I am a "satisfied customer," that is, I have found my celestial healing experiences to be enlightening, safe, and seemingly effective. I find I am most encouraged by the opportunity the celestial healing phenomenon has provided me for exploring a broader dimension of thinking and feeling, allowing me to expand the boundaries of my own reality. There is a strong sense of emotional and spiritual reassurance that accompanies the expanded cosmic view, in knowing that we are not alone in the universe and believing that there exist other intelligent, sentient beings who may, indeed, care about our welfare. It simply *feels better* to believe that there is more love "out there," and to accept my own role in this universal community. I have enjoyed my own celestial experiences and will continue to explore certain aspects of the extraterrestrial phenomenon in the future.

For some of us, this seems to be less a matter of free choice and more a kind of rude awakening to one's own hidden history. Some people just suddenly *remember:* I am an ET experiencer. Others may have vague hints, unconscious rumblings like dream imagery, only to discover *under hypnosis* during regression therapy: I am an ET experiencer. And certain people *consciously choose* to open themselves, their minds, and their lifestyles to the possibility of a bigger, much bigger community of beings with whom we can interact. When we open ourselves up to such a possibility, typically we will experience some effects, including actual interactions with other, nonhuman beings. We may then find ourselves saying: I am an ET experiencer.

ARE YOU AN ET EXPERIENCER?

As you may have noted in reading through the preceding accounts of extraterrestrial encounters, experiencers tend to report *specific effects*—physical, psychological, and emotional/spiritual—associated with their contact experiences. Ufologists and therapists who work with experiencers have discovered a number of signs that they can use as *indicators*, that is, signals to indicate that someone *may* have had ET-related experiences.

Not everyone can recall consciously their own history of extraterrestrial encounters. Some experiencers may notice one or more of the indicators, but fail to put them all together in their own minds, dismissing various signs as dreams, strange coincidences, or inexplicable events that are best forgotten. Some experiencers seem to suddenly "wake up" to their ET experience history after watching a television program on UFOs [like Lynne did in Chapter 1], or upon seeing an oddly familiar picture and realizing that the strange but well-known face is, in fact, extraterrestrial. And some experiencers begin to recall encounters after visiting a therapist for some other concern, which usually ends up being directly related to their ET contact history.

When I began to explore the celestial healing phenomenon, I did not suspect that I, too, might have a personal *history* of ET experiences. Now I would not be surprised to discover that I do. There are, indeed, a number of indicators that, in retrospect, could point to a history of some type of relationship with nonhuman beings. The strongest indicator is my current research and work on this particular project, certainly a topic outside of my purview as a health educator and author of exceedingly *practical* books on healthy living!

Then there was my calm acceptance of Nancy and her celestial healing practice, my open curiosity about the possibility of ETs as a source for human healings, my decision to follow the *very* alternative celestial healing path. Of course, all of this could just be due to a pronounced distrust or fear of modern medicine, rather than an actual unconscious relationship with otherworldly beings.

But then there were the odd dreams, exceedingly vivid and visionlike, often including strange beings. Of course, everybody has those lifelike dreams now and again, so this could mean very little in and of itself. Except that one time I awoke to find strange sparkly flakes on the palms of my hands. I was single at the time, sleeping alone in my apartment in Washington, D.C., sometime in 1986. When I spotted the shiny material on the inside of both hands—which reminded me of a wrinkly layer of Elmer's glue, something I used to spread on my hands as a child in grade school—I immediately jumped out of bed and rushed to the bathroom sink. I was totally freaked out because *I knew that there was absolutely no earthly explanation* for the sudden appearance of these sticky sparkles.

Yet, I ignored this very strange experience, telling no one for over a year. But then it happened *again*, around a year later, in a different bed, in a different apartment, in a different city! Still, I quickly "forgot" about these inexplicable bizarre incidents. Until I was researching this book, when a viable explanation became available: Perhaps the sparkles on my hands came "from elsewhere," a physical sign from another world, an indicator of celestial, extraterrestrial contact. I still am not sure whether this was indeed the case, but upon reading about the strikingly similar discovery by the famed healer Ze'ev [see page 236], I literally leaped out of my office chair and moaned out loud, "Oh, my God! That's what happened to *me*!"

So far, the only thing I can heal with my hands is a weak sentence on a page. But perhaps that is what I am supposed to be doing; that is, helping others to give voice to their celestial healing experiences, helping readers to learn about the potentially healing effects of extraterrestrial encounters.

Perhaps you, too, have experienced a close encounter, even a healing encounter you have not yet consciously recalled. You might want to turn to the Appendix on page 298 to examine the list of indicators for celestial experiences. Since I am not a psychotherapist or ufologist, I can only suggest that you look over the list I have prepared from my own research, including interviews with experiencers and studies conducted by investigators. If you then feel the desire to further investigate your own past, no matter how many YES answers, if any, you tallied up, there are places you can go for assistance in this search. Following the "Most Common Indicators for Extraterrestrial Encounter Experiences" is a second list, "Resources for Experiencers," which provides information on the major organizations to contact in seeking out therapists who work with experiencers, support groups for experiencers, and ufology research organizations that offer help to the general public.

In reading over these lists, remember that you may

actually stir up some very strong, repressed, unconscious material. If you feel at all frightened or upset, PLEASE PUT THE BOOK DOWN. This might not be the best time for you to explore this alone. You may want to seek out some support at this point, or simply put the whole topic out of your mind, at least for the time being. Please use your intuition and listen to your feelings: *You know what is right for you.*

MY FIRST CELESTIAL HEALING

After my first encounter with Nancy on the bench in front of the cancer center, her words flitted through my mind as I struggled with my frightening medical diagnosis and the idea of undertaking the complicated and intensive therapy the surgeon had prescribed for me. Late at night as I tossed and turned, sleepless and worrying obsessively about the upcoming surgery, drug therapy, and other invasive treatments, Nancy's comments echoed in my memory. Maybe, I finally decided, just *maybe* Nancy was right and the traditional medical approach to treating my thyroid cancer was wrong—for *me.*

Two weeks prior to my scheduled surgery for removal of my thyroid gland, I returned to the cancer center for a presurgical physical exam. I was hoping I would run into Nancy, and as I sat nervously in a hard-backed plastic chair in the waiting area, she sauntered by in her starched lab coat and caught my eye. When I grinned and asked her to sit for a minute, Nancy nodded her head as if to say, "Ah, *this person* listened to me."

We discussed my diagnosis as I waited for a nurse to escort me to the examining room. Although she did not suggest that I cancel my treatment plans, Nancy volunteered to perform a special healing on me with her associate, another celestial healer. "We will be using blue light," she informed me, "and we will look closely at the throat area for blockages." She told me that, with my permission, they would tap into and directly channel for me the extraterrestrial energies she and her partner often used in performing medical healings for emotionally and/or spiritually based imbalances. I immediately granted her permission to conduct a healing and gave her my phone number to call with any insights. After all, I reasoned, why not? What harm could a long-distance "healing" do?

When a stern-faced nurse bustled up to escort me to my exam, I thanked Nancy and hurried off, forgetting to ask for her phone number. I had not even asked her last name.

Nancy did not tell me exactly when she would be conducting the healing, but she did warn me that I would probably feel angry afterward. In the tedious hustle of the presurgical procedures, I completely forgot about our discussion. Otherwise, I might have grown curious about her forecast: "You will not feel any discomfort or pain, but after the healing you might find yourself flying into a fierce rage. We may be cutting some [spiritual or astral] ties and releasing some negative energies."

A few days later, I had a full-blown temper tantrum. After crashing around the kitchen, flinging a few pans, and vaulting a plastic bowl out an open window, I locked myself in the bedroom and buried my screams in a huge feather pillow. "Oh, my God," I bellowed. "I am becoming my mother!"

My mother, the "perfect Earth mother" with no life outside of her family, was first diagnosed with cancer when my younger sister was a year old. She died while still in her forties. She had undergone several surgeries, always following her doctor's orders and complying as only the most compliant, "perfect" patients do. Oftentimes, these are not the patients who thrive. In many cases, the patients who *create their own healing program*—typically in conjunction with a doctor or alternative healer—do the best at recovery and survival, remission and renewal.

All of these thoughts boomeranged around in my brain as I calmed myself and arrived at two simple but startling conclusions: 1) I did not *have* to become my mother as, in reality, I was a different person altogether and therefore did not need to follow in her footsteps on the path to premature death; and 2) I had flown into a rage *for absolutely no reason at all.* Hmmm, I wondered, remembering Nancy's prediction. Had some sort of healing taken place?

I made some radical decisions with my flushed face stuffed into that feather pillow. I would seek out alternatives to surgery and the traditional Western prescription for my type of cancer. I would stop being afraid of my cancer: I had it, I was living with it, it wasn't even *bothering* me! I decided I would *accept my cancer as part of me and learn from it.* And I would heal myself of what *was* really bothering me, that is, the unbalanced direction my life had taken. A surgeon could remove a whole pile of my body organs, but only I could repair my life.

I canceled the surgery and began to repair my life.

It took me a while to track down Nancy. She had not telephoned me, and I doubted I could contact a massive organization like the cancer center where she worked and simply ask for "Nancy." But one afternoon, I decided to try. So I called the cancer center and asked for Nancy. "Which one?" I was asked in return. "The one with all the jewelry," I explained. "Oh, Nancy Leggett," the secretary quickly responded. "She's in the billings department." Then she put me through.

"I was hoping you would call," Nancy admitted when she answered the phone. "I make it a policy not to interfere with the hospital patients, if you know what I mean." When I informed her that I had canceled my surgery and had developed my own healing program, she laughed. "When we took a look at your thyroid area during the healing session, there was nothing there. Nothing!" Nancy explained. "We cut some old ties with your mother, and focused a lot of blue light in your throat area. You will be talking about all this—and writing about it, writing stories, so *many* stories," Nancy stated.

At the time, I had no idea what she was talking about. Stories? I was a health writer, not a novelist. It took many months before I came to the realization that, in fact, I wanted to explore and *share stories of celestial healing*—my own experience, and that of many others with far more dramatic healing tales to tell.

As a follow-up, Nancy suggested some books I might want to read about extraterrestrial energies and the channeled information from beings from other worlds. Nancy also recommended that I next undertake a channeled celestial healing with a well-known channeler of extradimensional energies. She gave me David Miller's phone number.

MY CHANNELED CELESTIAL HEALING

The following transcript is from the channeled healing David Miller conducted with me two months after I was diagnosed with thyroid cancer. Since he lives in Arizona and I reside in South Florida, the most affordable way to conduct the session was by telephone, a method David employs on a regular basis with clients all over the U.S.

At an appointed time, I telephoned David and we began our session. As instructed, I sat comfortably on a soft couch in my family room, using pillows to support my back and head. It felt awkward to breathe deeply and enter a meditative state while clutching a portable phone, but David's voice was soothing and, with my eyes closed, I eventually relaxed. I listened as he/"they" talked, not thinking, not judging. I felt open to the experience and ready to learn from whomever or whatever David was channeling into my life.

(High frequency tone, tone, tone)

Good evening. I am Julliano. And we are the Arcturians. I am one of the Commanders with the Arcturians, who have come on a mission because there are so many like yourself who are awakening to their purpose, who are awakening to their past lifetimes when they have been in other planetary systems. Did you know, Virginia, that you have been on the Pleiades before, and that you have had very successful incarnations there? And now, you are in a "school," here on Earth, and you are at the point in this lifetime when you are going to remember what has occurred in the Pleiades. You are here to participate and assist in the transformation of the Earth and the transformation into the fifth dimension.

This is, you know, a phenomenal time to be on this planet. It is so phenomenal that there are beings from all over the galaxy who are coming to Earth. Some are observing, some beings (like yourself) have volunteered to come back into the incarnation process of the Earth, to actually come into a physical incarnation and thus to use that to have a direct experience. A direct experience means that you are a "student." You are studying what it is like to be in this evolutionary transition point on the Earth, studying how you and others you are observing are going through the transformation.

Your illness can be viewed as that activation energy, that activation point that is bringing you deeper into your subconscious, challenging you to come into touch with your true spiritual nature, your true spiritual light. Your illness has done this already in many ways, but now it is time to go into a deeper activation of your light-being. This is what we're going to work with you on this evening. This is going to require some guided exercises and guided meditations that we are going to suggest to you.

So I hope that you are comfortable and that you are ready to leave your body. We are very excited to have you come up, and there are friends here, guides who are waiting to greet you. First I will sing a tone that will get you into a different state, and then I will give you some instructions. (Tone, tone, tone.)

As you are sitting there, comfortably, allow your consciousness to rise above your body. We are aligning our special corridor of light over your house. This corridor of light is aligned over you. This corridor is a vestibule, a transition into a higher dimension. This is a special corridor because it will allow you to rise in consciousness, in your spiritual essence, in your etheric astral body, to come meet us in a higher dimension. If it was not for this corridor, you would not be able to do this. Feel this huge light corridor, a silver-blue light that is over you. In your consciousness, in your etheric sense, feel yourself rise up the corridor. It is a floating sensation as you are going up higher and higher, you are rising above your home, you are rising above the Earth. You can look down and see that you are above the Earth.

You continue to come up the corridor, and you are

coming into a huge ship. This is one of the command ships from the Arcturius system. You come into our healing room, our healing chamber. As you, in spirit, come into the room, you are comfortably seated in one of our arm-chairs and you are very relaxed. This healing chamber becomes like a phone booth around the chair. Now the booth is filling with a blue light, a special blue light that you have not seen before. It is a spiritual light and it is penetrating into your consciousness, it is penetrating into your spirit. All of this light that is coming into your spirit is going to be manifested as a healing feeling in your physical body.

Now I send one of our special healers to place his hands over the back of your head. (Tone, tone, tone.) We go deep inside your brain, your consciousness, your memories. There are activation points in your memories, waiting to be stimulated. As you hear these new sounds, your memo-ries from past lives are going to be stimulated. And your knowledge of the Pleiadians is going to be activated. (Sound, sound, sound; tone, tone, tone.)

There are bolts of this blue light that are going into your etheric brain, and you are being awakened. Awakened to some of the consciousness that you attained before, and to some of the knowledge that you attained before, as a Pleiadian.

So, you are in our healing chamber and we are sending you more light. We are going to spin you around in your chair now. This is a spinning like you've never experi-enced, there is no dizziness. This is a spinning where we are activating your consciousness. You must remember that consciousness is increased when the energy level of the person is increased, when their frequency increases. When you are at a higher frequency, then you are able to go into higher realms of consciousness. We are spinning the chair around, and you are going around faster and faster, but you are not feeling any dizziness. You are moving at an accelerated rate. You can feel yourself able to rise higher. And higher. And now, we can go into another realm.

Follow me as I hold your hand in etheric. We are going down a long corridor, a large tunnel. And we arrive at the Pleiades system. We come to one of the planets you have been to before, and we enter one of the temple libraries.

You are able to rest here as we look at volumes and volumes of information about the Earth and about the illnesses and diseases that occur there. We are going to align with a special volume that has information about the particular problem that your Earth body has now: Your Earth body problem is relatively minor, we will be able to find some points right now . . . We are taking in these points of information, we are identifying them, we are feeding the information telepathically into your system. (Whooshing sounds.)

You are going to be on a new thought-wave. A new thought-wave that will help you to eliminate any trace of discomfort. And when you return to the doctor's office, they will not be able to tell that anything was wrong. There is no longer anything there. (Whooshing sounds.)

Now we are going to a special Pleiadian temple, and we are entering a room filled with crystals. In this room, we see a beautiful heart-shaped crystal, a crystal like you have not seen before on Earth. We take this heart-shaped crystal and place it over the area of your etheric body that is the affected area of your Earth body. Now there is special music playing, a kind of music you have not heard on Earth, a music that vibrates with the heart-shaped crystal. And in the alignment of the crystal, we are able to complete the healing. (Tone, tone, tone.)

The Pleiadians enter, friends and healers. You are resting, lying down. We are standing over your etheric body, sending you light and singing you songs. We are placing a very light, very thin sheet over your body. This sheet is a stabilization cover that is going to enable you to hold the vibrations that you have encountered here. The sheet is floating over you, it is very comforting, it is very soothing.

Now, the sheet is removed. We are going to leave the temple, but before we do we thank all of the healers who have been with us. Now we are floating, floating back to the library. At the library, we pause so that you may continue to receive information . . .

Now we are leaving the library. We travel the beautiful light corridor back to the Arcturian ship, where you are comfortably seated again in the Arcturian healing chamber.

From this point, we can look down to see your Earth body below. We are sending light into your Earth body. And we are sending the information and knowledge you have attained, sending it down into your Earth body. We are projecting it down, and it is streaming into your Earth body through your head. So, when you return to your physical body, you will feel very highly charged, excited, and activated.

You are in the corridor now, going back down to your Earth body. We are sending you back down now. Slowly, you descend the corridor and reenter your body. This is comfortable, and you make the readjustment.

You have completed a short journey, but a very powerful journey, with us. We will continue to use the corridor to send you light. And we will continue to work with you in any way that you request. For you are surely shining very brightly in all aspects of your being. I am Julliano. We are the Arcturians. Good evening.

Whenever the high frequency tone interrupted the peacefulness of my guided channeling experience, a very sharp throbbing occurred in the back of my head. At first I felt alarmed, then strangely reassured: *Something* was happening.

After the channeling session ended, I felt exhausted and elated, as if I had indeed just returned from a fascinating trip to somewhere far away. There were no noticeable changes in my health, but there had not been any symptoms associated with my cancer anyway. I never again experienced the throbbing in my head, nor did I consciously recall any previous lifetime(s) as a Pleiadian. I do think I might be on a "new thought-wave," however. And my "illness" *has* helped me to remember the importance of my spiritual nature, and to focus more on the nonmaterial aspects of my life.

CANCER OR WAKE-UP CALL?

On the day the surgery to remove my thyroid gland was originally scheduled, I received an informative brochure in the mail from the Thyroid Foundation of America. I felt quite reassured that I had made the right decision in canceling all of the recommended aggressive treatments when I read the following statement: "Tiny areas of papillary cancer can be found in up to 10% of 'normal' thyroid glands when thyroid tissue is carefully examined with a microscope. The more carefully a pathologist looks for these tiny cancers, the more commonly they are found. These microscopic cancers seem to have *no clinical importance* and are *more a curiosity than a disease.*" (Emphasis mine.) "There are only about 12,000 new cases of papillary cancer in the United States each year, but because these patients have such a long life expectancy, we estimate that *one in a thousand people have or have had this form of cancer.*"[1] (Emphasis again mine.)

A curiosity rather than a disease? Perhaps papillary carcinoma of the thyroid is, in fact, one example of a true "little cancer," a type of cellular abnormality that actually exists in many (one out of every thousand) people who, blissfully unaware, simply live out their normal life spans.

According to Nancy Leggett and David Miller's *Arcturians,* whatever "curiosities" may have been residing in my thyroid gland are no longer there. Or at least, they are of no "clinical importance." My alternative doctor feels the same way. So do I. However, I would *not* recommend that anyone who receives a thyroid cancer diagnosis, or a diagnosis for any type of cancer or other serious illness, forgo all modern medical treatment in favor of celestial healing. My case was unusual in that I had no visible tumor on the thyroid and, after much independent research, was able to make the decision to seek alternative care with a relatively low risk of severe immediate repercussions. Only time will tell whether my decision was the right one with respect to my overall health and life span. All I can say at this time is, my particular choice of direction in this matter *felt right to me*. It still does.

Perhaps of most importance, my cancer diagnosis led me on a journey toward a new perspective of reality, ultimately changing *me* and my life. Although I would never suggest that you should do what I did and drop all of the proven miracles of Western medicine in favor of the possibility of a miracle healing from other worlds, I do think celestial healing is worth exploring—*in addition* to your doctor's guidance, your alternative health care program, *and* your religious or spiritual practice. Simply by opening yourself up to the otherworldly possibilities, you can expand your consciousness, thereby automatically improving your state of mental and physical well-being. As an addition to your current health plan, it certainly cannot hurt you. But it *will* change you.

ARE YOU CRAZY?

It is tempting to ignore the ET-healing phenomenon instead, and to dismiss all experiencers as "UFO nuts" or hysterics. When I first met Nancy Leggett outside the Florida cancer center, I questioned her sanity and, later, my own. But research into the extraterrestrial phenomenon indicates that *the majority of experiencers are intelligent, capable, high-functioning individuals with no history of symptoms of mental illness.* Except, of course, that they believe in UFOs and in the extraterrestrial or celestial beings who they say are communicating with them.

A number of psychological studies have been conducted on experiencers, and therapists who work with experiencers have compiled their clients' records, all of which seem to indicate quite clearly that the abduction or ET experience is *not* a form of repressed sexual or physical abuse, mass hysteria, personal fantasy, psychosis, multiple personality disorder, psychogenic fugue state (which is a prolonged state of amnesia due to emotional causes), or temporal lobe dysfunction in which the temporal lobe of the brain is somehow stimulated, resulting in hallucinations.[2]

While most experiencers wonder at some point if they are, as Connie Isele in Chapter 4 put it, "losing my marbles," *many never tell anyone of their ET experiences for fear of being labeled "crazy."* According to Virginia Bennett, a California hypnotherapist who works with ET contact experiencers, "Some researchers estimate that 95% of extraterrestrial contact is positive, but may go unreported since there is no need to seek professional assistance in dealing with the experience."[3] Yet, more and more therapists are working with high-functioning clients who are coming to them solely because of a history of extraterrestrial encounters. Dr. Courtney Brown, author of *Cosmic Voyage*, estimates that "approximately forty thousand individuals in the United States (to date) may have sought some form of professional help with regard to their abduction experiences."[4] For experiencers who have been healed of a medical problem, a visit to a therapist may feel unnecessary, even threatening, an invitation to being labeled "crazy."

Since there does not yet exist some kind of a "mental illness" label for this widespread phenomenon, we must proceed in one of two directions: Either we must create a new category of mental illness so that mental health practitioners can diagnose people with "ET personality disorder" or "UFO-related fugue state disorder," and begin to prescribe specific medications, hypnosis, and other treatments; or we must *accept that there exist other realities*, other realities as real as the three-dimensional state that currently serves as our consensual reality. If we are to acknowledge and accommodate the increasing numbers of people all over the world who are claiming that they have experienced UFO and/or extraterrestrial close encounters, healing and other, we must either expand our concept of mental illness or enlarge our perception of reality itself.

Personally, I do not believe that all experiencers are disillusioned or insane. None of the experiencers I talked to seemed crazy, although some did seek therapy to help them cope with and better understand their experiences. My most recent book included interviews with artists who had a history of mental illness, so I am able to differentiate (usually) between unusual experiences and madness.

It would be easier to tell ourselves that people who claim to have ET experiences are crazy than to accept the alternative: that *they are telling the truth.* It would be less threatening to assume that UFO/ET experiences are a radical new mental aberration, a nearly universal psychological phenomenon, than to recognize that *something is really going on* for experiencers with extraterrestrials. My research for this book has led me to believe that experiencers actually tend to be mentally *ahead* of the rest of us in that they seem to be *more evolved* on a psychospiritual level, often with advanced psychic, healing, and intuitive skills.

If John Hunter Gray can virtually halt the aging process, and if Ron Blevins can take instruction in healing telepathically, and if normal, everyday people can be healed of medical conditions *overnight*, well then, perhaps we are not so *many* light-years away from our own science fiction future. If normal, everyday people can learn and evolve *and heal* through their encounters with otherworldly beings, well then, perhaps *everybody* can change themselves—physically, emotionally, psychospiritually. Even you and me.

PART IV

It Could Happen
to *You*

"Healing is a matter of time, but it is also a matter of opportunity." —HIPPOCRATES

"Miracles happen, not in opposition to Nature, but in opposition to what we know of Nature." —ST. AUGUSTINE

"The main reason for healing is love." —PARACELSUS

CHAPTER 18

How to *Become* an Experiencer

I f you feel a strong desire to explore the ET experience for yourself for healing or other reasons, I can provide you with some simple guidelines and the specific resources to direct you on this journey. I would suggest, however, that you *first build yourself a good support system.* As with anything involving the unknown, some ET-related experiences can prove unsettling, even frightening. Sometimes simply the immersion in UFO materials, such as books and films, can result in nightmares and anxiety. Be sure that you have at least *one person with whom you can share your feelings* as you begin to explore the extraterrestrial phenomenon. Perhaps you can convince a spouse or a friend to join you on this adventurous journey.

If you are ready to begin your quest to make contact, consider the following step-by-step approach to opening up the lines of communication with the ET realms.

METHODS FOR ET CONTACT

1. Learn to meditate.
2. Contact an ET channeler or healer.
3. Contact CSETI to join their CE-5 initiative.
4. Do The Monroe Institute program(s).
5. Do the Farsight Institute program(s).

Each of these steps requires an increasing level of personal commitment, as well as a greater financial investment and degree of flexibility in lifestyle. You may simply learn to meditate and, in consciously opening yourself up to the extraterrestrial energies, find that this is enough to allow for the level of ET experience desired. Or you may wish to call in the services of an ET "professional," or join a group of other seekers attempting to make conscious contact. For the truly committed and deeply adventurous, The Monroe Institute and the Farsight Institute offer intensive programs for consciousness exploration and expansion, providing ready access to the other realms. Your path will ultimately depend on how you wish to accomplish your goal of personal ET contact experience.

Before undertaking any of these (or other) steps to making contact, however, it is *very important* that you learn how to protect yourself. There exist "good" unseen forces and "not so good" unseen forces, just as there is both good and bad in the "seen" three-dimensional everyday reality. If you were about to undertake a deep-sea journey, you would expect to encounter both friendly forms of sea life *and* you would be prepared just in case you happened to cross paths with some forms of not-so-friendly sea life. This holds true for a jungle journey, a desert trek, a mountain climb, a trip to a foreign city. Thus, it should be no surprise to learn that in preparing for ET encounters, one must take certain precautionary steps.

Bev Marcotte, the founder and coordinator of Lightkeepers Remote Viewing/Remote Healing Network [see Chapter 9], suggests the following steps for self-protection before opening oneself up to the other realms for healing or self-healing purposes.

PROTECTING YOURSELF[1]

- Before you begin, clean the air around you of negative energies by burning incense or sage.
- In a relaxed state, say to yourself: "I put on the mantle of pure white impenetrable light. It encloses and protects me from the top of my head to the soles of my feet. This seamless mantle of God's pure loving light protects me from anything that would harm me or influence me physically, spiritually, mentally, or emotionally, or become an obstacle to healing myself or healing anyone else."
- Now imagine God (or the Divine Source) pouring down pure white light, loving light. It pours into your head, filling your body

while pushing out any negative energy inside you.

- In your mind, pull this white light all through your body, from head to fingers and toes, flooding yourself with the white light as it pushes out all of the negative energies through the soles of your feet. See the negative dis-ease leave your body, disappearing through the floor beneath you to bury itself deep in the ground.
- See yourself full of God's pure white light.
- When the session is completed, cleanse the air around you once more.

This is what Bev calls a "mini-healing," a brief meditation that cleans your body of negative energies and sends out a clear message: *You are walking "in the light" on your journey* into the other realms. Your energy is good, positive, and you seek only good, positive ET energy with which to interact.

Ze'ev Kolman, the world-renowned healer in Dr. Hans Holzer's book *The Secret of Healing*, teaches people how to use what he calls "the Blue Shield" in order to construct a layer of defense around themselves before healing self or others:

THE BLUE SHIELD

- In a relaxed state with eyes closed, imagine yourself in the negative, as if you are looking at a photographic negative of your own image.
- Picture light surrounding your image, white, blue, or purple in color, but of a very light shade.
- With your eyes open, trace the outline of a protective shield around the contours of your body, but trace wider than your true physical form to thereby include the unseen layers of self (the aura).[2]

According to Ze'ev, the purpose of "the Blue Shield" is to protect your body and aura from others' emanations, the energies coming from other people that may or may not be negative. This could include energies from nonhuman life forms as well.

There are other methods for such self-protection, all of which seen to include the use of light surrounding the body, one's home and/or loved ones. In learning meditation, contacting an ET channeler or healer, or attending the CSETI, Monroe Institute, or Farsight Institute programs, further instructions will be provided for protecting yourself when venturing into the "psychic realms."

MEDITATION

There are a number of different types of meditation programs available to the public, and plenty of books for self-teaching purposes. The two meditation methods I am personally familiar with are Silva Mind Control and Transcendental Meditation (TM). I use a combination of these two techniques when I meditate each day.

The Silva Mind Control Method is taught by trained lecturers throughout the U.S. and in seventy-two other countries. The Basic Lecture Series is a thirty-two-hour program of lectures and training exercises, usually conducted over two consecutive weekends. It is not "brainwashing," but a scientific training program designed to teach you how to enter an altered level of consciousness in which you can control your own mind. In the altered state of mind, your brain waves are slowed but you are not asleep. Faculties considered to be unconscious become more conscious, allowing you to both control your body and expand your mind's reach. In this mental state, you can learn to heal yourself, possibly others. You can also find yourself interacting with the nonhuman beings who inhabit other realms, realms more accessible to the expanded consciousness.

The Silva Method was designed some thirty years ago by José Silva, and more than eight million people have graduated from his program. The main benefit of this method is easy access to an altered state of consciousness, which the program advises followers to access daily for the purposes of deep relaxation, stress reduction, improved learning, enhanced creativity, better health and well-being. You may choose to undertake the program and learn the Silva Mind Control Method for these reasons alone, and/or for the purpose of gaining access to the altered state of mind that allows for openness to celestial, extraterrestrial contact.

The Silva Method is simple and easy. To find out when a program is scheduled in your area, contact Silva Mind Control International, Inc. [See Resources on page 321.] You may want to pick up a copy of the book *You the Healer* by José Silva and Robert B. Stone, which provides an easy guide to learning and adopting the Silva Method at home on your own, and utilizing this meditation technique specifically for healing purposes.

Transcendental Meditation (TM) is a simple, effortless procedure that is practiced twice daily for fifteen to twenty minutes while sitting comfortably in a relaxed state. As your body becomes deeply relaxed, your mind can transcend the normal chatter of mental activity to what the TM method calls "Transcendental Consciousness," where consciousness is truly *open*. This is a scientific technique, not a religious practice. It is easy to learn and, the program promises, *anyone* can learn to do it. I found it to be extremely easy to do, very relaxing, and a great method for opening up to the celestial realms.

TM has been well studied by the scientific community during the last three decades to validate the claims that this meditation technique benefits the mind, body, behavior, and environment of practitioners. Research findings include increased happiness, reduced stress, increased intelligence, increased creativity, improved memory, improved health, improved relationships, increased energy, reduced insomnia, reversal of biological aging, reduced crime, and improved quality of life in society. TM practitioners on average have the biological age of a person five to twelve years younger, as well as a significantly reduced incidence of many illnesses and diseases.[3] According to Dr. Courtney Brown, a specialist in scientific remote viewing and controlled altered states of consciousness [more later in this chapter], "It is easier to tell people in our society that their blood pressure will improve with the practice of TM than it is to tell them that they will soon become aware of their own souls . . . Rather, *my personal observations* indicate to me that people who practice TM have a flavor to their consciousness that is much like that of advanced ETs and future humans."[4]

TM was introduced to the public over forty years ago by Maharishi Mahesh Yogi, but has been practiced by yogis for centuries. TM is taught in this country in Maharishi Vedic Schools, and in public and private locations in most cities in America. When I decided to learn TM, I only had to drive three miles from my own home to the home of a TM trainer, where three of us attended the sixteen-hour course in a very comfortable living room. Courses are often taught at colleges and universities, YMCAs and YWCAs, and other centers of higher learning. To find out where there is a TM course or trainer nearest you, call the

TM 800 number. If you have access to the Internet, you can listen to a twenty-three-minute lecture on the TM technique and download information on the alternative health programs and physicians recommended by the Maharishi. [See Resources, page 321.)

NOTE: Silva Mind Control and TM are not inexpensive courses. In my own case, however, both have proven to be wise investments in the long-term status of my own physical health, mental flexibility, and consciousness expansion.

ET CHANNELERS & HEALERS

David Miller, who you met in Chapter 13, is an example of a channeler of extraterrestrials and their healing energies. Peter Faust, in Chapter 10, is a professional healer, an acupuncturist and energy healer, who uses ET energies in his healing work. Bev Marcotte in Chapter 9 is one of a group of remote viewers/remote healers who are conducting healing work over distances, typically with the assistance and/or guidance of extraterrestrials. Nancy Leggett [Chapter 11] and Ingrid Parnell [Chapter 12] are laypersons who have developed their healing skills under the guidance of celestial, extraterrestrial contacts.

These five individuals are good examples of the increasing number of people who feel "called" to do healing work, healing others with the energies from celestial sources. You may contact these individuals directly [see Resources, page 322], or use the "Resources for Experiencers" list in the Appendix for referrals to individuals across the U.S. who do ET channeling and/or ET channeled healings. If you join ET experiencer support groups or attend UFO/ET seminars, you will undoubtedly learn about *many* ET channelers and healers. Ask around: Find out who is good, affordable, successful, accessible.

A single visit or session with a channeler may serve to introduce you to one or more groups of celestial beings or extraterrestrials, allowing you to communicate with these beings through the channeler. You may or not may "feel" anything. This is a passive interaction, but it can assist you in opening up to the possibility of a personal relationship with otherworldly beings. The channeler may be able to provide you with certain tools, such as Tachyon or crystals, to assist you in making contact on your own.

Be very careful in working with channelers and self-taught healers. Some are outright charlatans, others are not very adept at what they claim to be able to do. Judge for yourself, and do not overspend. I would advise you to investigate these relationships slowly and carefully, collecting as much information as you can from ET channelers and celestial healers regarding methods and techniques *for making contact on your own*. After all, the goal is to communicate directly with celestial beings without the costly services of an interpreter or go-between.

CSETI

The Center for the Study of Extraterrestrial Intelligence, a nonprofit, international educational organization headquartered in North Carolina, has an all-volunteer staff working to establish contact with extraterrestrial civilizations and to inform the public about their existence. The Rapid Mobilization Investigative Team of CSETI responds to reported incidents of significant ET activity all over the world. CSETI claims to have successfully established contact with ET spacecraft in Mexico, England, Belgium, and certain parts of the U.S., and they anticipate a full landing and boarding of a UFO within the next two to five years.[5]

According to CSETI, "A plan is in place to allow for gradually broader and deeper contact with human society and individuals so that humans may become accustomed to the reality of other intelligent beings in the universe, and so that needed research and observation may take place on both sides. Limited but increasing opportunities for bilateral and human initiated contact will occur in the reasonably near future."[6]

CSETI asks, "Are we alone in the universe, and have other intelligent life forms found their way to our small part of the galaxy? The best available evidence suggests that no, we are not alone, and yes, they have already found us. The real question at this point may be, 'What are we going to do about it?' "[7] CSETI has formed a project they call the "Close Encounters of the Fifth Kind Initiative," close encounters of the fifth kind (CE-5*) being defined as voluntary or human-initiated ET contact.

The CE-5 Initiative involves specific protocols in a multidisciplinary approach that combines technology with consciousness to facilitate human-ET contact. Some of the communication techniques utilized by CSETI include simple light or laser signals, telepathic projection, use of crop circles, and sound waves. A number of CE-5 working groups are currently meeting regularly in various locations, attempting to follow the CSETI protocols for contacting ETs. CSETI also conducts seminars to introduce the general public to the idea and invite participation. A recent weekend workshop scheduled for the South Florida area included information on fieldwork methodology (i.e., techniques to initiate contact), interpreting contact experiences, retaining memories of contact, and an evening of outdoor contact work. Advanced training retreats for exploring higher consciousness and initiating UFO/ET interaction are also offered by CSETI.

If you would like more information on CSETI and their CE-5 Initiative, contact them directly [see Resources, page 320). You must be willing to spend the night (or most of it) outside, often in remote areas, and have the flexibility to travel without much notice. Remember, the CSETI work is all volunteer, and therefore self-funded. Workshops can be expensive.

---

*A "close encounter-1" is defined as a close sighting of a UFO; CE-2 as seeing physical evidence from a UFO (e.g., burned grass, radioactive soil); CE-3 as seeing an ET in or near a UFO; CE-4 as an "abduction" by an ET; CE-5 as consensual contact with an ET.

But interplanetary communication may, after all, be worth the price of admission.

THE MONROE INSTITUTE

This nonprofit educational and research organization was established in 1956 by Robert A. Monroe, who worked with psychologists, psychiatrists, physicians, biochemists, electrical engineers, and physicists in the investigation of human consciousness. Using noninvasive methodology, including Monroe's invention called "Hemi-Sync," audio technology that can bring the two hemispheres of the brain into synchronization, The Monroe Institute (TMI) assists participants in learning how to achieve a highly productive altered state of consciousness, a focused and coherent brain-mind state. TMI offers a variety of week-long residential programs at their training center in Virginia, as well as home-study programs with training manuals and over two hundred audiotapes and CDs.

The Hemi-Sync process includes methods and techniques to support hemispheric synchronization of the brain, which enables access to beneficial states of consciousness. A combination of verbal instructions with special blends and sequences of sound patterns is designed to evoke specific brain wave states. There is no use of hypnosis or subliminal suggestion, nor is any particular belief system promoted. The Hemi-Sync programs can be used to help strengthen mental, emotional, and physical capabilities, improving health and memory, enhancing creativity and sleep, aiding meditative states with access to expanded states of consciousness.

Several years ago, I used a collection of Hemi-Sync tapes in a private setting to help me access my subconscious mind and collect ideas for a book I was writing. The experience was phenomenal! At that time, I did not meditate and had never even tried to achieve a meditative state. But by lying on a bed in a dark room, listening with head phones to audiotapes of odd, discordant sounds, I found myself in a *very* altered state of mind. With little effort on my part, I was able to recall deeply buried childhood memories in vivid flashes that felt more like brief dreams. I experienced lengthy, dreamlike sequences as well, explicit and often bizarre vignettes directly related to both my personal life and the concept I was attempting to explore in my writing. I even "saw" my future self, my potential futures revealing themselves in filmlike clips with several different versions of "me" some years hence.

The Hemi-Sync experience was, for me, powerfully insightful and consciousness expanding, allowing me to look at myself and my life in a series of three-dimensional sound bites. I felt transported to a broader, more spiritual reality, a state of mind beyond the time/space continuum we inhabit. A lot of fear was dispelled, and I began to realize the accessibility of consciousness itself, my own and a more universal aspect beyond the here-and-now state to which I had limited myself.

The Hemi-Sync process can be utilized for a wide variety of purposes, and specific tapes are available for a number of different applications including allergies, anger, attention deficit disorder, blood pressure, breathing, changing behavior patterns, death and dying, energy tuning, expanded awareness, financial success, fitness and sports, general wellness, immune system function, learning and memory, meditation and spiritual development, pain management, personal growth, pregnancy and childbirth, problem solving and creativity, self-confidence, sensory improvement, sleep and dreams, stress, surgery, and weight control.[8] There is also a specific program designed for healing purposes: The Dolphin Energy Club provides members with training in both self-healing and the healing of others through accessing specific, altered states of consciousness.

People who attend The Monroe Institute residential programs and those who use the tapes and CDs, either at home or in clinical or educational settings, are able to explore an expanded consciousness that includes other planets, worlds, dimensions, realms, and realities. With time and practice, you could use the Hemi-Sync process to open communication avenues with the otherworldly beings you are interested in meeting because one of TMI's discoveries is the brainwave frequencies that allow us to perceive an area of nonphysical existence where nonhuman life thrives. Thus, Hemi-Sync practitioners can "travel" into this "subspace," where they are able to interact with humans who are no longer living, as well as with nonhuman entities from a variety of celestial, extraterrestrial sources.

Therapists trained at TMI offer Hemi-Sync programs to clients, as do physicians and educators who have attended The Monroe Institute. If you wish to have guidance in your exploration of the Hemi-Sync process for consciousness expansion, you might want to contact TMI for referral to professional practitioners in your area, or to learn how you can attend the Institute in the foothills of the Blue Ridge Mountains. Or you may choose to venture forth on your own, as I did, using the Hemi-Sync training programs available for home study. To contact TMI, see Resources on page 321 for their phone number, address, E-mail, and Web site.

THE FARSIGHT INSTITUTE

Professional training in scientific remote viewing (SRV) was developed by the U.S. military for the purposes of psychic spying. SRV training is currently offered to the public by private companies and by Dr. Courtney Brown, an associate professor of political science at Emory University and director of the Farsight Institute in Atlanta. SRV is not like mediumistic or psychic "seeing," but is an exacting discipline involving a precise set of protocols to be practiced by a rigorously trained viewer.

A trained remote viewer can "travel" into the past or the future to collect data. SRV sessions always focus on a specific "target," including places, events, and people or beings. Trained viewers have been providing reports for over a decade about a variety of extraterrestrial locations including planets and other realms, and on the ETs who have been seen and sometimes contacted during remote viewing sessions. Unlike military remote viewing, SRV as taught at Farsight enables two-way communication between viewer and telepathic beings. Thus, SRV provides a scientific method for contacting and communicating with extraterrestrials.

According to Dr. Brown, remote viewers were consistently "blocked," unable to view ET abductions in progress, until quite recently. Dr. Brown believes that the ETs only placed limitations on remote viewers in order "to prevent us from interfering with ET activities, or to protect us from something for which we are not fully prepared."[9] In his fascinating book *Cosmic Voyage*, Dr. Brown summarizes and shares his SRV reports on his own ET encounters. In an attempt to develop a more complete picture of the phenomenon by focusing less on the well-publicized trauma of abductions, Dr. Brown expands our concept of ET-human interaction by providing us with the viewpoint of a voluntary participant via SRV. His experiences in this regard are largely positive in nature, and he is encouraging in his belief that we all should—and *can*—"enter the realm of galactic diplomacy" as cosmic citizens aware of and involved in our cosmic neighborhood.[10]

Dr. Brown's Farsight Institute offers intensive training in SRV for those interested in developing this skill, a skill that the U.S. military has basically proven anyone can learn to use with accuracy exceeding that of natural psychics. This training is not inexpensive and requires a background in meditation and consciousness work. You can write to Dr. Brown at the Farsight Institute for information on their Atlanta-based training programs* [see Resources, page 320] if you are interested in opening yourself up to what Dr. Brown refers to as "all sorts of activities and areas of awareness that are not typical of the standard human set of experiences in a lifetime."[11]

This includes, of course, ET contact.

Simply by becoming open to the existence of alternate realities and celestial realms, you can open yourself up to otherworldly experiences. And as anyone who prays to the Divine Source knows, communicating with the other realms can be, in and of itself, a healing experience. You already know how to pray: Just communicate in your own way, saying what is in your heart.

Now you have a set of steps you can take toward establishing a relationship with celestial, extraterrestrial beings. It is up to *you* to decide if and when you are ready to begin.

---

*TransDimensional Systems (TDS) is another Georgia-based institute offering training in SRV and other paranormal skills such as telepathic communication. Programs include basic training, intermediate skills, and an advanced remote viewing seminar, as well as specialized training in medical remote viewing. Provided to students in intimate groups of two to four, training programs can be made available off-site if a number of individuals in a specific geographic location express interest in TDS. [See Resources on page 321 for address and Web site information.]

PART V

What *Is* Happening?

"It is precisely because I believe theologically that there is a being called God, and that He is infinite intelligence, freedom, and power, that I cannot take it upon myself to limit what He might have done."

—FATHER THEODORE M. HESBURGH, former president of Notre Dame[1]

CHAPTER 19

Putting It All in Perspective

In Chapter 2, John Hunter Gray mentions the "cursory medical exams" he underwent with his son during two encounter experiences. Mary Kerfoot [Chapter 3] states candidly that she has *never* experienced the typical "abduction" medical exams as reported in the media. None of the participants in this book project complain of trauma due to invasive medical procedures conducted during their encounter experiences. Despite a lack of understanding as to the motives and the purpose of ET medical intervention, the people I talked to were quite grateful for the results. As Melanie Green [Chapter 6] explains, "You will not be hearing any complaints from me!"

The standard abduction experience publically presented by certain UFO researchers and commonly depicted in the media almost always includes a highly traumatic medical-type scenario in which the abductee is immobilized on an otherworldly operating table while frightening-looking creatures poke and probe with scary instruments, usually culminating in a rectal exam, sperm or ovum removal. Because so many experiencers do report this type of ET-related experience, it is undoubtedly one aspect of the encounter phenomenon. Unfortunately, this one aspect of the encounter experience has received the preponderance of media and public attention, while there exists a virtual ignorance of most of the other aspects of ET-human interaction. Barbara Lamb [Chapter 15] sees the medical exam as the most traumatic and therefore *most easily recalled* part of the ET encounter experience, sometimes the *only* thing an experiencer is able to remember. However, it seems there is usually much more involved in the typical encounter experience, much of it less traumatic and more positive, enlightening, even healing in nature.

Whenever I brought my infant and, later, toddler son for his regular "well-baby" medical checkups, he would scream incessantly as soon as he spotted the large, bearded, very jolly physician. One of the nurses told me that with certain children she had resorted to bringing their vaccination shots out into the parking lot because they were too fearful to enter the pediatrician's office and sat screeching in their parents' cars.

Of course, a baby or young child does not understand that a medical exam, including those dreaded immunization shots, is what we adults regard as positive, necessary "preventive medicine." As adults, we are all (hopefully) less fearful in visiting the doctor, dentist, chiropractor, acupuncturist, and other medical professionals *because we understand the purpose of the interaction*, and are therefore able to accept any associated discomfort as just one aspect of *a relationship essential to our well-being.*

My son used to fall apart in the shoe store, too. He was afraid of the shoe salesman, who sat on a very low stool and fiddled with my son's feet. But when my son turned three, he began to play a game called "Arthur, the Shoe Store Man," pretending to fit himself with a variety of styles of "new shoes." When his real shoes grew snug, he asked his father, "When can we go get some new shoes?" The trip was easy, fun. My son finally understood that the stranger at his feet was performing tasks that were in everyone's best interest. He slapped Arthur's palm, gave him the "high five" sign, and raced out of the store in his new white sneakers.

The trauma of a strange place with strange creatures who perform strange tasks is certainly very real. As Connie Isele points out in Chapter 4, it is uncomfortable enough when the doctors you visit are human; it is even more so when they are not! But if the preceding accounts of medical healings are to be believed, the ET medical plan has, at the very least, certain *beneficial* effects. We do not know the purpose of these mysterious visits from other realms, but it seems that if we are able to move past the trauma of the *uncomfortable strangeness*, the trauma of *not knowing*, we may boost our potential for recognizing the positive, healing aspects of the ET encounter experience. Perhaps the ET medical plan is not a self-serving "attack" on human "victims" but is, as John

Hunter Gray believes, an experience that combines the self-interest of the ET doctor/researchers with the best interest of a civilization lagging in medical knowledge and expertise.

John G. Miller, an emergency-room physician who practices in the Los Angeles area, has investigated ET abduction cases as a doctor treating medical trauma (without hypnosis). In viewing the phenomenon from the perspective of a human doctor, Miller points out, "The most consistent impression I get from accounts of alleged alien examination techniques and 'medical' procedures, whether from written reports or my own witnesses, is that I'm not hearing about our kind of medicine. The most consistent feature in these reports is the *difference* between reported alien techniques and procedures and our own. The differences are great enough to invalidate any theory of origin of these reports that is based on the idea that they somehow originate in the witnesses' own past medical experience or knowledge."[1]

Miller points out these differences: The ET medical exam tends to overlook the cardiovascular, respiratory, lymphatic, and certain other internal systems "often of great concern to the human physician," while focusing on the head, skin, and reproductive organs. "Everywhere you look in these abductees' accounts," Miller concludes, "they are fundamentally different from human medicine."[2] He suggests that the *absence* of certain things is as important for us to consider as those things that are noted by experiencers during the encounter.

Perhaps modern medicine could learn from experiencers about certain ET medical techniques that do seem to work. Experiencers often recall the use of light and sound, laserlike instruments, and cold jellylike substances. Needle marks and puncture wounds are commonly reported. But where are the stethoscopes, rubber gloves and thermometers, scales and blood pressure cuffs? Hair samples are clipped, fingernail and skin samples are taken. No chest X rays? No urine samples?

What do the ET medical exam techniques indicate? Are they looking for the effects of the Earth environment on the human body, examining our hair and nails for pollutants and contaminants? This would explain the commonly reported interest in the neck area and thyroid gland,[3] where damage from overexposure to radiation could be noted.

All of this is, of course, supposition only. We cannot be sure of the purpose for the ETs' methods and techniques for examining the human body. We could, however, *accept as important* the various accounts of medical healings reported by experiencers. And we could begin to consider how celestial beings are curing diseases that Western medicine is unable to cure. If the ETs know how to speed up recovery from wounds and surgery, boost immunity to colds and flus, eradicate depression and cancer cells overnight, perhaps we should stop complaining about their bedside manner and begin to study what they are accomplishing in the field of medicine. As the preceding chapters illustrate, the extraterrestrial approach to health and healing seems nothing short of miraculous. Certainly, they are light-years ahead of us in their medical knowledge and technology. Perhaps they can assist us in catching up. Perhaps they are attempting to do exactly that.

HOW HEALING HAPPENS

If celestial beings are real, if they are coming here from somewhere else "out there," no matter where that may turn out to be, how is it that they can perform such amazing medical healings? Is there something we might learn from the various cases of ET-related cures about our own bodies, our own abilities for healing? And if it turns out that, in fact, there are no ETs after all, might there *still* be something we could learn from the case histories presented in this book? ETs or no ETs, exactly *how did all of these people heal?*

Healing seems to be a highly individualistic process that varies from person to person. One person's rare steak may indeed by another's poison, your aunt's "surefire" cold cure of warm apple cider vinegar and vitamin C may make *you* feel worse. But current medical research does seem to point to the possibility that we all possess an innate "healing system," a mind-body-spirit complex of natural self-repair that may be stimulated into action by a variety of factors.

In their well-researched and inspirational book, *Re-*

markable Recovery, Caryle Hirshberg and Marc Ian Barasch explore what they refer to as "the UFOs of medicine": spontaneous remission.[4] Such healings are generally considered to be extremely rare and lacking in "proof." Inexplicable in terms of modern medicine, spontaneous healings often go unreported in the medical literature because of the attending physicians' fear of criticism from their peers. How could an inoperable tumor be threatening a patient's life one day, and simply gone the next? Such cases make doctors extremely ill at ease because they cannot even begin to explain how these patients heal themselves.

In researching these kinds of cases, talking to people who have spontaneously recovered from a variety of supposedly incurable, supposedly fatal diseases, Hirshberg and Barasch note the following: "There are no medical journals devoted to the study of remarkable recovery, those odd instances when a disease such as terminal cancer vanishes almost exorcismally from the body. There are no medical school courses explaining how, on certain irreproducible occasions, a malignant tumor disappears from a CT scan like a glitch from a radar screen. Though there are institutions devoted to the study of most major diseases, and nationwide networks that trace epidemiology and treatment efficacies, there is no national remissions registry to track unexplained healings. It is not known how often they occur, in what diseases, and in what kinds of people, much less why . . . Remarkable recovery is a phenomenon so spectacular, elusive, and almost scientifically disreputable that few researchers have bothered to look for it, let alone pursue its implications."[5]

The authors propose the likely possibility that spontaneous cures of incurable diseases occur when the body's *innate healing system is turned on high*, jacked up due to one or, more often, a combination of specific, individualized factors including emotions, belief systems, dreams and altered states of consciousness, self-hypnosis, dissociative states, love and relationship, visualization, artistic and creative pursuits, biofeedback, nutrition, "unknown 'energy' effects."[6] They cite "existential shifts," a sweeping change in worldview, as another probable factor.[7] Trauma-induced trancelike states are also cited as a possible immune system enhancer.[8] According to the authors, "Accounts of remarkable recovery are fraught with descriptions of symbolic processes, altered states, high emotion, special physical movements, and forms of social congregation that seem part and parcel of healing ceremonies everywhere."[9]

Including encounter experiences "out there," on other planets, in other dimensions or realms.

It would seem that the typical celestial healing, if we can say that any celestial experience is "typical," mimics the non-ET spontaneous healing in both the associated factors and the most profound end result: The individual who is healed is a changed person afterward, not only physically but mentally and emotionally, spiritually and even socially. I would like to suggest that the celestial or extraterrestrial encounter experience should be added to the list of possible reasons for unexplained remarkable recoveries. Perhaps celestial healings are the source of those "unknown 'energy' effects." Celestial healings are, in fact, the UFOs of the "UFOs of medicine." They need to be acknowledged, recognized for what they may be revealing about our innate ability to heal ourselves of illnesses, including incurable, even fatal conditions.

It is possible that if one believes one is experiencing an encounter with otherworldly beings, whether or not the event is "real," the body's mind-body-spirit complex can respond to this consciousness-expanding state by *changing*, boosting one's immune system function, even altering the body's cells on some subatomic level. The result is recovery from illness, healing the body-mind-spirit, and changing the experiencers in ways seen and unseen.

WHY DON'T THEY HEAL EVERYBODY?

Of course, ET experiencers are not all in a perfect state of health and well-being. Most get ill, just like the rest of us. Experiencers die of cancer and heart disease, car accidents and other common and not so common fates. Many experiencers actually suffer from sensitivities and ills they believe may be directly or indirectly related to their extraterrestrial encounters. For example, experiencers may report symptoms of what is sometimes called a "generalized sensitivity effect," including heightened sensitivities to environmental conditions such as light, sound, or humidity, and to alcohol, caffeine, medications, certain foods and chemicals. Allergies may appear or worsen, and chronic, vague symptoms may occur. Some experiencers report an "electrical sensitivity syndrome" in which their bodies seem to interfere with electrical function, causing the malfunction of televisions, watches and clocks, lamps and streetlights, computers and cars. It may be that experiencers of close encounters have an increased sensitivity to electromagnetic fields.* It may be that their experiences have reprogrammed their nervous systems, making them both more environmentally sensitive *and* more open to other realities, other dimensions, other worlds.

So, why don't the celestials save all the humans they have contacted or communicated with? Why will one experiencer suffer from arthritis or diabetes, while another will be cured overnight? Why do some experiencers become physically and emotionally ill after an encounter, while others are miraculously healed?

We just do not know the answer to these questions. Perhaps it has something to do with our individual soul's destiny on Earth, maybe it's simply a matter of

---

*The temporal lobe of the brain is very sensitive to electrical disturbances, and may be ultrasensitive in the "encounter-prone" person. The temporal lobe acts as a transducer of electromagnetic energy, and stimulation of this area of the brain with magnetic fields can produce out-of-body, psychic, and mystical experiences.

luck. As with many things in life, the reasons remain unknown. These particulars of individual fate may be part of God's plan, not ours, not the celestials'. All we can do is attempt to open ourselves up to the possibility that we, too, may be fortunate enough to be healed, healing ourselves, possibly others.

FEAR: OBSTACLE TO HEALING

One night a few months after I had begun to explore the celestial healing phenomenon, my son, who was barely two at the time, caught his first cold. Because he was feverish and did not understand why he was unable to breathe normally, he was fitful at bedtime and wide awake at midnight. We settled in together on the couch in the family room, where I let him lie on my chest while I meditated. This seemed to relax him, and he quickly fell asleep.

After meditating, I was relaxed but fully awake. I began to think about how exciting it would be to have an ET encounter experience. At this point, I had not developed any fear around the phenomenon as my few experiences (with Nancy Leggett, and with the channeler David Miller) had been secondhand, pleasant, and very positive.

Suddenly, a humming noise filled the room and I could hear what sounded like a radio playing. It sounded strange, as if I were listening to my old AM/FM transistor radio from the 1960s with the tiny plastic earplug. The music was somehow familiar, from my childhood, but fuzzy, not quite tuned in. *Cool*, I thought to myself as I hugged my sleeping baby a little bit tighter. *Here we go!* I knew that *something* was happening.

I felt as if we were being drawn up and out the window next to the couch, which was closed. And then I felt as if we were outside in the cool night, my son still on my chest. We were moving very rapidly, sucked upward into the star-studded sky. The air was bracing, strangely silent. The stars surrounding us were very bright, and there seemed to be more of them than could normally be seen in the Florida night sky. I was excited, and held my son close.

Then it seemed as if my son was looking at the sky, too, craning his neck to stare up at all the beautiful stars. I could see him smile. Yet, I could still feel his warm forehead resting against my chest. How could this be?

The dichotomy seemed to snap something inside my head, and suddenly we were back on the couch, the baby still sleeping peacefully on my chest. I felt quite disappointed, as if we had been returned prematurely, before reaching our distant destination.

When I finally put my son to bed and crawled in beside my husband, he noted the time: four o'clock. Had we spent four hours on the couch, or did my son and I actually go somewhere "out there" during that chunk of time? I do not have any other memories from the experience, but I cannot help but wonder: Was my son awake on the way "there," watching the sky and grinning, and asleep on the way home, resting comfortably against my chest? I do not know and my son isn't telling.

He did say later that at night sometimes he will "fly up, up, up" to what he calls "the City of Knowledge." Recently, my son informed me that "the teacher" there had taught him "how to go to the City of Knowledge without closing my eyes."

I wish that I, too, had maintained this curious, fearless attitude. Instead, a series of nighttime awakenings began to startle and upset my husband and me, culminating in a preventive approach of self-protective mental images of white lights used to turn away the night visitors, like hanging a NO SOLICITING sign above our bed. The humming noises soon stopped, the fuzzy images of strange-looking creatures no longer appeared, we slept quietly through the night once again.

As quickly and easily as I had opened the door to the other realms, I closed it back up again. Because I was afraid.

EVOLUTION TO HEALTH

When I first conceived the idea for this book, my intent was to interview experiencers of ET-related medical healings in order to derive a specific *program for healthy living*, a kind of ET-prescribed diet and lifestyle for the new millennium. I fully expected that this program, the "ET health plan," would entail specific dietary practices, possibly the use of herbs and supplements, some sort of exercise and stress-reduction methods, and a spiritual/emotional component of some kind. I pictured this "ET health plan" as being an environmentally conscious, spiritually conscious, and mind-body conscious method for living in the twenty-first century. I imagined that I would first make some deep mind and body alterations, radical changes in my own lifestyle, and then advise others on how to do the same, all of us following in the footsteps of the ET encounter experiencers, the experiencers who had been healed by celestial beings.

Well, I was wrong. There is no "ET health plan." The changes we need to make are both simpler and much more involved than eating differently and practicing deep-breathing exercises. According to the ET encounter experiencers I talked to, the people you met in the preceding chapters, the celestial healers and those healed by celestial beings, we need to do the following if we wish *to be healed, that is, to change ourselves* in making an important, life-saving, potentially Earth-saving evolutionary step forward:

---

1. Stop being afraid of the unknown, including death, the afterlife, the other realms.
2. Expand consciousness to see the Oneness of *all* life.
3. Love ourselves, one another, the planet, the Cosmos.

Not exactly what *I* had in mind when I began writing this book. It would be easier, certainly, to devise an "ET health plan" with a low-fat organic diet, a daily nature walk, and a meditation program. The ETs told Diane Tai [in Chapter 16] to "eat foods with the highest vibration on the planet."[10] Now *that* would make an interesting diet program. But the ETs also advised someone else that she "must only eat cow things," and when this experiencer ate anything other than beef or dairy products, she actually became quite ill![11]

None of the celestial healers responded to my queries about diet and lifestyle habits with any advice more specific than "Don't worry about it." As Nancy Leggett explained, "People will start to change what they eat and how they live *naturally*, as their vibrations increase. They will be drawn to certain foods and will *intuitively* know what to eat and how to live in balance. This will begin to happen as consciousness evolves."[12]

So much for my "ET health plan."

Actually, this is where the consciousness expansion comes in: We need to stop focusing on and obsessing about the physical body, our fears of illness, pain, and death. This is a *much more important* step on the journey to well-being than changing our diets or buying organic produce! In fact, this is where the transformation lies: in the *transcending of the physical self.* And this is one of the primary messages the extraterrestrial visitors seem to be attempting to share.

So what do we *do*, exactly?

In lieu of the down-to-Earth "ET health plan" I had naively intended to share, I suggest that you consider doing the following, as I am struggling to do:

- *Purify your mind* using meditation and/or prayer, clearing out anxiety, worries, and fears.
- *Simplify your life* as much as possible, reducing your dependence on the material to focus more on your spiritual life.
- Find the time to *serve others* more by focusing less on amassing material desires.
- *Open yourself up* to the multitude of possibilities that exist in a multidimensional multiverse teeming with life and an infinite variety of intelligent, sentient beings.
- *Replace fear with love.*

My guess is that making these changes in attitude could help us all to take the first step in an evolutionary journey toward cosmic consciousness. The otherworldly beings may just be a little farther along on the universal path, popping up now and then—from other planets, other dimensions, other realms—to give us some much-needed assistance and advice. Some encounter experiencers are beginning to listen. Some are being healed, some are healing others.

Perhaps *you*, too, are ready now, willing to listen to those who have been healed by beings from "out there," able to turn to those who can help us heal ourselves with guidance from other, more evolved worlds. Celestial healing: What an extraordinary way to get our attention! Maybe now we can all begin to move beyond the fear, stepping bravely along the path to *soul* healing, cosmic awareness, and a more evolved perspective.

CELESTIAL HEALING 101

In the preceding chapters, we have met a wide selection of credible people with incredible accounts of medical healings that they attribute to celestial sources. I do not think that the individuals I talked to about celestial healing are lying. I do not believe they are all crazy. They have encountered *something* extraordinary, something that has changed their health, changed their perspective on reality.

Because I believe these experiencers, I, too, have dramatically altered my view of the world we live in, the known world and the vast, extraordinary unknown world. Dr. Mark Plotkin, a Harvard ethnobiologist who studies the medicinal and healing effects of shamanism and other primitive rituals, shares this wisdom: Do not be afraid to cast your lot with a small band of people who are determined to change the world because that is often the only way that change takes place.

I do not want to be afraid anymore.

Do you?

How to Tell if *You're* an Experiencer

The following list of *indicators* includes the most common signs of close encounter experiences. You can use this list to conduct a quick self-appraisal. Some ufology experts would advise that if you answer YES to four or more of these statements, it is possible that you are an experiencer. Other experts believe that a YES answer to even *one* of these questions points to a potential history of close encounter experiences.

MOST COMMON INDICATORS FOR EXTRATERRESTRIAL ENCOUNTER EXPERIENCES

Answer YES or NO to the following questions, checking in with your heart and gut (instincts) as well as with your memory:

1. I have experienced an *unexplained healing* of some type(s) of illness, ailment, affliction, or condition, medical or psychiatric; this healing might be

associated with strange dreams or nightmares, vague memories of odd experiences just beyond my recall.

2. I have noticed the following *unexplained markings* on my body: scooped-out skin tissue that heals quickly, a straight-line cut that does not bleed, a puncture wound that resembles a needle mark, burn marks; any of these markings might appear in shapes such as triangles or circles.

3. I have noticed the following *unexplained body symptoms:* nose bleeds; ringing in the ear(s); lowered metabolism with reduced body temperature; reduced need for sleep with an increase in energy; sudden strong aversion to alcohol, caffeine, sugar, meat, or other foods; sudden hair loss or gain; noticeable boost in immune system function with reduced/eliminated colds and flus; onset of "chemical sensitivity" with allergic-type reactions to individual chemicals; chronic fatigue syndrome, fibromalagia.*

4. I have experienced *sleep disorders* such as persistent insomnia without medical explanation, or waking up at the same time every night (e.g., 3:00–3:30 A.M.) for no apparent reason, or feeling a strong desire to stay awake all night (and doing so, even to the detriment of my health, job, and/or lifestyle).

5. I have experienced *persistent nightmares and/or*

---

*Some experiencers report chemical sensitivities they believe may be related to their encounters, and certain researchers claim a link, as yet unproven, between a history of "abductions" and the two autoimmune disorders, chronic fatigue syndrome and fibromalagia.[1] Note: IF YOU HAVE CHRONIC FATIGUE SYNDROME OR FIBRO-MALAGIA, THIS DOES NOT MEAN THAT YOU ARE AN ET EXPERIENCER. *Any relationship is, at this point, highly speculative.*

dreams of UFOs, extraterrestrials, weird monsters, or strange nonhuman beings; these dreams may be so vivid they resemble visions, and might occur during waking hours as well as during sleep.

6. I have *awakened to unusual body sensations* such as tingling, numbness, dizziness, heaviness, or temporary paralysis, often accompanied by disorientation; I have checked with my doctor and these symptoms *do not have a medical explanation*.

7. I have experienced *periods of missing time*, that is, the inability to account for sizable chunks of time, from one hour to many hours or even days; this has occurred in an otherwise normal situation, such as while taking a walk, driving somewhere, or simply sitting in my house.

8. I have experienced a strong reaction or *overreaction of fear or anxiety* with persistent restlessness, after seeing books, films, objects, or pictures associated with UFOs and/or ETs.

9. I have one or more *particular phobia(s)* for which I have no rational explanation; these phobias may include a fear of being alone, driving alone, and/or driving past certain locations; a strong aversion to bright lights, shiny floors, medical offices, hospitals, airports, and/or all public facilities with bright lights and shiny floors; a fear of falling, flying, falling *up*; a fear of falling asleep; a strong feeling of being watched, possibly with a fear of being "taken away" by unseen forces; a fear of creatures with large eyes, such as owls; an aversion to small children and/or babies; or other unusual, inexplicable phobias.

10. I have experienced *obsessive behavior with UFO and/or ET*-related materials, immersing myself in books, films, and lectures on the topic.

11. I believe I have experienced one or more *UFO sightings*, with or without any side effects or associated ET experience memories.*

12. I have found myself inexplicably but irresistibly drawn to an *alternative career path* (such as body work, energy balancing, "hands on" healing, deep tissue massage, psychospiritual counseling), while losing interest in my lifelong/current work.

13. I believe I have developed newfound, enhanced, and/or pronounced *psychic abilities;* these skills may include precognition, precognitive dreaming, clairvoyance, telepathy, clairaudience, and/or telekinesis.

14. I have developed a new *cosmic awareness*, a uni-

---

*Ufologist Richard J. Boylan, Ph.D., claims: "My personal rule of thumb, which comes from examining many cases with this circumstance present, is that anyone who has had a UFO approach within a quarter-mile has probably had concurrent close encounters, whether the person consciously remembers or not."[2] There have been a number of negative physical effects associated with close encounters with UFOs. Some people who report sighting a flying object close up have claimed to experience one or more of the following symptoms: feeling of heat, hair standing on end, disorientation, pain, headache, temporary paralysis, marks, burns, lumps, bumps, growths, sores, loss of appetite, diarrhea, lethargy, eye problems (e.g., redness, itchiness), hair loss, tooth damage, and/or psychological problems.[3] Many of these symptoms appear to be the result of radiation exposure, possibly from exposure to the flying objects themselves.[4] Chronic health problems experienced after UFO close encounters have even been referred to as "flying saucer disease."[5] In certain instances, such UFOs are believed to be human-engineered test models that are unsafe for observers within a specific distance.

versal spiritual awareness that is providing me with a different view of my life in general; this awareness may include the strong belief that we are not alone in the universe and that *all* beings are connected as part of the Divine Creation.

If you answered YES to one or more of the above statements, this does not mean that you are an extraterrestrial encounter experiencer. You may have an undiagnosed medical condition, a non-ET-related phobia, or a quirk in your personality. Then again, if you feel a strong urge to explore the *possibility* of a history of unconscious extraterrestrial contact experiences, chances are quite good that you just might *be* an experiencer. As Budd Hopkins once told a group of scientific researchers assembled at a meeting to discuss the potential validity of the contact experience: "The reason why we are all here today and have this great interest in the phenomena is that most likely we all have had an abduction or a contact experience at some time in our life."[6]

If you choose to explore further, the following resources may prove helpful, offering direct counsel and support or general guidance about how to obtain any specific information you may desire.

RESOURCES FOR EXPERIENCERS

To contact any of the following, see Resources on pages 320–21 for addresses and phone numbers, E-mail and Web sites.

*1. Program for Extraordinary Experience Research (PEER): This nonprofit organization was founded in 1993 by John Mack, M.D., of Harvard Medical School, to study the scientific research *and* the reports by experiencers of unexplained phenomena. PEER offers referrals to a nationwide network of therapists, as well as public education forums in the Boston area and a very interesting newsletter.

2. The Academy of Clinical Close Encounter Therapists (ACCET): An association of health and mental health professionals "who are developing special expertise in understanding and professionally working with experiencers of extraterrestrial encounters," this nonprofit organization offers workshops for clinicians and lists over one hundred therapists in its membership directory.[7] You might find a trained therapist through ACCET if PEER is unable to refer you to someone in your area.

3. Intruders Foundation (IF): Established by Budd Hopkins, perhaps the best-known hypnotist working with experiencers, IF accepts private clients and conducts research on the abduction phenomenon. It may be difficult to schedule an appointment with this popular speaker and advocate for the validity of abductions, "grays," and interbreeding/hybridization with ETs.

*4. Contact Forum: An interesting bimonthly newsletter full of first-person accounts of ET experiences, open exchange of research concepts and information, and a listing of therapists and support groups all over the U.S.

*5. Mutual UFO Network (MUFON): Established in 1967, this nonprofit organization boasts over five thousand members, including scientists and experiencers, and offers a national network of support groups, public education programs, a monthly magazine, and "field investigators" who will take a close look at your reports of UFO sightings or abductions.

6. Project Awareness: This group organizes conferences to disseminate information to the public regarding UFOs, ET encounters, and related experiences. Seminars often include well-known speakers from the UFO research community, as well as panels of abductees and experiencers.

7. Fund for UFO Research: Established in 1979, this is the "first and only organization dedicated to providing financial support for scientific research into all aspects of the UFO phenomenon," including "continuing support for the scientific study of abductions," according to their informational brochure.[8] Reports on the abduction studies they have funded may be of interest.

8. Center for the Study of Extraterrestrial Intelligence (CSETI): An international, nonprofit, scientific research and education organization, CSETI studies the ET-human relationship, attempting to foster ET-human communication and exchange through training workshops, conferences, and projects. Their "Close Encounter-5 Initiative," for example, is an ongoing long-term project involving scientists, investigators, and other interested individuals using

specially designed protocols for making contact with ETs.

9. Universal Vision: This San Francisco-based organization established by Scott Mandelker, Ph.D., offers counseling, lectures, workshops, and a newsletter for individuals interested in exploring their "cosmic identity," including ET contact and ET dual or self-identity. Mandelker is the author of *From Elsewhere: Being E.T. in America*.

10. Communion Network (CN): A clearinghouse for information on encounter experiences, this organization was founded by Whitley Strieber, author of *Communion* and a number of other popular books on extraterrestrial contact. Strieber lectures frequently all over the U.S. on his own encounter experiences and reports on the latest research on topics such as implants and videotaped UFO sightings. He encourages experiencers to write or E-mail to share their stories as he compiles a massive data base on human-extraterrestrial contact. Information on lecture sites and new CN materials are available on the CN Web site.

The organizations marked with an asterisk (*) may be the best places for you to contact first, as you can tap in quite quickly to ongoing programs, support groups, and lectures in your area, and obtain referrals to therapists, hopefully local, who work with extraterrestrial experiencers. *Be careful* in aligning yourself with any group and/or individual(s), as there seem to be a variety of factions, with specific slants to their agendas, within the UFO/ET research community. Some researchers/hypnotherapists and their advocates appear to have a strong bias in certain areas, such as the all-experiencers-are-*abducted*-purely-for-interbreeding-purposes school of thought. Thus, it is always a wise idea to talk to other experiencers about their *therapy* experiences when deciding on an appropriate counselor, and to explore the psychology of any support group you might consider joining. If the general philosophical attitude of a therapist or support group is that all ETs are "evil," for example, you might seek alternatives with a more open, less fear-driven approach to the encounter phenomenon.

If you are unable to locate support in your area, you may want to explore the Internet, as there are a number of Web sites and chat rooms for those interested in the extraterrestrial contact experience. Again, *be wary:* Just because it is on the Internet does not mean it is accurate or well researched. I found some very misleading ET "information" on the Internet, but was able to network readily with good results.

If you wish to specifically pinpoint information about or make connections with those who have experience with extraterrestrial *healing*, your search can seem more difficult, as this particular aspect of the UFO phenomenon is less commonly and less publically recognized. But if you are interested in exploring your own possible ET healing encounter, you can join a support group for experiencers, where it is possible that you will find others reporting similar experiences. You might seek out a therapist trained to work with experiencers, even though most people who find themselves suddenly healed of a painful and/or chronic medical condition typically do not feel the need for counseling. However, a trained hypnotherapist can assist you in consciously recalling hidden memories associated with your healing encounter experience(s), and possibly other information from encounters that you do not consciously remember.

If you are interested in contacting *healers* who work with celestial or extraterrestrial energies, you may find it difficult at first to locate such specialized practitioners. However, increasing numbers of people are finding themselves drawn to do this type of healing work. A good way to start your research is to network through the following organizations (addresses and phone numbers provided on page 320–21).

1. The Barbara Brennan School of Healing: As mentioned by ET energy healer Peter Faust in Chapter 10, this school is one of the premier educational facilities for practitioners of energy healing work. They may be able to refer you to graduates who, like Peter, offer extraterrestrial energy therapy.

2. National Federation of Spiritual Healers: This is another practitioner organization you might call for referral, although "spiritual healing" is not necessarily the same as ET energy healing work so you will have to be specific about what type of energy work you are seeking.

Please be aware that there is *no guarantee* that a person who claims to be a healer is, in reality, honest, reputable, or successful. Just like when you make an appointment with a psychic or a medium, a channeler or other New Age practitioner, you are taking your chances when you put yourself in the hands of any self-proclaimed ET or celestial energy healer. *You* must decide if it is worth the money, time, effort, and risk.

So, do you think you might be an extraterrestrial contact experiencer? A celestial healing experiencer? If it does seem that you just might be, you need not feel alone. More and more people all over the world are "waking up" to find that they suddenly remember a long-forgotten self, a part of themselves that has led a "secret life," interacting with beings from other worlds, other dimensions. This self-discovery can turn out to be the most enlightening, most exciting step on your life journey. It can prove to be the most *healing* self-discovery you ever make.

Notes

Prologue

1. Fred Alan Wolf, *The Dreaming Universe* (New York: Simon and Schuster, 1994), pp. 347–48.

Part I
Chapter 1

1. Alexandra M. Levine et al., "Successful Therapy of Convoluted T-Lymphoblastic Lymphoma in the Adult," *Blood*, vol. 61, no. 1 (January 1983), p. 92.
2. According to Helen Burstin, M.D., "There could be a scar on the lung from a tumor that had been treated and disappeared, but it may not necessarily be visible on X rays"; personal files.

Chapter 2

1. John R. Salter, Jr., "No Intelligent Life Is Alien to Me," *Contact Forum*, vol. 1, no. 1 (July/August 1993), pp. 1–2.
2. "Professor Says Humanoids 'Intercepted' Him, Son, on Trip through Coulee Region," *La Crosse Tribune* (July 13, 1997), p. 1.
3. Personal files.

4. "Professor Says . . ." *La Crosse Tribune*, p. 1.
5. Personal files.
6. John Hunter Gray, "Thoughts on Fear, Extraterrestrials, and Healthy Minds," *When Cosmic Cultures Meet: Proceedings*, Human Potential Foundation (1996), p. 189.
7. Salter, *Contact Forum*, p. 3.

Chapter 5

1. Excerpt from a series of communications to Ron Blevins from the tall beings, "Communications From the Collective" #02: "Manifest in the nature of our existence is that knowledge which affirms the undeniable truth that it is the soul that gives life and personage to the body, rather than the body to the soul. For the soul is not dependent on the body for its existence, but is oriented to the nature and essence of Creative Order which is its source . . . Increased in wisdom and going forth in the purpose of that conceived in the Mind of All Knowing. End of Communication."
2. References to the use of quartz stones in traditional ceremonies, including healing rites, can be found in the following: Helen C. Roundtree, *The Powhatan Indians of Virginia, Their Traditional Culture* (Norman, OK: University of Oklahoma Press, 1944), p. 136; James Mooney, *Myths of the Cherokee* and *Sacred Formulas of the Cherokees*, Bureau of American Ethnology, Annual Report, vol. 19 (1900), pp. 460–61; Bruce Power, "Sacred Secrets of the Caves," *Science News*, vol. 153, no. 4 (January 24, 1998), p. 50.

Chapter 7

1. Ruth Montgomery, *Aliens Among Us* (New York: G. P. Putnam's Sons, 1985), p. 139.

2. "Arcturian Groups of Forty Newsletter," no. 22 (March 12, 1998), p. 2.

Chapter 8

1. Philip J. Imbrogno and Marianne Horrigan, *Contact of the Fifth Kind* (St. Paul, Minnesota: Llewellyn Publications, 1997), pp. 91–93.
2. Ibid., p. 98.

Part II
Chapter 10

1. Roger K. Leir, "Alien Implants—A 1998 Update," *MUFON Journal* (June 1998), pp. 3–8.

Chapter 13

1. Norma Milanovich, *We, the Arcturians* (Albuquerque, NM: Athena Press, 1990).
2. Personal files.

Part III
Chapter 16

1. Preston Dennett, *UFO Healings* (Mill Springs, N.C.: Wild Flower Press, 1996), p. 159.
2. Ibid., p. 160.
3. Ibid., pp. 17–18.
4. Ibid., pp. 19–20.
5. Ibid., pp. 118–20.
6. Ibid., pp. 122–23.
7. Ibid., p. 96.
8. Ibid., p. 146.
9. John F. Schuessler, *UFO-Related Human Physiological Effects* (Houston, TX: John F. Schuessler, 1996), p. 12.
10. Ibid., p. 15.

11. Ibid., p. 48.
12. Edith Fiore, *Encounters: A Psychologist Reveals Case Studies of Abductions by Extraterrestrials* (New York: Ballantine Books, 1989), p. 2.
13. Ibid., pp. 34–35.
14. Ibid., p. 39.
15. Ibid., p. 47.
16. Ibid., p. 51.
17. Ibid., pp. 219–22.
18. Ibid., pp. 72–83.
19. Ibid., pp. 131–34.
20. Ibid., pp. 130.
21. Ibid., pp. 143–44.
22. John E. Mack, *Abduction: Human Encounters with Aliens* (New York: Ballantine Books, 1994), p. xiii.
23. Ibid., pp. 230–32.
24. Ibid., pp. 81–82.
25. Ibid., p. 97.
26. C.D.B. Bryan, *Close Encounters of the Fourth Kind* (New York: Penguin Books USA, 1995), p. 447.
27. Ibid., pp. 19–20.
28. Ibid., p. 26.
29. Ibid., p. 41.
30. Scott Mandelker, *From Elsewhere: Being ET in America* (New York: Dell Publishing, 1995), pp. 1–10.
31. Ibid., pp. 24–25.
32. Ibid., p. 27.
33. Ibid., p. 162.
34. Paul David Pursglove, *Zen in the Art of Close Encounters* (Berkeley, CA: The New Being Project, 1995), pp. 94–96.
35. Ibid., p. 114.
36. Hans Holzer, *The Secret of Healing* (Hillsboro, OR: Beyond Words Publishing, Inc., 1995), pp. 13–14.

37. Ibid., p. 17.
38. Ibid., pp. 30, 53.
39. Ibid., pp. 18, 92.
40. Ibid., pp. 20, 130.

Chapter 17

1. The Thyroid Foundation of America, Inc., and The American Thyroid Association, Inc., "Thyroid Topics: Cancer of the Thyroid" (Boston, MA: The Thyroid Foundation of America, Inc., 1995), p. 2.
2. David Jacobs, *Secret Life: Firsthand Documented Accounts of UFO Abductions* (New York: Simon and Schuster, 1992), pp. 285–97.
3. Virginia Bennett, *A UFO Primer* (Berkeley, CA: Regent Press, 1993), p. 17.
4. Courtney Brown, *Cosmic Voyage* (New York: Penguin Books USA, 1996), p. 54.

Part IV
Chapter 18

1. Personal files, revised.
2. Hans Holzer, *The Secret of Healing*, p. 170.
3. The TM program (introductory brochure) ©TM.
4. Courtney Brown, *Cosmic Voyage*, pp. 369–70.
5. Steven M. Greer, M.D., *The CSETI Project: An Introduction* (Asheville, NC: CSETI, 1992, 1996), pp. 1–2.
6. Ibid., p. 5.
7. Ibid., p. 10.
8. *The Hemi-Sync Catalog* (Interstate Industries, P.O. Box 505, Lovingston, VA 22949, 1997), pp. 4–6.
9. Brown, *Cosmic Voyage*, p. 52.
10. Ibid., p. 363.
11. Ibid., p. 366.

Part V

1. Howard Blum, *Out There* (New York: Simon and Schuster, 1990), pp. 193–94.

Chapter 19

1. C.D.B. Bryan, *Close Encounters of the Fourth Kind*, pp. 34–35.
2. Ibid., p. 35.
3. David Jacobs, *Secret Life*, p. 92.
4. Caryle Hirshberg and Marc Ian Barasch, *Remarkable Recovery* (New York: Riverhead Books, 1995), p. 7.
5. Ibid., pp. 1–2.
6. Ibid., p. 245.
7. Ibid., p. 251.
8. Ibid., p. 259.
9. Ibid., p. 267.
10. Edith Fiore, *Encounters*, p. 223.
11. Bryan, *Close Encounters of the Fourth Kind*, pp. 308–11.
12. Personal files.

Appendix

1. Personal files; and Katherina Wilson, "Fibromalagia and Abductees" series (Portland, OR: Puzzle Publishing, 1993–1998). Wilson is not a medical researcher, but networks with experiencers who, like herself, suffer from musculoskeletal pain and fatigue for which a cause is unknown.
2. Richard J. Boylan, *Close Extraterrestrial Encounters* (Tigard, OR: Wild Flower Press, 1994), p. 30.
3. John F. Schuessler, *UFO-Related Human Physiological Effects*, p. 5.
4. Jenny Randles and Peter Hough, *The Complete Book of*

UFOs (New York: Sterling Publishing Co., 1996), pp. 219–22.

5. Patrick Huyghe, *The Field Guide to Extraterrestrials* (New York: Avon Books, 1996), p. 86.

6. Philip J. Imbrogno and Marianne Horrigan, *Contact of the Fifth Kind*, pp. 222–23.

7. "ACCET Membership Information Form" (Sacramento, CA: Academy of Clinical Close Encounter Therapists), p. 1.

8. Fund for UFO Research, Inc., Bulletin (Mount Rainier, MD: Fund for UFO Research, Inc.), pp. 1–2.

References

Becker, Robert O. *The Body Electric*. New York: William Morrow & Co., 1985.

Bennett, Virginia. *A UFO Primer*. Berkeley, CA: Regent Press, 1993.

Bloecher, Ted, Aphrodite Clamar, and Budd Hopkins. *Final Report on the Psychological Testing of UFO "Abductees."* Mt. Rainier, MD: Fund for UFO Research, Inc., 1985.

Blum, Howard. *Out There*. New York: Simon and Schuster, 1990.

Boylan, Richard. *Close Extraterrestrial Encounters: Positive Experiences with Mysterious Visitors*. Mill Spring, NC: Wild Flower Press, 1994.

Brennan, Barbara. *Hands of Light*. New York: Bantam Books, 1987.

———. *Light Emerging*. New York: Bantam Books, 1993.

Brown, Courtney. *Cosmic Voyage*. New York: Penguin Books USA, 1996.

Bryan, C.D.B. *Close Encounters of the Fourth Kind*. New York: Penguin Books USA, 1995.

Bullard, Thomas E. *Comparative Analysis of UFO Abduction Reports and Catalog of Abductions*. Mt. Rainier, MD: Fund for UFO Research, Inc., 1987.

Chopra, Deepak. *Quantum Healing.* New York: Bantam Books, 1989.

Dennett, Preston. *One in Forty: The UFO Epidemic.* Commack, NY: Kroshka Books, 1996.

———. *UFO Healings: True Accounts of People Healed by Extraterrestrials.* Mill Spring, NC: Wild Flower Press, 1996.

Dossey, Larry. *Healing Words: The Power of Prayer and the Practice of Medicine.* New York: Harper San Francisco, 1993.

———. *Prayer Is Good Medicine: How to Reap the Healing Benefits of Prayer.* New York: Harper San Francisco, 1996.

Fiore, Edith. *Encounters: A Psychologist Reveals Case Studies of Abductions by Extraterrestrials.* New York: Doubleday, 1989.

Fuller, John G. *Incident at Exeter and the Interrupted Journey.* New York: Fine Communications, 1966.

Goldberg, Bruce. *Time Travelers From Our Future: Explanation of Alien Abductions.* St. Paul, MN: Llewellyn Publications, 1998.

Good, Timothy. *Above Top Secret: The Worldwide UFO Coverup.* New York: William Morrow & Co., 1988.

———. *Alien Contact: Top-Secret UFO Files Revealed.* New York: William Morrow & Co., 1993.

Haines, Richard F. *CE-5: The Chronicle of Human-Initiated Contact.* Naperville, IL: Sourcebooks, Inc., 1998.

Hirshberg, Caryle and Marc Ian Barasch. *Remarkable Recovery: What Extraordinary Healings Tell Us About Getting Well and Staying Well.* New York: Riverhead Books, 1995.

Holzer, Hans. *The Secret of Healing.* Hillsboro, OR: Beyond Words Publishing, Inc., 1996.

Huyghe, Patrick. *The Field Guide to Extraterrestrials.* New York: Avon Books, 1996.

Imbrogno, Phillip and Marianne Horrigan. *Contact of the Fifth Kind.* St. Paul, MN: Llewellyn Publications, 1997.

Jacobs, David. *Secret Life: Firsthand Documented Accounts of UFO Abductions.* New York: Simon and Schuster, 1992.

Jho, Zoev. *ET 101: The Cosmic Instruction Manual to Planetary Evolution*. New York: Harper San Francisco, 1995.

Lewels, Joe. *The God Hypothesis: Extraterrestrial Life and Its Implications for Science and Religion*. Mill Spring, NC: Wild Flower Press, 1997.

Mack, John E. *Abduction: Human Encounters with Aliens*. New York: Scribner, 1994.

Mandelker, Scott. *From Elsewhere: Being ET in America*. New York: Dell Publishing, 1995.

Marciniak, Barbara. *Bringers of the Dawn: Teachings from the Pleiadians*. Santa Fe, NM: Bear & Company, 1992.

Milanovich, Norma. *We, the Arcturians*. Albuquerque, NM: Athena Press, 1990.

Miller, David. *Connecting With the Arcturians*. Pine, AZ: Planetary Heart Publications, 1998.

Monroe, Robert A. *Far Journeys*. New York: Doubleday, 1987.
———. *Journeys Out of Body*. New York: Doubleday, 1971.
———. *Ultimate Journey*. New York: Doubleday, 1994.

Montgomery, Ruth. *Aliens Among Us*. New York: G. P. Putnam's Sons, 1985.

Morehouse, David. *Psychic Warrior*. New York: St. Martin's Press, 1996.

Pursglove, Paul David. *Zen and the Art of Close Encounters: Crazy Wisdom and UFOs*. Berkeley, CA: The New Being Project, 1995.

Randles, Jenny and Peter Hough. *The Complete Book of UFOs*. New York: Sterling Publishing Co., 1996.

Ring, Kenneth. *The Omega Project: Near-Death Experiences, UFO Encounters, and the Mind at Large*. New York: William Morrow & Co., 1992.

Roth, Robert. *Transcendental Meditation*. New York: Donald I. Fine Books, 1988.

Schuessler, John F. *UFO-Related Human Physiological Effects*. P.O. Box 58485, Houston, TX 77258-8485, 1996.

Silva, José and Robert B. Stone. *You the Healer.* Tiburon, CA: H. J. Kramer, Inc., 1989.

Strieber, Whitley. *Communion.* New York: Beech Tree Books, 1987.

———. *The Secret School: Preparation for Contact.* New York: Harper Collins Publishers, 1997.

———. *Transformation.* New York: Beech Tree Books, 1988.

Talbot, Michael. *The Holographic Universe.* New York: Harper Collins Publishers, 1991.

Vallée, Jacques. *Dimensions: A Casebook of Alien Contact.* New York: Contemporary Books, 1988.

Wolf, Fred Alan. *The Dreaming Universe.* New York: Simon and Schuster, 1994.

JOURNALS, MAGAZINES, AND NEWSLETTERS

Contact Forum (bimonthly magazine): Blue Water Publishing, Inc., P.O. Box 190, Mill Spring, NC 28756. Web site at http://www.5thworld.com.

The ET Journal (bimonthly magazine): Universal Vision, 2130 Fillmore Street, #201, San Francisco, CA 94115.

FATE Magazine: True Reports of the Strange and Unknown (published monthly): P.O. Box 64383, St. Paul, MN 55164-0383. Web site at http://www.llewellyn.com.

The Leading Edge Newspaper (bimonthly): Box 1359, Pisgah Forest, NC 28768.

MUFON Journal (monthly magazine): Mutual UFO Network, Inc., 103 Oldtowne Road, Seguin, TX 78155-4099.

The Pleiadian Times (quarterly newsletter): Bold Connections Unlimited, P.O. Box 782, Apex, NC 27502.

Resources

Organizations for Support, Education, Referral

- The Academy of Clinical Close Encounter Therapists (ACCET), 2826 O Street, Suite 3, Sacramento, CA 95816; (916) 455-0120.
- The Barbara Brennan School of Healing, P.O. Box 2005, East Hampton, NY 11937; 0-700-HEALERS.
- The Center for the Study of Extraterrestrial Intelligence (CSETI), P.O. Box 15401, Asheville, NC 28813; (704) 274-5671.
- Communion Network (CN), 5928 Broadway, San Antonio, TX 78209; E-mail: Whitley @ Strieber.com; Web site: http://www.strieber.com.
- Contact Forum (bimonthly magazine), c/o Wild Flower Press, P.O. Box 190, Mill Spring, NC 28756; (704) 894-8444; Web site: http://www.5thworld.com.
- The Farsight Institute, P.O. Box 49243, Atlanta, GA 30359.
- Fund for UFO Research, Inc., P.O. Box 277, Mount Rainier, MD 20712.
- Intruders Foundation (IF), P.O. Box 30233, New York, NY 10011.
- Mutual UFO Network (MUFON), 103 Oldtowne Road, Seg-

uin, TX 78155-4099; (830) 379-9216; Web site: http://mufon.com.

- National Federation of Spiritual Healers, 1137 Silent Harbor, P.O. Box 2022, Mount Pleasant, SC 29465; (803) 849-1529.
- Program for Extraordinary Experience Research (PEER), P.O. Box 398080, Cambridge, MA 02139; (617) 497-2667; Web site: http://www.peer-mack.org.
- Project Awareness, P.O. Box 730, Gulf Breeze, FL 32562; E-mail: crumble @ telapex.com.
- Silva Mind Control International, Inc., P.O. Box 2249, Laredo, TX 78044-2249; (512) 722-6391.
- TransDimensional Systems (TDS), P.O. Box 1883, Duluth, GA 30096; (770) 814-9410; E-mail: TDS @ largeruniverse.com; Web site: http://www.largeruniverse.com.
- Transcendental Meditation (TM), 1-800-888-5797; call for course listings available in your area; Web site: http://www.wholeness.com.
- The Monroe Institute (TMI), 62 Roberts Mountain Road, Faber, VA 22938; (804) 361-1252; E-mail: MonroeInst @ aol.com; Web site: http://www.monroe-inst.com/. Ask about Dolphin Energy Club, a healing service for TMI members: (804) 361-9132.
- Universal Vision (UV), 2130 Fillmore Street, #201, San Francisco, CA 94115; (415) 567-2190; E-mail: starborn @ sirius.com.

Products (as mentioned by healers, experiencers)

- Ascension Alchemy, 8810 Gross Point Road, Suite 74D, Skokie, IL 60077; (847) 673-3431. Products like "Etherium Gold," recommended by some healers for increasing cellular vibration to assist ascension into a higher dimension. *Please note:* I did not try any of these products myself, and I cannot vouch for their safety or efficacy.

- Advanced Tachyon Technologies, Inc., 435 Tesconi Circle, Santa Rosa, CA 95401; (707) 573-5800. Products include "Tachyonized" water, wrist and head bands, pendants and disks, and other items used "to balance and rejuvenate the body" by harnessing the faster-than-light, free energy form known as tachyon energy. Tachyonized products have been altered at the subatomic level to create a conductor for Tachyon energy, which is theorized as capable of reversing the aging process, improving cellular and organ function, increasing mental and physical health and vitality. *Please note:* I cannot vouch for the effectiveness of these products, although I did test out the water, wrist bands, and a disk. Whether these items actually worked or not earned a subjective assessment of "possibly." My husband swears by the tachyonized wrist band for writer's cramp.

Healers (included in this book)

- Healing Arts of Belmont, Belmont, MA; (617) 484-HEAL (Peter Faust).
- InGrace, 11065 S.W. 70th Terrace, Miami, FL 33173 (Ingrid Parnell).
- Nancy Leggett, 9363 Fontainbleu Boulevard, #226H, Miami, FL 33172; (305) 220-6819.
- Lightkeepers Remote Viewing/Remote Healing Network, 2628A Colonel Glenn Highway, Suite 119, Fairborn, OH 45324; E-mail: GSTURGESS @ aol.com; Web site: http:// hometown.aol.com/deerl/LightkeepersDec 98/page1.html
- David Miller, P.O. Box 4074, Prescott, AZ 86302; (520) 776-1717; E-mail: Zoloft @ cybertrails.com; Web site: cybertrails.net/groupofforty.